St. George's (Old Spesutia) Parish

Harford County Maryland

Church and Cemetery Records 1820–1920

Henry C. Peden, Jr.

HERITAGE BOOKS
2012

HERITAGE BOOKS
AN IMPRINT OF HERITAGE BOOKS, INC.

Books, CDs, and more—Worldwide

For our listing of thousands of titles see our website
at
www.HeritageBooks.com

Published 2012 by
HERITAGE BOOKS, INC.
Publishing Division
100 Railroad Ave. #104
Westminster, Maryland 21157

Copyright © 2002 Henry C. Peden, Jr.

All rights reserved. No part of this book may be reproduced or transmitted in any form or by any means, electronic or mechanical, including photocopying, recording or by any information storage and retrieval system without written permission from the author, except for the inclusion of brief quotations in a review.

International Standard Book Numbers
Paperbound: 978-1-58549-742-3
Clothbound: 978-0-7884-9397-3

FOREWORD

St. George's Parish was one of three parishes laid out in Baltimore County by the Act of 1692 passed by the Maryland Assembly. In colonial times, St. George's Protestant Episcopal Church was also known as Spesutia Church and was under the perview of the Church of England.

When Harford County was created in 1773, St. George's Parish fell entirely within the new county and occupied the upper and eastern two-thirds thereof. The lower and western one-third of the county fell within the bounds of St. John's Parish in Baltimore County. With respect to St. George's, "the old parish is the mother of many churches in Harford County, the oldest is St. James' Chapel at Trappe, 1751; Rock Spring, 1805; St. John's Havre de Grace, 1809; Deer Creek Parish, Darlington (in which is old St. James' at the Trappe), 1859; Emmanuel, Bel Air, 1868; Holy Trinity, Churchville, 1869." {Ref: Historical Sketch of St. George's Parish (1953), p. 11}

In 1987 when I compiled and published my first book of church records entitled *St. John's and St. George's Parish Registers, 1696-1851*, I mentioned that there were other records for St. George's Parish between 1681 and 1799 that were also available. I had planned to abstract them "in the near future" and was glad that Bill and Martha Reamy found the time in 1988 to publish the next volume entitled *St. George's Parish Registers, 1689-1793*.

I have now put together another volume of St. George's Parish records that span the years 1820 to 1920. These records were taken from microfilm copies of the original records in the Maryland State Archives (Special Collections), viz., St. George's Parish, Church Records, 1834-1903 (MSA M419) and St. George's Church, Parish Register, 1903-1958 (MSA M681).

While there is a gap in the registers from 1800 to 1834, the later records do contain some information for that time period, mainly birth dates and/or ages. To help fill this gap, I decided to include all the data for the hundred year period from 1820 to 1920 that pertained to births, baptisms (including sponsors), marriages, confirmations, communicants (received and removed), deaths and burials. From cemetery records maintained at the Historical Society of Harford County, plus several visits I made to the Old Spesutia Church Cemetery in Perryman, I supplemented the aforementioned data with information copied from tombstone inscriptions.

It should be noted that one of the parish registers had a unique section entitled "Families" which listed the members of many of the families that belonged to St. George's Church circa 1893-1903. Although no dates or relationships were given, that information has been included herein as well. The only records not included are the vestry proceedings; perhaps they will be another book for someone to do "in the near future."

Essentially, the information found in the registers and cemetery records has been gleaned, alphabetized by the person's last name, and in many cases combined when they pertain to a specific individual. In other words, instead of having several entries scattered throughout the book for one person's baptism, confirmation, marriage, and burial, this information has been pulled together into one paragraph about that individual.

I thought that doing the book in an alphabetical format would be helpful to researchers in that it spares one from the tedious flipping back and forth between the index and the text. There is a name cross reference built into the text that negates the necessity for an index anyway. And, of course, every entry in the book is followed by the source and/or page number in the event the researcher wants to see the original record.

Henry C. Peden, Jr.
Bel Air, Maryland
December 1, 2001

Dedicated to the memory of

Walter Remington Frank III

(1945-2001)

ST. GEORGE'S (OLD SPESUTIA) PARISH
HARFORD COUNTY, MARYLAND
CHURCH AND CEMETERY RECORDS, 1820-1920

AARONSON, Ambrose Palmer, born 13 Apr 1849, died 27 Jul 1878. {Ref: Tombstone inscription}

AARONSON, Annie Jane, wife of Ambrose Palmer Aaronson and also of Bennett Osborn, born 31 Jan 1849, died 21 Oct 1899. {Ref: Tombstone inscription}

AARONSON, James Edward, age 56 years, 11 months and 26 days, buried 3 Sep 1917. {Ref: Parish Register, 1903-1958, p. 159}

AARONSON, William F., born 1848, died 1910. {Ref: Tombstone inscription}

ABBOTT, Moses J., of Havre de Grace, buried 8 Mar 1855. {Ref: Church Records, 1834-1903, p. 92}

ABRAMS, Gertrude E., married Benjamin F. Johnson on 20 Feb 1889 at the Church of the Epiphany in Philadelphia; also see "Benjamin F. Johnson," q.v. {Ref: Church Records, 1834-1903, pp. 154-155}

ABT, Matthew B., born 24 Aug 1871, died 25 Apr 1912, age 41 years, 8 months and 1 day, buried 28 Sep 1912. {Ref: Parish Register, 1903-1958, p. 158; Tombstone inscription}

AIREY, Ella Barker, daughter of G. G. and F. B. Airey, born 1 Aug 1880, baptized 11 Sep 1881 (sponsors: the parents and Mrs. Ella C. Barker). {Ref: Church Records, 1834-1903, pp. 2-3}

AIREY, Fannie B., buried 28 Dec 1883. {Ref: Church Records, 1834-1903, p. 100}

AIREY, George, married Fannie B. Patterson on 21 Jun 1870; also see "Ella B. Airey," q.v. {Ref: Church Records, 1834-1903, p. 147}

AIREY (ARY), Sarah, married Samuel B. Ivans on 20 Oct 1859. {Ref: Church Records, 1834-1903, p. 142}

ALANDER, Henry, see "Henry Allender," q.v.

ALL, Rachel, died -- Jun 1851 in her 73rd year. {Ref: Tombstone inscription}

ALLEN, Brasseys, wife of Rev. John Allen, died 29 Dec 1831 in her 69th year. {Ref: Tombstone inscription}

ALLEN, Eben N., see "Elecia Allen," q.v.

ALLEN, Edward, see "Mary W. Allen," q.v.

ALLEN, Elecia M., wife of Eben N. Allen, died 13 Jan 1823 in her 28th year. {Ref: Tombstone inscription}

ALLEN, John (reverend), rector from 1795 to 1815; "For 20 years the faithful and untiring minister of this church, died 16 Mar 1830, age 69" [and] buried in the church yard; also see "Brasseys Allen" and "William H. Allen," q.v. {Ref: Tombstone inscription; Historical Skecth of St. George's Parish (1953), pp. 9, 13}

ALLEN, Mary Wilson, daughter of Edward and Sallie Allen, born 27 Nov 1853, baptized 22 Aug 1854. {Ref: Church Records, 1834-1903, pp. 26-27}

ALLEN, Mathew Johnson, M.D., died in Tallahassee, Florida on 27 Dec 1851 in his 51st year. {Ref: Tombstone inscription}

ALLEN, Sallie, see "Mary W. Allen," q.v.

ALLEN, William Henry, son of Rev. John Allen, age 12, died 29 Sep 1836. {Ref: Tombstone inscription}

ALLENDER (ALENDER), Henry, married Frances Hopkins on 28 Oct 1860. {Ref: Church Records, 1834-1903, p. 143}

ALLENDER (ALANDER), Leone, daughter of Henry and Frances Alander, born 8 May 1860, baptized 28 Oct 1860. {Ref: Church Records, 1834-1903, pp. 30-31}

ALRICH, Anner Moss, married Bailey Tyler on 6 Oct 1897; sponsored the baptism of David Daniel Alrich (colored) on 28 Jan 1891. {Ref: Church Records, 1834-1903, pp. 11, 160-161}

ALRICH, Mary B. (Mrs.), sponsored the baptism of Pearson Chapman on 18 Apr 1897; removed 2 Jul 1900. {Ref: Church Records, 1834-1903, pp. 13, 203}

ALRICH, Mary L. (Miss), removed 2 Jul 1900. {Ref: Church Records, 1834-1903, p. 203}

ALRICH, Susan Berkeley (Miss), confirmed 27 Oct 1894, removed 2 Jul 1900. {Ref: Church Records, 1834-1903, pp. 204-205, 302}

ALRICH, W. A., sponsored the baptism of Hugh Bush Malcolm on 5 Jan 1890; also see "Savington W. Crampton," q.v. {Ref: Church Records, 1834-1903, p. 9}

ALRICH, W. Rosalie (Miss), sponsored the baptism of David Daniel Alrich (colored) on 28 Jan 1891; removed 2 Jul 1900. {Ref: Church Records, 1834-1903, pp. 11, 203}

ALRICH, William A. (reverend), born 23 Apr 1836, died 25 Mar 1903. {Ref: Tombstone inscription}. The following was recorded in the church register on Saturday, March 28, 1903:
"Rev. Wm. A. Alrich, for over ten years Rector of St. George's Parish: from May 1st 1890 to July 1st 1900. He died in the surf at Palm Beach, Fla. from paralysis of the heart on Wednesday March 25. He was laid to rest today in the cemetery surrounding the church which was the last charge he held, & whose rectorship he had resigned on account of ill health." {Ref: Church Records, 1834-1903, p. 104}

ANDERSON, Christina W., married John Howard Shalburg ---- 1877. [*Ed. Note:* The date was blank, but the marriage was listed between June and December in the register]. {Ref: Church Records, 1834-1903, p. 148}

ANDERSON, Ellen (colored), married Samuel Clark (colored) on 6 Oct 1870. {Ref: Church Records, 1834-1903, p. 147}

ANDERSON, Mary Lena (neé Palmer), member in 1904, transferred to St. Paul's Chapel, Severn Parish, on 4 Apr 1905. {Ref: Parish Register, 1903-1958, p. 109}

ANDERSON, Rachel, married Bradford Stokes on 18 May 1889. {Ref: Church Records, 1834-1903, pp. 154-155}

ANDREWS, Viva Irene, daughter of ---- [blank], born 20 Apr 1892. {Ref: Parish Register, 1903-1958, pp. 34-35}

ANSALVICH, Emanuel, died 6 Sep 1918. {Ref: Tombstone inscription}

ANSALVICH, Rosana S., age 27, buried 20 Jan 1904. {Ref: Parish Register, 1903-1958, p. 158}

ARCHER, Howe Davis, son of Robert H. and Ellen H. Archer, born 14 Sep 1855, baptized 17 Sep 1855, buried 4 Nov 1855. {Ref: Church Records, 1834-1903, pp. 26-27, 92}

ASHER, Margaret C., born 1882, died 1920. {Ref: Tombstone inscription}

ATKINSON, Sallie A. E. (Miss), age 52, died 13 Jul 1879, buried 15 Jul 1879. {Ref: Church Records, 1834-1903, p. 98; Tombstone inscription}

AVERY(?), Corrie Patterson, child of George and Fannie B. Avery(?). [*Ed. Note:* No date of birth or baptism was given, but the baptism was listed among several others in the register between 1872 and 1876. The name also had a question mark after it]. {Ref: Church Records, 1834-1903, pp. 40-41}

AVERY(?), Eugenia Goldsborough, daughter of George and Fannie B. Avery(?). [*Ed. Note:* No date of birth or baptism was given, but the baptism was listed among several others in the register between 1872 and 1876. The name also had a question mark after it]. {Ref: Church Records, 1834-1903, pp. 40-41}

BACON, James, died 15 Mar 1817 in his 45th year. {Ref: Tombstone inscription}

BAKER, Cornelia Stockham, wife of John H. Baker, born 1833, died 1916. {Ref: Tombstone inscription}

BALDWIN FAMILY.
The following family information was entered in the church records under the heading of "Families" circa 1893-1903, but no relationships or ages were indicated, just names:
Mrs. Florence O. Baldwin, Mary Virginia Baldwin, Blanch Eugenia Baldwin, and Mary Baldwin. {Ref: Church Records, 1834-1903, p. 259}

BALDWIN, Blanch (Blanche) Eugenia, daughter of William M. and Florence O. Baldwin, born 29 Apr 1895, baptized 27 Oct 1895 (sponsors: the mother and Blanch Eugenia Michael), confirmed 11 Dec 1910, later dropped [date not given]; also see "Marshall W. Baldwin" and "Baldwin Family," q.v. {Ref: Church Records, 1834-1903, pp. 12-13; Parish Register, 1903-1958, p. 87}

BALDWIN, Florence Olivia (neé Thompson), received from St. Mathias' Church in Philadelphia on 22 Apr 1894; sponsored the baptisms of David Ray Morris on

25 May 1902 and Edward Alfred Cullum and Edna Matilda Cullum on 26 Apr 1903; church member in 1903, later removed [date not given]; also see "Baldwin Family," q.v. {Ref: Church Records, 1834-1903, pp. 15, 17, 204; Parish Register, 1903-1958, p. 106}

BALDWIN, Howard, see "Katherine Baldwin," q.v.

BALDWIN, Katherine Elizabeth, daughter of Howard and Rosie Baldwin, born 11 Jan 1917, baptized 28 Jul 1917 in the church rectory (sponsors: Mrs. Lacey Schofield and Rosie Baldwin). {Ref: Parish Register, 1903-1958, pp. 32-33}

BALDWIN, Lacey, married William Schofield on 25 Sep 1912. {Ref: Parish Register, 1903-1958, pp. 138-139}

BALDWIN, Laura M. E., married Carroll C. Hopkins on 1 Jan 1914 at the residence of the bride's father (also noted in record was "See Register of Deer Creek Parish"). {Ref: Parish Register, 1903-1958, pp. 138-139}

BALDWIN, Marshall William, son of ---- [blank] and Blanche Baldwin, born 29 Apr 1913, baptized 16 Sep 1913 (sponsor: Mrs. H. S. Holloway); died -- Sep 1913, age 5 months, buried 29 Sep 1913. {Ref: Parish Register, 1903-1958, pp. 32-33, 159}

BALDWIN, Mary, see "Baldwin Family," q.v.

BALDWIN, Mary Virginia, age 14, confirmed 29 Dec 1901, church member in 1903, later removed [date not given]; also see "Baldwin Family," q.v. {Ref: Church Records, 1834-1903, p. 303; Parish Register, 1903-1958, p. 107}

BALDWIN, Rosie, sponsored the baptism of Katherine Elizabeth Baldwin on 28 Jul 1917; also see "Katherine Baldwin," q.v. {Ref: Parish Register, 1903-1958, pp. 32-33}

BALDWIN, William Marshall, buried 8 Nov 1901, age 44 years, 2 months and 19 days; also see "Blanch Baldwin," q.v. {Ref: Church Records, 1834-1903, p. 104}

BANKS, Andrew, married Cassey Richardson on 8 Aug 1863; also see "George W. Banks," q.v. {Ref: Church Records, 1834-1903, p. 145}

BANKS, George Washington, son of Andrew and Cassey Banks, born 30 Sep 1862, baptized 28 Apr 1864. {Ref: Church Records, 1834-1903, pp. 34-35}

BANKS, Isaac Alexander, married Mary J. Washington on 27 Jun 1862. {Ref: Church Records, 1834-1903, p. 144}

BARKER, John A., married Ella C. Patterson on 18 Jun 1874. {Ref: Church Records, 1834-1903, p. 148}

BARKER, Ella C., sponsored the baptism of Ella Barker Airey on 11 Sep 1881. {Ref: Church Records, 1834-1903, p. 3}

BARNES, Elizabeth, see "Mary Garrettson," q.v.

BARNES, George W. (Mrs.), of Havre de Grace, buried 22 Jan 1857. {Ref: Church Records, 1834-1903, p. 93}

BARON, Anna Mary, buried 24 Oct 1860. {Ref: Church Records, 1834-1903, p. 93}

BARON, Catharine Ann Baron, married William Elliott on 13 Dec 1836. {Ref: Church Records, 1834-1903, p. 138}

BARRON, Albert Worrell, son of Samuel Howell and Rebecca A. Barron, born 1 Oct 1854, baptized 7 Jun 1861. {Ref: Church Records, 1834-1903, pp. 30-31}

BARRON, Lucretia C., born 12 Apr 1818, confirmed 14 May 1865, died 11 Nov 1887. {Ref: Church Records, 1834-1903, p. 294; Tombstone inscription}

BARRON, Rebecca A., confirmed 10 May 1860; also see "Albert W. Barron," q.v. {Ref: Church Records, 1834-1903, p. 294}

BARRON, Samuel H., see "Albert W. Barron," q.v.

BARTIE, William L., married Annie Lamdin on 25 Feb 1868. {Ref: Church Records, 1834-1903, p. 146}

BARTOL, Emma Augusta, daughter of Barney and Mary A. Bartol, born 12 Jul 1844, baptized 5 Oct 1856. {Ref: Church Records, 1834-1903, pp. 28-29}

BASS, Mary Eliza (colored), married George H. Read (colored) on 14 Dec 1882. {Ref: Church Records, 1834-1903, p. 150}

BATEMAN, Anna, confirmed 6 Aug 1879. {Ref: Church Records, 1834-1903, p. 298}

BAUER, Cornelia, granddaughter of James T. and Marion Ford, born 1915, died 1917. {Ref: Tombstone inscription}

BAY, John W., born 19 Jun 1842, died 28 Apr 1891. {Ref: Tombstone inscription}

BEATY, Frances, died 6 Sep 1826, age 76. {Ref: Tombstone inscription}

BECK, Harry, married Mary DeBruler on 19 May 1880. {Ref: Church Records, 1834-1903, p. 149}

BEEMAN, Florence (Miss), confirmed 10 Oct 1882. {Ref: Church Records, 1834-1903, p. 299}

BEEMAN, M. Florence, daughter of T. J. and M. L. Beeman, age 27, died 1 Sep 1886, buried 3 Sep 1886. {Ref: Church Records, 1834-1903, p. 101; Tombstone inscription}

BEEMAN, Maggie L., daughter of T. J. and M. L. Beeman, age 25, died 22 Mar 1887. {Ref: Tombstone inscription}

BEEMAN, T. J., see "M. Florence Beeman" and "Maggie L. Beeman," q.v.

BELLINGHAM, Hallie, see "Hannah Bellingham," q.v.

BELLINGHAM, Hannah, born 1834, died 1916. {Ref: Tombstone inscription}

BELLINGHAM, Hannah, daughter of William and Hannah Bellingham, died 23 Jan 1885 in her 15th year. {Ref: Tombstone inscription}. The church records indicate Hallie W. Bellingham died 22 Jan 1885, age 14 years, 3 months and 5 days]. {Ref: Church Records, 1834-1903, p. 100}

BELLINGHAM, William, son of William and Hannah Bellingham, died 5 Nov 1892, age 28. {Ref: Tombstone inscription}

BELLINGHAM, William, died 25 Jun 1895, age 65. {Ref: Church Records, 1834-1903, p. 103}

BELLOMY, Margaret, married William Spangler on 20 Nov 1889. {Ref: Church Records, 1834-1903, pp. 156-157}

BIAYS, James, see "Ann B. Hoke," q.v.

BIDDLE, Thomas A., of Spesutia Island, buried 24 Feb 1852. {Ref: Church Records, 1834-1903, p. 92}

BINKLY, ----, infant child (still born) of George and Catherine Binkly, buried 21 Oct 1897 in Lutheran Cemetery. {Ref: Church Records, 1834-1903, p. 103}

BIRCKHEAD, Sarah E., married Henry T. Martin on 4 Jun 1868. {Ref: Church Records, 1834-1903, p. 146}

BLACK, John Merryman, married Alice M. Jay on 28 May 1918. {Ref: Parish Register, 1903-1958, pp. 138-139}

BOARDLEY, Alexander (colored), son of Fanny Boardley, born -- Oct 1861, baptized 21 Jun 1865. {Ref: Church Records, 1834-1903, pp. 34-35}

BOARDLEY, George William (colored), son of Fanny Boardley, born -- Oct 1861, baptized 21 Jun 1865. {Ref: Church Records, 1834-1903, pp. 34-35}

BOARMAN, Robert R., married M. Isabel Wetheral on 15 Oct 1867 at Grace Church in Baltimore. {Ref: Church Records, 1834-1903, p. 146}

BOLTON, Frank C., confirmed 30 Sep 1876. {Ref: Church Records, 1834-1903, p. 298}

BOLTON, Ida C., confirmed 30 Sep 1876. {Ref: Church Records, 1834-1903, p. 298}

BOLTON, Lee Blacklar, son of Daniel K. and Eliza C. Bolton, born 16 Mar 1868, baptized 18 Jul 1869. {Ref: Church Records, 1834-1903, pp. 38-39}

BOND FAMILY.
The following family information was entered in the church records under the heading of "Families" circa 1893-1903, but no relationships or ages were indicated, just names. Additional information shown in parenthesis was entered subsequently in the register:
George J. Bond (removed) and Mrs. ---- [blank] Bond (removed). {Ref: Church Records, 1834-1903, p. 256}

BOND, Clara, married William Wilmer on 6 Nov 1872. {Ref: Church Records, 1834-1903, p. 148}

BOND, George James (Mr. and Mrs.), removed to Baltimore on 6 Nov 1890; also see "Bond Family," q.v. {Ref: Church Records, 1834-1903, p. 202}

BOND, Mary, sponsored the baptism of Mary G. M. Larkin on 17 May 1885; also see "Mary E. Bond" and "Thomas Bond" and "William G. Bond," q.v. {Ref: Church Records, 1834-1903, p. 5}

BOND, Mary Elizabeth, daughter of Thomas and Mary Bond, born ---- [blank] at Furnace and baptized 12 Sep 1841 in church. {Ref: Church Records, 1834-1903, pp. 20-21}

BOND, Sarah (Mrs.), born in County Wicklow, Ireland -- Jan 1793, died at Cheltonham, Pennsylvania 31 Oct 1868 in her 75th year. {Ref: Tombstone inscription}

BOND, Sarah W. Washington, married James Rhodes on 27 Dec 1856. {Ref: Church Records, 1834-1903, p. 141}

BOND, Thomas, see "Mary E. Bond" and "Thomas Bond" and "William G. Bond," q.v.

BOND, Thomas, son of Thomas and Mary Bond, born ---- [blank] at Furnace and baptized 12 Sep 1841 in church. {Ref: Church Records, 1834-1903, pp. 20-21}

BOND, William Gregory, son of Thomas and Mary Bond, born ---- [blank] at Furnace and baptized 12 Sep 1841 in church. {Ref: Church Records, 1834-1903, pp. 20-21}

BONN, Honoria Blake, married Louis T. Michael on 20 Jan 1887. {Ref: Church Records, 1834-1903, pp. 152-153}

BONN, Mary Elizabeth, married James Street Mitchell on 16 Feb 1887. {Ref: Church Records, 1834-1903, pp. 152-153}

BONN, Samuel G., sponsored the baptism of Edwin Bonn Michael on 8 Feb 1891. {Ref: Church Records, 1834-1903, p. 11}

BOOTH, Esther, daughter of Harry S. and Margaret E. Booth, age 8 weeks, private baptism on 14 Jun 1892 at home; died at age 6 months, buried 23 Oct 1892 in Lutheran Cemetery. {Ref: Church Records, 1834-1903, pp. 10-11, 102}

BOOTH, Harry S., see "Esther Booth," q.v.

BOOTH, James, see "John Booth" and "Mary E. Booth," q.v.

BOOTH, John, infant son of James and Mary H. Booth, born 4 May 1864, died 8 May 1864, buried 9 May 1864. {Ref: Church Records, 1834-1903, p. 94; Tombstone inscription}

BOOTH, Mary Emma, daughter of James and Mary Howell Booth, born 18 Mar 1861, baptized 3 Nov 1861, died 10 Sep 1864, buried 11 Sep 1864. {Ref: Church Records, 1834-1903, pp. 30-31, 94; Tombstone inscription}

BOOTH, Mary Howell, born 23 Nov 1826, died 25 Jun 1864, buried 27 Jun 1864. {Ref: Church Records, 1834-1903, p. 94; Tombstone inscription}

BOOTHE, Laurance Coal, buried 17 Sep 1864. {Ref: Church Records, 1834-1903, p. 94}

BOTTS FAMILY.
The following family information was entered in the church records under the heading of "Families" circa 1893-1903, but no relationships or ages were indicated, just names. Additional information shown in parenthesis was entered subsequently in the register:
John Botts (died 23 Jan 1896), Mrs. ---- [blank] Botts, and Miss Eliza Hattie Kimball (married Joseph Steele). {Ref: Church Records, 1834-1903, p. 257}

BOTTS, Alice A., born 21 Aug 1852, died 21 May 1920. {Ref: Tombstone inscription}

BOTTS, Elizabeth, see "William R. Botts," q.v.

BOTTS, Elizabeth J., born 8 Nov 1853, died 14 Sep 1912. {Ref: Tombstone inscription}

BOTTS, Florence D., daughter of J. and H. A. Botts, died 21 Apr 1873 in her 14th year. {Ref: Tombstone inscription}

BOTTS, Harriet A., died 4 May 1915 in her 87th year; also see "Florence D. Botts" and "John B. Botts" and "William S. Botts," q.v. {Ref: Tombstone inscription}

BOTTS, J. Wesley, see "William R. Botts," q.v.

BOTTS, John, born 1 Nov 1819, died 23 Jan 1896, buried 26 Jan 1896; also see "Botts Family" and "Hall Family," q.v. {Ref: Church Records, 1834-1903, pp. 103, 200; Tombstone inscription}

BOTTS, John B., son of J. and H. A. Botts, died 3 Nov 1865 in his 15th year. {Ref: Tombstone inscription}

BOTTS, William, confirmed 30 Sep 1876. {Ref: Church Records, 1834-1903, p. 298}

BOTTS, William Robert, son of J. Wesley and Elizabeth (Lizzie J.) Botts, born 20 Jun 1889, baptized 21 Jul 1889, died 26 Jul 1889, buried 29 Jul 1889. {Ref: Church Records, 1834-1903, pp. 8, 101; Tombstone inscription}

BOTTS, William S., son of J. and H. A. Botts, died 3 Nov 1865 in his 20th year. {Ref: Tombstone inscription}

BOWERS, Leroy, age 1 year, buried 6 Oct 1918 in Angel Hill Cemetery [in Havre de Grace]. {Ref: Parish Register, 1903-1958, p. 159}

BOWIE, Thomas F. (general), married Virginia Griffith on 24 Jul 1855. {Ref: Church Records, 1834-1903, p. 140}

BOWLYER, Charles William, married Sophia Wheeler ---- [blank, prob. January] 1872. {Ref: Church Records, 1834-1903, p. 147}

BOWMAN, ---- [blank], buried 27 Mar 1884. {Ref: Church Records, 1834-1903, p. 100}

BOWSER, George Henry, married Eliza Jane Lizby on 26 Dec 1861. {Ref: Church Records, 1834-1903, p. 143}

BOWZER, Maria, married John L. Stevenson on 24 Dec 1856. {Ref: Church Records, 1834-1903, p. 140}

BOYD, Isabella (Miss), confirmed 27 Apr 1856 at St. John's Church in Havre de Grace. {Ref: Church Records, 1834-1903, p. 297}

BOYD, Mary, buried 24 Feb 1866. {Ref: Church Records, 1834-1903, p. 94}

BOYER, Carrie (neé Watts), Methodist, confirmed 18 Jun 1916. {Ref: Parish Register, 1903-1958, pp. 88, 111}

BOYER, Henry Hanson, Methodist, confirmed 18 Jun 1916. {Ref: Parish Register, 1903-1958, pp. 88, 111}

BOYER, Oliver Porter, Methodist, confirmed 17 May 1914, married Effie Louise Nelson on 13 Nov 1920. {Ref: Parish Register, 1903-1958, pp. 88, 110, 138-139}

BOYER, Sarah S. (mother), born 5 Jul 1813, died 13 Nov 1878. {Ref: Tombstone inscription}

BRADBERRY, Mary M., wife of John T. Bradberry, age 38, died 10 Feb 1862. {Ref: Tombstone inscription}

BRADFIELD, John Henry, married Mary Susan Kimble on 10 Aug 1869. {Ref: Church Records, 1834-1903, p. 147}

BRADFORD FAMILY.
The following family information was entered in the church records under the heading of "Families" circa 1893-1903, but no relationships or ages were indicated, just names. Additional information shown in parenthesis was entered subsequently in the register:
Mr. ---- [blank] Bradford (removed), Mrs. ---- [blank] Bradford (removed), Miss Helen Nelson, and Miss Edith Nelson. {Ref: Church Records, 1834-1903, p. 252}

BRADFORD, B. (Mrs.), sponsored the baptism of Isabel Nelson on 24 Feb 1884. {Ref: Church Records, 1834-1903, p. 3}

BRADFORD, Fannie P., wife of C. N. Bradford, confirmed 10 Oct 1882, died 31 Jan 1883 in her 69th year, buried 2 Feb 1883. {Ref: Church Records, 1834-1903, p. 100, 229; Tombstone inscription}

BRANDT, Edwin (colored), married Margaret Monk (colored) on 8 Feb 1872. {Ref: Church Records, 1834-1903, p. 147}

BROCK FAMILY.
The following family information was entered in the church records under the heading of "Families" circa 1893-1903, but no relationships or ages were indicated, just names. Additional information shown in parenthesis was entered subsequently in the register:
George W. Brock (Aberdeen), Mrs. Rosa Brock (Aberdeen), Miss Iris G. Brock (Aberdeen), and George Edmund Brock (Aberdeen, removed to Buffalo, New York). {Ref: Church Records, 1834-1903, p. 258}

BROCK, George Edmund, received from St. Anne's Church in Annapolis on 30 Mar 1902 and removed to St. Paul's Church in Buffalo, New York on 27 Nov 1902; also see "Brock Family," q.v. {Ref: Church Records, 1834-1903, pp. 208-209}

BROCK, Iris G. (Miss), received from St. Anne's Church in Annapolis on 3 Aug 1902; church member in 1903 [name misspelled "Bock" in one register], later removed [date not given]; also see "Brock Family," q.v. {Ref: Church Records, 1834-1903, p. 208; Parish Register, 1903-1958, p. 106}

BROCK, Rosa (Mrs.), received from St. Anne's Parish in Annapolis on 31 Mar 1893; sponsored the baptism of Mildred Louise Morgan on 31 Jul 1897; church member in 1903 [name misspelled "Bock" in one register], later removed [date not given] also see "Brock Family," q.v. {Ref: Church Records, 1834-1903, p. 204; Parish Register, 1903-1958, p. 106}

BROOKINGS, Henry G., married Eliza P. Lamdin on 4 Dec 1867. {Ref: Church Records, 1834-1903, p. 146}

BROOKS, Laura, confirmed 3 Oct 1858. {Ref: Church Records, 1834-1903, p. 294}

BROOKS, Mary, confirmed 3 Oct 1858. {Ref: Church Records, 1834-1903, p. 294}

BROOKS, Sophia, confirmed 27 Apr 1856. {Ref: Church Records, 1834-1903, p. 297}

BROOKS, ---- (Mr.), a hand killed on R.R., buried 22 Jan 1846. [*Ed. Note:* In another Parish Register, 1696-1851, it indicates he was "a hand on the railroad, caught between the cars and instantly killed"]. {Ref: Church Records, 1834-1903, p. 91}

BROWN, Amelia (colored), married Solomon Giles (colored) on 26 Jun 1879. {Ref: Church Records, 1834-1903, p. 149}

BROWN, Belle (colored), married Jacob A. Tinson (colored) on 2 Aug 1882 at Colored M. E. Church. {Ref: Church Records, 1834-1903, p. 150}

BROWN, Billy (colored), buried 23 Oct 1870. {Ref: Church Records, 1834-1903, p. 96}

BROWN, Caroline (colored), married Levin Collins (colored) on 15 Nov 1883 at Colored M. E. Church. {Ref: Church Records, 1834-1903, p. 151}

BROWN, Carrie (Corrie) *[sic]* A., married Charles W. Pitt on 30 Dec 1880. {Ref: Church Records, 1834-1903, p. 149}

BROWN, Charles H. (colored), married Annie Winchester (colored) on 11 Jun 1868. {Ref: Church Records, 1834-1903, p. 146}

BROWN, Fenton M., eldest daughter of Jacob and Mary Brown, died 3 Apr 1879 in her 70th year. {Ref: Tombstone inscription}

BROWN, Frenetta Jane, daughter of Solomon and Semelia Brown, born 15 Aug 1861, baptized 26 Dec 1861. {Ref: Church Records, 1834-1903, pp. 30-31}

BROWN, Harriet Cassandra (servant of Mrs. Chauncey of "Primrose"), daughter of ---- [blank], born -- Jun 1827, baptized 30 Jun 1837. {Ref: Church Records, 1834-1903, pp. 18-19}

BROWN, Isaac William, son of James and Maria Brown, born 3 May 1863, baptized 14 Jul 1863. {Ref: Church Records, 1834-1903, pp. 32-33}

BROWN, J. William, married Martha C. Brown on 13 Jan 1881. {Ref: Church Records, 1834-1903, p. 149}

BROWN, Jacob, died 2 Mar 1827 (1828?), age 53 (55?) years and 1 month; also see "Mary Brown" and "Fenton Brown" and "Thomas Brown," q.v. {Ref: Tombstone inscription}

BROWN, James, see "Isaac W. Brown," q.v.

BROWN, Janetta, married Samuel Ramsy on 29 Dec 1863. {Ref: Church Records, 1834-1903, p. 145}

BROWN, Maria, see "Isaac W. Brown," q.v.

BROWN, Martha C., married J. William Brown on 13 Jan 1881. {Ref: Church Records, 1834-1903, p. 149}

BROWN, Mary, wife of Jacob Brown, died 2 Feb 1845 in her 69th year; also see "Fenton Brown" and "Thomas Brown," q.v. {Ref: Tombstone inscription}

BROWN, Mary (colored), married John Christie (colored) ---- 1877. [*Ed. Note:* The date was blank, but the marriage was listed between June and December in the register]. {Ref: Church Records, 1834-1903, p. 148}

BROWN, Mary Lizzie (colored), married Lloyd Preston (colored) ---- 1877. [*Ed. Note:* The date was blank, but the marriage was listed between June and December in the register]. {Ref: Church Records, 1834-1903, p. 148}

BROWN, Philip, married Martha Ringgold on 16 Jan 1848. [*Ed. Note:* In another Parish Register, 1696-1851, it indicates Philip T. Brown, a free man, married Martha Ringgold, a servant woman of Mr. M. Hawkins, on January 16, 1847, both "persons of color"]. {Ref: Church Records, 1834-1903, p. 139}

BROWN, Rebecca (colored), married Caleb McComas (colored) ---- 1877. [*Ed. Note:* The date was blank, but the marriage was listed between June and December in the register]. {Ref: Church Records, 1834-1903, p. 148}

BROWN, Richard A. (colored), married Sarah Wilmore (colored) on 1 Jan 1883 at Colored M. E. Church. {Ref: Church Records, 1834-1903, p. 150}

BROWN, Semelia (colored), married Philip Monk (colored) on 12 Nov 1876; also see "Frenetta Brown," q.v. {Ref: Church Records, 1834-1903, p. 148}

BROWN, Solomon, see "Frenetta Brown," q.v.

BROWN, Sophia (colored), married Stephen Stansbury (colored) on 11 May 1877. {Ref: Church Records, 1834-1903, p. 148}

BROWN, Susan (of "Primrose"), married John Luster Webster on 19 Dec 1839. {Ref: Church Records, 1834-1903, p. 138}

BROWN, Thomas, son of Jacob and Mary Brown, age 48, died 23 Mar 1858, buried 24 Mar 1858. {Ref: Church Records, 1834-1903, p. 93; Tombstone inscription}

BUCK, Charles E. (Mrs.), sponsored the baptism of Annie Taylor on 24 Jun 1883 and witnessed the baptism of Emily Augusta Michael (adult) on 17 Jun 1884. {Ref: Church Records, 1834-1903, pp. 3, 5}

BUCK, Harry Herbert, son of Rev. C. E. and E. C. Buck, born 26 Sep 1882, baptized 16 Nov 1882 (sponsors: the parents, Henrietta Shriver and C. W. Michael). {Ref: Church Records, 1834-1903, pp. 2-3}

BUCK, Mrs., sponsored the baptism of Martha Laurinda Gallup (adult) on 20 Jul 1884. {Ref: Church Records, 1834-1903, p. 5}

BUDD, Elizabeth, buried 15 Nov 1871. {Ref: Church Records, 1834-1903, p. 96}

BUDD, Milcah (Miss), buried 9 Apr 1855. {Ref: Church Records, 1834-1903, p. 92}

BUDD, Milcah, see "Eliza Lewis" and "Josias W. Lewis" and "Susan Lewis" and "John Lewis" and "Maria Ann Lewis" and "Mary M. Lewis," q.v.

BUGGY, Charles Noah, son of Robert and Lydia Buggy, born 2 Nov 1880, private baptism on 1 Nov 1881, age 11 months and 10 days, buried 6 Nov 1881 at Garrettson Chapel. {Ref: Church Records, 1834-1903, pp. 2-3, 100}

BURCH, Mary Letitia (Mrs.), age not indicated, buried 14 Mar 1916 at Loudon Park Cemetery in Baltimore. {Ref: Parish Register, 1903-1958, p. 159}

BURKITT, Lavinia, confirmed 14 May 1865. {Ref: Church Records, 1834-1903, p. 294}

BURNS, Margaret, married Thomas B. Quillan on 28 May 1912. {Ref: Parish Register, 1903-1958, pp. 138-139}

BURRELL, William Cleaver, son of Andrew J. and Mary B. Burrell, born 21 Jan 1908. {Ref: Parish Register, 1903-1958, pp. 38-39}

BURTON, William C., married Lizzie Low on 15 Jan 1889. {Ref: Church Records, 1834-1903, p. 154}

BUTLER, Mary, married James Matthews on 17 Oct 1863. {Ref: Church Records, 1834-1903, p. 145}

BUTTRICK, Winthrop Parkhurst, son of Capt. Winthrop P. and Catherine S. Buttrick, born 15 Aug 1918, baptized 19 Oct 1919 (sponsors: St. Louis Reese, Capt. Buttrick and Sydney Clark). {Ref: Parish Register, 1903-1958, pp. 34-35}

BYRD, Charles W., married Ida May Taylor on 15 Dec 1898 at "Union Farm" near Perryman. {Ref: Church Records, 1834-1903, pp. 160-161}

BYRD, I. May, sponsored the baptism of Raymond Rouse Taylor and William Henry Taylor on 26 Apr 1908. {Ref: Parish Register, 1903-1958, p. 31}

BYRD, Ida Taylor, church member in 1903; sponsored the baptism of Isabel Frances Taylor on 4 Jul 1906; removed to Baltimore [date not given]. {Ref: Parish Register, 1903-1958, p. 106}

BYRD, Mrs., sponsored the baptism of Asa Carr Taylor, John Robert Keen, III, and Ida Virginia Taylor on 1 Apr 1916; see "Taylor Family," q.v. {Ref: Parish Register, 1903-1958, p. 33}

CAGE, James Leonard, son of James Samuel and Mary Jane Cage, born 30 Dec 1868, baptized 4 Nov 1869. {Ref: Church Records, 1834-1903, pp. 38-39}

CAGE, Vertinda Elizabeth, daughter of James Samuel and Mary Jane Cage, born 24 Dec 1866, baptized 4 Nov 1869. {Ref: Church Records, 1834-1903, pp. 38-39}

CAIN (CANN?), Sallie, married Welton Curtis on 25 Sep 1879. {Ref: Church Records, 1834-1903, p. 149}

CAIN, Harriet (colored), married Benjamin Christy (colored) on 1 Nov 1888. {Ref: Church Records, 1834-1903, pp. 154-155}

CANON, John Abraham, son of John W. and Mary Canon, born 11 Sep 1842, baptized 23 Jan 1849. {Ref: Church Records, 1834-1903, pp. 22-23}

CANON, John, died 2 May 1855, age 62. {Ref: Tombstone inscription}

CANON, John William, married Mary Ann Cole on 23 Aug 1838, died 22 Dec 1856, age 42; also see "John A. Canon" and "Thomas W. Canon," q.v. {Ref: Church Records, 1834-1903, pp. 93, 138; Tombstone inscription}

CANON, Thomas William, son of John W. and Mary Canon, born 6 Jun 1848, baptized 23 Jan 1849. {Ref: Church Records, 1834-1903, pp. 22-23}

CARLISLE, J. Howard (captain and brevet major, U.S.A.), born 11 Jul 1822, died 16 Dec 1866, buried 19 Dec 1866. {Ref: Church Records, 1834-1903, p. 95; Tombstone inscription}

CAROL, Lucinda, married Benjamin Coleman on 14 Feb 1867. {Ref: Church Records, 1834-1903, p. 146}

CARR, Josiah, infant of I. and Mary(?) Carr, buried 19 Jan 1840 at "The Dairy." [*Ed. Note:* The names were entered in the register as "Josiah Carr, inft. of I. and Mary?"]. {Ref: Church Records, 1834-1903, p. 90}

CARR, Mary Elizabeth, confirmed 26 Jun 1853. {Ref: Church Records, 1834-1903, p. 296}

CARR, Sarah (colored), married William Nelson (colored) on 10 May 1877. {Ref: Church Records, 1834-1903, p. 148}

CARRY, Mary L. (colored), married John Henry Hinson (colored) on 17 Jun 1894 at "Medford" near Perryman. {Ref: Church Records, 1834-1903, pp. 158-159}

CARTER, Amanda, married Solomon Tolever on 21 Oct 1880. {Ref: Church Records, 1834-1903, p. 149}

CARTER, John Wesley (colored infant), son of ---- [blank], born ---- [blank], baptized 13 Aug 1878. {Ref: Church Records, 1834-1903, pp. 42-43}

CARTER, William (colored), married Amanda Giles (colored) ---- 1878. [Ed. Note: The date was blank, but the marriage was listed between March and June in the register]. {Ref: Church Records, 1834-1903, p. 148}

CASEY, Elizabeth (Mrs.), buried 2 Apr 1849. [Ed. Note: In another Parish Register, 1696-1851, it indicates she was about 85 years old]. {Ref: Church Records, 1834-1903, p. 91}

CATOR, George William, son of William D. and Annie E. Cator, born 27 Dec 1864, baptized 21 Aug 1865 at Bush. {Ref: Church Records, 1834-1903, pp. 34-35}

CATTLE, Margaret Grace, age 15, buried 25 Apr 1907 in Abingdon Graveyard (St. Mary's Church). {Ref: Parish Register, 1903-1958, p. 158}

CHANDLEE, Mary, wife of Benjamin Chandlee, died 6 Jan 1827, age 73. {Ref: Tombstone inscription}

CHANEY, Rebecca, buried 29 Mar 1863. {Ref: Church Records, 1834-1903, p. 94}

CHAPMAN FAMILY.
The following family information was entered in the church records under the heading of "Families" circa 1893-1903, but no relationships or ages were indicated, just names. Additional information shown in parenthesis was entered subsequently in the register:

Dr. P. Chapman, Norval P. Chapman, Charles Chapman, Mrs. Fannie C. Chapman (died, name lined out), and Pearson Chapman, Jr. (dead, 14 Apr 1898, name lined out). {Ref: Church Records, 1834-1903, p. 254}

CHAPMAN, Charles Blincoe Ward, age 18, confirmed 30 Apr 1899; church member in 1903, later removed [date not given]. {Ref: Church Records, 1834-1903, p. 302; Parish Register, 1903-1958, p. 106}

CHAPMAN, Edmonia, see "Norval P. Chapman," q.v.

CHAPMAN, Fanny C., wife of Dr. Pearson Chapman and daughter of J. G. and S. Michael, born 21 Apr 1855, died 5 Jan 1908, age 52, buried 7 Jan 1908; also see "Pearson Chapman, Jr." and "Chapman Family," q.v. {Ref: Parish Register, 1903-1958, pp. 106, 158; Tombstone inscription}

CHAPMAN, Norval (Norvell) Pearson, son of Dr. Pearson and Edmonia Chapman, born ---- [blank], baptized 2 May 1880, confirmed 9 Jun 1893; sponsored the baptism of Pearson Chapman on 18 Apr 1897; church member in 1903, later removed [date not given]; also see "Chapman Family," q.v. {Ref: Church Records, 1834-1903, pp. 13, 42-43, 301; Parish Register, 1903-1958, p. 106}

CHAPMAN, Pearson (doctor), age 75+ years, died 18 Dec 1915, buried 19 Dec 1915; also see "Fanny C. Chapman" and "Norval P. Chapman" and "Chapman Family," q.v. {Ref: Parish Register, 1903-1958, pp. 106, 159}

CHAPMAN, Pearson, M.D., married Fanny Cordelia Michael on 16 Oct 1895. {Ref: Church Records, 1834-1903, pp. 160-161}

CHAPMAN, Pearson, Jr., son of Pearson and Fanny C. Chapman, born 20 Jan 1897, baptized 18 Apr 1897 (sponsors: the parents, Norvell P. Chapman and Mrs. Mary B. Alrich); buried 16 Apr 1898, age 1 year, 2 months and 25 days; also see "Chapman Family," q.v. {Ref: Church Records, 1834-1903, pp. 12-13, 104}

CHARSHEE, Catharine Virginia, daughter of Bennett and Catherine V. Charshee, born 2 Feb 1856, baptized 22 Jun 1856. {Ref: Church Records, 1834-1903, pp. 28-29}

CHARSHEE, Corrilla Offord, daughter of Bennett and Catherine V. Charshee, born 15 May 1851, baptized 22 Jun 1856. {Ref: Church Records, 1834-1903, pp. 26-27}

CHASE, Cecilia Catharine (colored), daughter of William and Mary Chase, born 12 Nov 1898, private baptism on 17 Sep 1899 in the church rectory. {Ref: Church Records, 1834-1903, pp. 14-15}

CHASE, David Daniel (colored), son of William and Mary Chase, age 1 year and 2 months, baptized 28 Jan 1891 (sponsors: Anner M. and W. Rosalie Alrich). {Ref: Church Records, 1834-1903, pp. 10-11}

CHASE, George Robert, son of William and Mary Chase, born 14 Sep 1891, baptized 15 Sep 1892, child sick. {Ref: Church Records, 1834-1903, pp. 10-11}

CHASE, John Edward (colored), son of William and Mary Florence Chase, born 30 May 1900, baptized 7 Oct 1900 at church rectory (sponsors: William Chase and James W. Malcolm). {Ref: Church Records, 1834-1903, pp. 14-15}

CHASE, Mary F., see "John E. Chase," q.v.

CHASE, William C., married Margaret (Mary?) F. Harrison on 24 Dec 1885; see "John E. Chase," q.v. {Ref: Church Records, 1834-1903, pp. 152-153}

CHAUNCEY, Ann Eliza, died 1 Jul 1837 in her 36th year, buried 2 Jul 1837. {Ref: Church Records, 1834-1903, p. 90; Tombstone inscription}

CHAUNCEY (CHANCEY), Benjamin, died 5 Jul 1858, age 62, "fell dead in harvest field;" also see "Elizabeth Chauncey" and "S. Rebecca Chauncey," q.v. {Ref: Church Records, 1834-1903, p. 93; Tombstone inscription}

CHAUNCEY, Benjamin, buried 27 Mar 1896, age 51. {Ref: Church Records, 1834-1903, p. 103}

CHAUNCEY, Elizabeth, died 2 Feb 1845, age 69. {Ref: Tombstone inscription}

CHAUNCEY (CHANCEY), Elizabeth (Eliza Ann, Lizzie A.), daughter of Benjamin and Rebecca Chauncey, born 14 Sep 1846, baptized 6 Dec 1846, died 28 Aug 1864 in her 18th year, buried 31 Aug 1864. {Ref: Church Records, 1834-1903, pp. 22-23, 94; Tombstone inscription}

CHAUNCEY, George Henry, son of John Henry and Mary A. Chauncey, born 10 Aug 1836, baptized 21 Aug 1837. {Ref: Church Records, 1834-1903, pp. 18-19}

CHAUNCEY, John Henry, married Mary Amanda Henderson on 12 May 1835; also see "George H. Chauncey," q.v. {Ref: Church Records, 1834-1903, p. 138}

CHAUNCEY, John Henry, died 23 Aug 1837 at George Henderson's. {Ref: Church Records, 1834-1903, p. 90}

CHAUNCEY, Lizzie, see "Elizabeth Chauncey," q.v.

CHAUNCEY, Mary A., see "George H. Chauncey," q.v.

CHAUNCEY, Miranda, died 17 Oct 1834 in her 30th year. {Ref: Tombstone inscription}

CHAUNCEY, Mrs., see "Harriet C. Brown" and "James H. Ramsay" and "Susan E. Hollingsworth," q.v.

CHAUNCEY, Mrs. M. A., married Henry Nelson on 4 Apr 1839. {Ref: Church Records, 1834-1903, p. 138}

CHAUNCEY, S. Rebecca, wife of Benjamin Chauncey, died 27 Mar 1863, age 51; also see "Elizabeth Chauncey," q.v. {Ref: Tombstone inscription}

CHESLEY, Etta Harry, daughter of Rev. J. Harry and Claudia W. Chesley, born 19 Sep 1888, baptized 24 Oct 1888 by J. W. Chesley, Rector of Miles River Parish, Diocese of Easton. {Ref: Church Records, 1834-1903, p. 8}

CHESNEY, Adeline E. (Mrs.), buried 23 Jan 1855. {Ref: Church Records, 1834-1903, p. 92}

CHESNEY, Lelia Oliver, age 20, Presbyterian affiliation, confirmed 7 Dec 1902; church member in 1903, later removed [date not given]. {Ref: Church Records, 1834-1903, pp. 261, 303; Parish Register, 1903-1958, p. 106}

CHEW, Mary (Mrs. W. P.), buried 22 Apr 1837. {Ref: Church Records, 1834-1903, p. 90}

CHRISTIAN, Bettie C., confirmed 19 Feb 1874. {Ref: Church Records, 1834-1903, p. 297}

CHRISTIE, Ann, see "Jarrett Christie" and "Frank Christie" and "James M. Christie" and "Joseph R. Christie" and "Marshall R. Christie" and "Mary J. Christie," q.v.

CHRISTIE, Cornelia (Mrs.), age 80, buried 1875 or 1876 [exact date not given]. {Ref: Church Records, 1834-1903, p. 97}

CHRISTIE, Elmira (colored), married John Horsey (colored) on 25 Dec 1864. {Ref: Church Records, 1834-1903, p. 145}

CHRISTIE, Frank Amos (colored), son of Ann Christie, born 7 Dec 1856, baptized 27 Nov 1857. {Ref: Church Records, 1834-1903, pp. 28-29}

CHRISTIE, Gabriel, died 1 Apr 1808.
"Gabriel Christie, Esq., departed this life in the City of Baltimore on the 1st day of April 1808 in the 53rd year of his age. He was at decease Collector of the Port of Baltimore and had for a number of years served in the Congress of the United States as well as the Senate of the State of Maryland." {Ref: Tombstone inscription}

CHRISTIE, George, see "Marshall Christie," q.v.

CHRISTIE, Henry, buried 16 Feb 1855. {Ref: Church Records, 1834-1903, p. 92}

CHRISTIE, Jacob H. (colored), married Sabina Rumsey (colored) on 21 Dec 1865. {Ref: Church Records, 1834-1903, p. 146}

CHRISTIE, James, see "Mary J. Christie," q.v.

CHRISTIE, James McClung, son of James and Ann Christie, born 12 Mar 1849, baptized 26 Dec 1852. {Ref: Church Records, 1834-1903, pp. 24-25}

CHRISTIE, Jarrett (colored), son of Ann Christie, born 5 Nov 1858, baptized 5 Feb 1866. {Ref: Church Records, 1834-1903, pp. 36-37}

CHRISTIE, John (colored), married Mary Brown (colored) ---- 1877. [*Ed. Note:* The date was blank, but the marriage was listed between June and December in the register]. {Ref: Church Records, 1834-1903, p. 148}

CHRISTIE, Joseph H., married Mary A. Dallam on 11 Jun 1878. {Ref: Church Records, 1834-1903, p. 148}

CHRISTIE, Joseph Robert, son of James and Ann Christie, born 6 Aug 1852, baptized 26 Dec 1852, buried 28 Jan 1853. {Ref: Church Records, 1834-1903, pp. 24-25, 92}

CHRISTIE, Louisa (colored), married Isaac J. Monk (colored) on 21 Jul 1895. {Ref: Church Records, 1834-1903, pp. 160-161}

CHRISTIE, Margaret, married Henry S. J. McClay on 31 Aug 1854. {Ref: Church Records, 1834-1903, p. 140}

CHRISTIE, Marshall Roosevelt (colored), son of George H. and Annie E. Christie, born 11 Feb 1902, baptized 26 Aug 1902 (sick) at the church rectory (sponsors: the parents). {Ref: Church Records, 1834-1903, pp. 14-15}

CHRISTIE, Martha (colored), married Alexander Garrettson (colored) on 15 Jan 1891. {Ref: Church Records, 1834-1903, pp. 156-157}

CHRISTIE, Mary E. (colored), married John Webster (colored) ---- 1877. [Ed. Note: The date was blank, but the marriage was listed between June and December in the register]. {Ref: Church Records, 1834-1903, p. 148}

CHRISTIE, Mary Josephine, daughter of James and Ann Christie, born 11 Sep 1846, baptized 25 Oct 1846. {Ref: Church Records, 1834-1903, pp. 22-23}

CHRISTIE, Priscilla C., married John Sidney Hall on 19 Feb 1856. {Ref: Church Records, 1834-1903, p. 140}

CHRISTIE, Sarah, married Frank Johnson on 28 Dec 1861. {Ref: Church Records, 1834-1903, p. 144}

CHRISTY, Benjamin (colored), married Harriet Cain (colored) on 1 Nov 1888. {Ref: Church Records, 1834-1903, p. 154}

CHURCHILL, Fannie E. (colored), married John T. Pitt (colored) on 9 Feb 1882. {Ref: Church Records, 1834-1903, p. 150}

CLARK FAMILY.
The following family information was entered in the church records under the heading of "Families" circa 1893-1903, but no relationships or ages were indicated, just names:
Mrs. Chapman S. Clark, Margaret Clark, Eleanor Clark, Lawrence Clark, and Chapman S. Clark, Jr. {Ref: Church Records, 1834-1903, p. 255}

CLARK, Albert (colored), married Mary Ozburn (colored) on 30 Dec 1865; also see "John H. Clark" and "Thomas E. Clark," q.v. {Ref: Church Records, 1834-1903, p. 146}

CLARK, Calvin, married Dinah Dennison on 21 Feb 1861. {Ref: Church Records, 1834-1903, p. 143}

CLARK, Chapman (Mr.), sponsored the baptism of Nannie Moore Smith on 10 Jul 1892. {Ref: Church Records, 1834-1903, p. 11}

CLARK, Chapman Stuart, son of Chapman S. and Nannie M. Clark, born 24 Dec 1903, baptized 11 Sep 1910 (sponsors: Margaret B. Clark, Phillips M. Hall and John Dowell Smith); also see "Clark Family," q.v. {Ref: Parish Register, 1903-1958, pp. 30-31}

CLARK, Dinah (colored), married Jacob Rice (colored) on 27 Dec 1883. {Ref: Church Records, 1834-1903, p. 151}

CLARK, Eleanor Donnell, confirmed 10 Nov 1912; also see "Clark Family," q.v. {Ref: Parish Register, 1903-1958, pp. 88, 110}

CLARK, Jacob Henry (colored), son of Albert and Mary Clark, born 12 Jun 1866, baptized 15 Aug 1866. {Ref: Church Records, 1834-1903, pp. 36-37}

CLARK, John Alexander, son of William R. and Sarah Ann Clark, born 29 Nov 1853, baptized 4 Sep 1859. {Ref: Church Records, 1834-1903, pp. 30-31}

CLARK, Katherine Moore, confirmed 13 Jun 1915, later noted as "living near Annapolis" [date not given]. {Ref: Parish Register, 1903-1958, pp. 88, 111}

CLARK, Lawrence, see "Clark Family," q.v.

CLARK, Margaret Baldwin, sponsored the baptism of Chapman Stuart Clark on 11 Sep 1910; confirmed 10 Nov 1912; also see "Clark Family," q.v. {Ref: Parish Register, 1903-1958, pp. 31, 88, 110}

CLARK, Mary, see "Jacob H. Clark" and "Thomas E. Clark," q.v.

CLARK, Mary Ann, married Joseph Frisby on 28 Aug 1859. {Ref: Church Records, 1834-1903, p. 142}

CLARK, Mrs., of Bush River Neck, buried 20 Dec 1880. {Ref: Church Records, 1834-1903, p. 98}

CLARK, Nannie, see "Chapman S. Clark," q.v.

CLARK, Samuel (colored), married Ellen Anderson (colored) on 6 Oct 1870. {Ref: Church Records, 1834-1903, p. 147}

CLARK, Sarah Ann, see "John A. Clark," q.v.

CLARK, Sarah Elizabeth, daughter of William R. and Sarah Ann Clark, born 18 May 1856, baptized 4 Sep 1859. {Ref: Church Records, 1834-1903, pp. 30-31}

CLARK, Susannah Rebecca, daughter of William R. and Sarah Ann Clark, born 26 Jul 1850, baptized 4 Sep 1859. {Ref: Church Records, 1834-1903, pp. 30-31}

CLARK, Sydney, sponsored the baptism of Winthrop Parkhurst Buttrick on 19 Oct 1919. {Ref: Parish Register, 1903-1958, pp. 34-35}

CLARK, Sydney Peyton, confirmed 13 Jun 1915. {Ref: Parish Register, 1903-1958, pp. 88, 111}

CLARK, Thomas Edward (colored), son of Albert and Mary Clark, born 15 Sep 1865, baptized 15 Aug 1866. {Ref: Church Records, 1834-1903, pp. 36-37}

CLARK, William (captain), buried 10 Aug 1864. {Ref: Church Records, 1834-1903, p. 94}

CLARK, William (colored), married Charlotte Rice (colored) on 5 Dec 1867. {Ref: Church Records, 1834-1903, p. 146}

CLARK, William R., see "John A. Clark" and "Sarah E. Clark" and "Susannah R. Clark," q.v.

CLARKE, Frances T. (Mrs.), sponsored the baptisms of Thomas Hartley Marshall, Jr. on 26 Dec 1914 and Louise Trezevant Wigfall Marshall on 12 Sep 1916. {Ref: Parish Register, 1903-1958, p. 33}

CLAY, James Alexander, son of Joseph M. and Louisa Clay, born 20 Dec 1861, baptized 27 Aug 1865 at home. {Ref: Church Records, 1834-1903, pp. 34-35}

CLAY, Joseph M., married Louisa Wilson on 1 Jul 1855 and buried on 23 Feb 1871; also see "Thomas W. Glass," q.v. {Ref: Church Records, 1834-1903, pp. 96, 140}

CLAY, Josephine (Josaphine), daughter of Joseph M. and Louisa Clay, born 16 Apr 1858, baptized 27 Aug 1865 at home, confirmed 9 Feb 1872. {Ref: Church Records, 1834-1903, pp. 34-35, 297}

CLAY, Louisa, see "James A. Clay" and "Josephine Clay" and "Mary Ann Clay" and Sarah Jane Clay" and "William H. Clay," q.v.

CLAY, Mary Ann, daughter of Joseph M. and Louisa Clay, born 20 Nov 1864, baptized 27 Aug 1865 at home. {Ref: Church Records, 1834-1903, pp. 34-35}

CLAY, Sarah (Miss), buried 1875 or 1876 [exact date not given]. {Ref: Church Records, 1834-1903, p. 97}

CLAY, Sarah Jane, daughter of Joseph M. and Louisa Clay, born 11 Jun 1856, baptized 24 Sep 1857, confirmed 9 Feb 1872. {Ref: Church Records, 1834-1903, pp. 29-29, 297}

CLAY, William Henry, son of Joseph M. and Louisa Clay, born 2 May 1860, baptized 27 Aug 1865 at home. {Ref: Church Records, 1834-1903, pp. 34-35}

CLOMAN, Anna Elizabeth, confirmed 9 Dec 1906, later removed [date not given]. {Ref: Parish Register, 1903-1958, p. 87, 109}

COALE, Isaac Webster, "for Churchville," confirmed 13 Jun 1915. {Ref: Parish Register, 1903-1958, p. 88}

COALE, Susan (Mrs.), buried 20 Nov 1857. {Ref: Church Records, 1834-1903, p. 93}

COBOURN, Angeline Taylor, daughter of Hiram and Mary Cobourn, born 8 May 1857, baptized 1 May 1861. {Ref: Church Records, 1834-1903, pp. 30-31}

COBOURN, Benjamin Huntington, son of Hiram and Mary Cobourn, born 24 Dec 1854, baptized 1 May 1861. {Ref: Church Records, 1834-1903, pp. 30-31}

COBOURN, Hiram Cloud Gorby, son of Hiram and Mary Cobourn, born 26 Mar 1851, baptized 1 May 1861. {Ref: Church Records, 1834-1903, pp. 30-31}

COBOURN, Irene Elizabeth, daughter of Hiram and Mary Cobourn, born 8 May 1857, baptized 1 May 1861. {Ref: Church Records, 1834-1903, pp. 30-31}

COBOURN, Mary Josephine, daughter of Hiram and Mary Cobourn, born 21 Jan 1847, baptized 1 May 1861. {Ref: Church Records, 1834-1903, pp. 30-31}

COBOURN, Rachel McClure, married William Richardson on 1 May 1861. {Ref: Church Records, 1834-1903, p. 143}

COBOURN, Samuel McClure Norton, son of Hiram and Mary Cobourn, born 22 Jun 1844, baptized 1 May 1861. {Ref: Church Records, 1834-1903, pp. 30-31}

COCHRAN, J. H., M.D., married Ida Morean on 28 Nov 1888 at the residence of A. C. Morean. {Ref: Church Records, 1834-1903, p. 154}

COCKEY(?), E. M. (Mrs.), sponsored the baptism of Mary Virginia Taylor on 26 Nov 1914. {Ref: Parish Register, 1903-1958, p. 33}

COE, Mrs., buried 28 May 1871 in Philadelphia. {Ref: Church Records, 1834-1903, p. 96}

COLBURN, James Lawrence, born 10 Dec 1852, died 16 Sep 1864. {Ref: Tombstone inscription}

COLE FAMILY.

The following family information was entered in the church records under the heading of "Families" circa 1893-1903, but no relationships or ages were indicated, just names. Additional information shown in parenthesis was entered subsequently in the register:
Cornelius Cole, Mrs. Sarah Cole, Sarah Cole (name lined out), Miss F. May Cole, and Sarah Elizabeth Cole. {Ref: Church Records, 1834-1903, p. 253}

COLE, Abraham, born 12 Apr 1809, died 29 Apr 1890, buried 1 May 1890; also see "Sarah E. Cole," q.v. {Ref: Church Records, 1834-1903, p. 101; Tombstone inscription}

COLE, C., sponsored the baptism of Charles Wesley Michael on 6 Jul 1884. {Ref: Church Records, 1834-1903, p. 5}

COLE, Cornelius, confirmed 19 Feb 1878; sponsored the baptism of Norvell Chapman Taylor on 22 Nov 1891; church member in 1903; sponsored the baptisms of Douglas Elliott Kennedy, Jr. on 2 Sep 1917 and Herbert Malcolm Owens on 14 Oct 1917; removed to Baltimore in 1917; also see "Sarah E. Cole" and "Cole Family," q.v. {Ref: Church Records, 1834-1903, pp. 11, 298; Parish Register, 1903-1958, pp. 33, 106}

COLE, Cornelius B., died 6 Nov 1894, age 71. {Ref: Tombstone inscription}

COLE, F. May, confirmed 30 Sep 1876; sponsored the baptisms of Sarah Elizabeth Cole on 12 Oct 1890 and Louise Raymond Pentz on 4 Oct 1903; church member in 1903, removed to Baltimore in 1917; also see "Cole Family," q.v. {Ref: Church Records, 1834-1903, pp. 11, 17, 298; Parish Register, 1903-1958, p. 106}

COLE, Fannie (Miss), sponsored the baptism of Herbert Harlan Michael on 11 Sep 1881. {Ref: Church Records, 1834-1903, p. 3}

COLE, Fannie Nelson, confirmed 14 Mar 1871. {Ref: Church Records, 1834-1903, p. 297}

COLE, Harriet (slave of Garrett and Elizabeth Nelson), born 14 Jan 1832, baptized 13 Aug 1838. {Ref: Church Records, 1834-1903, pp. 18-19}

COLE, John, sponsored the baptism of Mary Frances Noble, James Noble, William Henry Noble and John Thomas Noble on 21 Jan 1841. {Ref: Church Records, 1834-1903, pp. 20-21}

COLE, Mary Ann, married John William Canon on 23 Aug 1838. {Ref: Church Records, 1834-1903, p. 138}

COLE, Sallie Cordelia (Mrs.), confirmed 9 Oct 1887. {Ref: Church Records, 1834-1903, p. 300}

COLE, Sarah, see "Cole Family," q.v.

COLE, Sarah E., wife of Abraham Cole, born 18 Sep 1821, died 16 Mar 1890. {Ref: Tombstone inscription}

COLE, Sarah E., wife of Cornelius Cole, born 17 Aug 1831, died 28 Jun 1878. {Ref: Tombstone inscription}

COLE, Sarah Elizabeth, confirmed 15 Nov 1885, church member in 1903, [removed to] "Hamilton, Baltimore, 1917." {Ref: Church Records, 1834-1903, p. 299; Parish Register, 1903-1958, p. 107}

COLE, Sarah Elizabeth, daughter of Cornelius and Sarah C. Cole, born 6 Aug 1890, baptized 12 Oct 1890 (sponsors: the parents and Miss F. May Cole), confirmed 25 Apr 1908, married Douglas Elliott Kennedy on 13 Jun 1914. {Ref: Church Records, 1834-1903, pp. 10-11; Parish Register, 1903-1958, pp. 87, 109, 138-139}

COLE, Susanna, married George Walker, Jr. on 2 Nov 1837. {Ref: Church Records, 1834-1903, p. 138}

COLEMAN, Benjamin, married Lucinda Carol on 14 Feb 1867. {Ref: Church Records, 1834-1903, p. 146}

COLLINS, Carrie (colored), married John Lewis Pinion (colored) on 24 Jan 1884 at the residence of Mr. John H. Michael in Perryman. {Ref: Church Records, 1834-1903, p. 151}

COLLINS, Levin (colored), married Caroline Brown (colored) on 15 Nov 1883 at Colored M. E. Church. {Ref: Church Records, 1834-1903, p. 151}

COLLINS, Levin H. (colored), married Mary Jane Welch (colored) on 8 Dec 1864. {Ref: Church Records, 1834-1903, p. 145}

CONRAD, Andrew, see "William H. Conrad," q.v.

CONRAD, Francisco Louisa, married Charles Henry Eden on 10 Feb 1891. {Ref: Church Records, 1834-1903, pp. 156-157}

CONRAD, William Henry, son of Andrew and Elizabeth Conrad, born 30 Jun 1880, private baptism on 20 Jun 1882. {Ref: Church Records, 1834-1903, pp. 2-3}

COOK, Charles, see "William F. Cook," q.v.

COOK, Elizabeth, see "Mary Sutor," q.v.

COOK, Ellennora, of Havre de Grace ("parents not known"), born 30 Jan 1856, baptized 9 Mar 1856, buried 9 Aug 1856. {Ref: Church Records, 1834-1903, pp. 26-27, 92}

COOK, Henrietta, see "Mary Sutor," q.v.

COOK, Susanna E., married Franklin D. Pearson on 14 Dec 1858. {Ref: Church Records, 1834-1903, p. 142}

COOK, Susannah S., born 1803, died 1905. {Ref: Tombstone inscription}

COOK, Thomas, see "Mary Sutor," q.v.

COOK, William Frederick, son of Charles and Catharine Cook, born 25 Mar 1856, baptized 30 Nov 1856. {Ref: Church Records, 1834-1903, pp. 28-29}

COOLEY, Catharine Elliott (Miss), confirmed 20 Nov 1889, married Benedict Keen Michael on 6 Jun 1894. {Ref: Church Records, 1834-1903, pp. 158-159, 301}

COOLEY(?), E. M. (Mrs.), sponsored the baptism of Mary Virginia Taylor on 26 Nov 1914. {Ref: Parish Register, 1903-1958, p. 33}

COOLEY, Kate E., see "Hollis Family," q.v.

COOPER, James, buried 27 Sep 1894, age 57. {Ref: Church Records, 1834-1903, p. 102}

COOPER, James (colored), married Martha Murphy (colored) on 2 Jun 1870. {Ref: Church Records, 1834-1903, p. 147}

COOPER, Susie Virginia, daughter of James and Martin G. Cooper, born 16 Apr 1871, baptized 18 Jun 1871. {Ref: Church Records, 1834-1903, pp. 38-39}

COOPER, ----, see "Mabel S. Osborn," q.v.

CORD, John, married Ellen Deaver on 12 Mar 1857. {Ref: Church Records, 1834-1903, p. 141}

CORNELL, William, Methodist, confirmed 17 May 1914, later removed to Eastern Shore [date not given]. {Ref: Parish Register, 1903-1958, pp. 88, 110}

COURTENEY, Abraham, married Alice Ann Wilmer on 7 Dec 1880. {Ref: Church Records, 1834-1903, p. 149}

COVER, Ira J., buried 19 Sep 1898, age 5½ months. {Ref: Church Records, 1834-1903, p. 104}

COWAN, John, sponsored the baptism of Sarah Elizabeth Cowan on 1 Aug 1841; died 12 Jan 1857, age 53, buried 13 Jan 1857; also see "John Cowen" and "Priscilla A. Cowan," q.v. {Ref: Church Records, 1834-1903, pp. 21, 93; Tombstone inscription}

COWAN, Mary Veazey (Veasey), daughter of John and Priscilla Ann Cowan, born 22 Dec 1845, baptized 6 Dec 1846, buried 20 Sep 1847. {Ref: Church Records, 1834-1903, pp. 22-23, 91}

COWAN, Priscilla A., wife of John Cowan, sponsored the baptism of George Anna Nelson on 1 Aug 1841; died 17 Jun 1877, age 66. {Ref: Church Records, 1834-1903, pp. 20-21; Tombstone inscription}

COWAN, Sarah Elizabeth, daughter of John and Priscilla Ann Cowan, born 6 Jan 1840, baptized 1 Aug 1841 (sponsors: the parents, Sarah Henderson, and J. Cowan. {Ref: Church Records, 1834-1903, pp. 20-21}

COWEN, John, married Priscilla Ann Henderson (of Spesutia) on 16 Jan 1840. {Ref: Church Records, 1834-1903, p. 138}

COX, Belle E., married Walter M. H. Palmer on 9 Sep 1869. {Ref: Church Records, 1834-1903, p. 147}

CRAMPTON, Annie Franklin, daughter of Rev. Savington W. and Isabella Crampton, born 21 Jun 1866, baptized 23 Sep 1866 at Woodlawn. {Ref: Church Records, 1834-1903, pp. 36-37}

CRAMPTON, Isabella (neé Perryman), wife of Rev. Savington W. Crampton, born 24 Jul 1841, died 2 Jun 1919, age 79 [sic], buried 3 Jun 1919. {Ref: Parish Register, 1903-1958, p. 159; Tombstone inscription}

CRAMPTON, Isabella (Isabel), daughter of Rev. Savington W. and Isabella (Belle) Crampton, born 9 Mar 1861, baptized 14 Jun 1861, died 3 Jan 1917, age 55 [sic], buried 5 Jan 1917. {Ref: Church Records, 1834-1903, pp. 30-31; Parish Register, 1903-1958, p. 159; Tombstone inscription}

CRAMPTON, Mary, daughter of Rev. Savington W. and Isabella Crampton, born 24 Apr 1859, baptized 10 Aug 1859, died 18 Dec 1919, age 61 [sic], buried 20 Dec 1919. {Ref: Church Records, 1834-1903, pp. 28-29; Parish Register, 1903-1958, p. 160; Tombstone inscription}

CRAMPTON, Oscar Philpott, born 4 Jan 1829, died 9 Mar 1913, age 85 [sic], buried 11 Mar 1913. {Ref: Parish Register, 1903-1958, p. 158; Tombstone inscription}

CRAMPTON, Savington Warren (priest), born 27 Sep 1810, married Belle Perryman on 2 Feb 1858, and died 19 Jan 1898; also see "Isabella Crampton," q.v. {Ref: Church Records, 1834-1903, p. 141; Tombstone inscription). The following was recorded in the church register:
"It seems fitting that the burial of The Rev. Savington Warren Crampton should be recorded in this Book, which contains the record of his Rectorship of St.

George's Parish from 1845 to 1872, 27 years. He died of paralysis in Baltimore on Wednesday, January 19, 1898, and was buried in Spesutia Cemetery on Friday, January 21st, aged 87 years. W. A. Alrich, Rector of St. George's Parish." {Ref: Church Records, 1834-1903, p. 98). The following was recorded subsequently: "The Rev. Savington Warren Crampton, age 87, for 27 years Rector of St. George's Parish from Nov. 1, 1845 to Sept., 1872. He died in Baltimore on Wednesday, January 19th of paralysis. Under his Rectorship the present church building was erected. He was of blameless life, and faithfully fulfilled the sacred duties of his calling. A man full of the Holy Ghost, and of faith. He was laid to rest in old Spesutiae Cemetary, in the spot which he had selected, Friday, January 21, 1898." {Ref: Church Records, 1834-1903, p. 102}

CRAMPTON, Warren Johnson, son of Rev. Savington W. and Isabella (Belle) Crampton, born 18 Dec 1868, baptized 27 Jan 1869, died 15 Sep 1870 of scarlet fever. {Ref: Church Records, 1834-1903, pp. 38-39, 96; Tombstone inscription}

CRONIN FAMILY.
The following family information was entered in the church records under the heading of "Families" circa 1893-1903, but no relationships or ages were indicated, just names:
Robert Clinton Cronin, Mrs. Mary C. Cronin, E. Lee Cronin, and Robert Clinton Cronin, Jr. {Ref: Church Records, 1834-1903, p. 254}

CRONIN, Clinton, married Mollie C. Gallup on 8 Jan 1885. {Ref: Church Records, 1834-1903, pp. 152-153}

CRONIN, Edgar Lee, son of Clinton and Mollie Cronin, born 28 Nov 1885, baptized 31 Oct 1886; also see "Cronin Family," q.v. {Ref: Church Records, 1834-1903, p. 6}

CRONIN, Mary C., sponsored the baptism of Flora Michael Gallup on 9 Oct 1898; also see "Cronin Family," q.v. {Ref: Church Records, 1834-1903, p. 13}

CRONIN, Mollie, see "Edgar L. Cronin," q.v.

CRONIN, Robert Clinton (Mr.), confirmed 9 Jun 1893; sponsored the baptism of John Randolph Denham on 30 Apr 1905 and James Llewellyn Owens on 1 Aug 1915; also see "Cronin Family," q.v. {Ref: Church Records, 1834-1903, p. 301; Parish Register, 1903-1958, pp. 31, 33}

CRONIN, Robert Clinton, Jr., son of Robert Clinton and Mary C. Cronin, born 9 Oct 1894, baptized 24 Feb 1895 (sponsors: the parents and Miss Isabella O'Brien), confirmed 21 Nov 1909; also see "Cronin Family," q.v. {Ref: Church Records, 1834-1903, pp. 12-13; Parish Register, 1903-1958, pp. 87, 109}

CRONIN, William Thomas, buried 11 Dec 1891, age 65(?). [*Ed. Note:* His age was written as such in the register, but in a different handwriting]. {Ref: Church Records, 1834-1903, p. 102}

CROSEN, John (colored), married Sidney Steward (colored) on 19 Aug 1869. {Ref: Church Records, 1834-1903, p. 147}

CRUIKSHANK, Lucy Calvert, confirmed 25 Apr 1908. {Ref: Parish Register, 1903-1958, pp. 87, 109}

CULLUM FAMILY.
The following family information was entered in the church records under the heading of "Families" circa 1893-1903, but no relationships or ages were indicated, just names. Additional information shown in parenthesis was entered subsequently in the register:
Vinton Cullum (near Aberdeen), Mrs. Margaret Cullum, Bessie Cullum, Lily Isabel Cullum, Edward Alfred Cullum, and Edna Matilda Cullum. {Ref: Church Records, 1834-1903, p. 261}

CULLUM, Amos Franklin, son of Jesse J. and Martha S. Cullum, born 12 Nov 1884, private baptism on 14 Jun 1885. {Ref: Church Records, 1834-1903, pp. 4-5}

CULLUM, Bessie, see "Cullum Family," q.v.

CULLUM, Dolly May, daughter of Samuel Wesley and Effie Cullum, born 17 Jul 1900, baptized 21 Sep 1902 (sponsors: Mrs. Florence O. Baldwin and Miss Emma J. Moulsdale). {Ref: Church Records, 1834-1903, pp. 14-15}

CULLUM, Edna Matilda (twin of Edward), daughter of Joseph Vinton and Margaret B. Cullum, born 11 Jan 1903, baptized 26 Apr 1903 (sponsors: Phillips M. Hall, Mrs. Matilda C. Hall and Mrs. Florence C. Baldwin); also see "Cullum Family," q.v. {Ref: Church Records, 1834-1903, pp. 16-17}

CULLUM, Edward Alfred (twin of Edna), son of Joseph Vinton and Margaret B. Cullum, born 11 Jan 1903, baptized 26 Apr 1903 (sponsors: Phillips M. Hall, Mrs. Matilda C. Hall and Mrs. Florence C. Baldwin); also see "Cullum Family," q.v. {Ref: Church Records, 1834-1903, pp. 16-17}

CULLUM, Effie, see "Dolly May Cullum" and "Grace A. Cullum" and "Hazel V. Cullum" and "Mollie C. Cullum" and "Raymond F. Cullum," q.v.

CULLUM, George, married Minnie Thompson on 31 May 1904 in the church rectory. {Ref: Parish Register, 1903-1958, pp. 138-139}

CULLUM, Grace Alberta, daughter of Samuel and Effie Cullum, born 13 Jul 1909, baptized 5 Sep 1909 in the church rectory (sponsors: the parents), "ill, died" [no date given]. {Ref: Parish Register, 1903-1958, pp. 30-31}

CULLUM, Harry William, son of Harry W. and Sarah Jane Cullum, born 6 Jun 1915, private baptism on 13 Aug 1915 near Perryman (sponsors: the parents). {Ref: Parish Register, 1903-1958, pp. 32-33}

CULLUM, Hazel Virginia, daughter of Samuel W. and Effie Cullum, born 10 Jun 1896, baptized 7 Jun 1898 (sponsor: the mother), confirmed 21 Nov 1909, later removed [date not given]. {Ref: Church Records, 1834-1903, pp. 12-13; Parish Register, 1903-1958, pp. 87, 109}

CULLUM, Jesse, see "Amos F. Cullum," q.v.

CULLUM, Joseph, see "Edna M. Cullum" and "Edward A. Cullum" and "Lily I. Cullum" and "Mary E. Cullum," q.v.

CULLUM, Lily Isabel, daughter of Joseph Vinton and Margaret B. Cullum, born 22 Apr 1899, baptized 8 Sep 1901 (sponsors: the mother, Miss Martha P. Hall and Mr. James W. Malcolm); also see "Cullum Family," q.v. {Ref: Church Records, 1834-1903, pp. 14-15}

CULLUM, Margaret, see "Edna M. Cullum" and "Edward A. Cullum" and "Lily I. Cullum" and "Mary E. Cullum" and "Cullum Family," q.v.

CULLUM, Margaret B. (Mrs.), sponsored the baptism of Wilford Jennings Bryan Denham on 10 Oct 1902. {Ref: Church Records, 1834-1903, p. 15}

CULLUM, Mary Edith, daughter of Joseph Vinton and Margaret B. Cullum, born 22 Jul 1901, baptized 8 Sep 1901 (sponsors: the mother, Miss Martha P. Hall and Mr. James W. Malcolm). {Ref: Church Records, 1834-1903, pp. 14-15}

CULLUM, Mollie Catherine, daughter of Samuel and Effie Cullum, born 19 Sep 1906, private baptism on 17 Feb 1907 (ill). {Ref: Parish Register, 1903-1958, pp. 30-31}

CULLUM, Nora Mary, daughter of Harry W. and Sarah Jane Cullum, born 12 May 1914, private baptism on 13 Aug 1915 near Perryman (sponsors: the parents). {Ref: Parish Register, 1903-1958, pp. 32-33}

CULLUM, Raymond Franklin, son of Samuel and Effie Cullum, born 27 Jan 1912, private baptism on 9 Oct 1912 at Perryman (ill). {Ref: Parish Register, 1903-1958, pp. 30-31}

CULLUM, Samuel, see "Dolly May Cullum" and "Grace A. Cullum" and "Hazel V. Cullum" and "Mollie C. Cullum" and "Raymond F. Cullum," q.v.

CULLUM, Sarah, see "Harry W. Cullum" and "Nora M. Cullum," q.v.

CULLUM, Vinton, see "Cullum Family," q.v.

CUMMINS, Sophia, confirmed 26 Jun 1853. {Ref: Church Records, 1834-1903, p. 296}

CURTIS, Harriet Ellen (colored), married Charles Jarret (colored) on 26 Apr 1867. {Ref: Church Records, 1834-1903, p. 146}

CURTIS, Mary C., married William Henry Williams on 23 May 1861. {Ref: Church Records, 1834-1903, p. 143}

CURTIS, Welton, married Amy Rumsey on 18 May 1862. {Ref: Church Records, 1834-1903, p. 144}

CURTIS, Welton, married Sallie Cain (Cann?) on 25 Sep 1879. {Ref: Church Records, 1834-1903, p. 149}

DALLAM, Alfred Rush, son of John Paca and Mary A. G. Dallam, born 10 Oct 1869, baptized 10 May 1870. {Ref: Church Records, 1834-1903, pp. 38-39}

DALLAM, Benjamin Rush, son of Dr. William Dallam, age 46, died 8 Nov 1866 of dysentery. {Ref: Church Records, 1834-1903, p. 95}

DALLAM, Caroline Elizabeth Bayne, daughter of John Paca and Mary Dallam, born 8 Jan 1865, baptized 28 Apr 1865, died 21 Jan 1871, buried 22 Jan 1871. {Ref: Church Records, 1834-1903, pp. 34-35, 96; Tombstone inscription}

DALLAM, Doctor, see "John L. Rhodes," q.v.

DALLAM, Edward, died in 1874 [exact date not given]. {Ref: Church Records, 1834-1903, p. 97}

DALLAM, Elizabeth (colored), married Peter Pitt (colored) on 11 Dec 1885. {Ref: Church Records, 1834-1903, pp. 152-153}

DALLAM, Ella (colored), married Lloyd Rice (colored) on 22 Dec 1887. {Ref: Church Records, 1834-1903, pp. 154-155}

DALLAM, Jacob, married Mary Rumsey on 15 Oct 1863. {Ref: Church Records, 1834-1903, p. 145}

DALLAM, John Paca, confirmed 26 Jun 1853; also see "Benjamin R. Dallam" and "Caroline E. B. Dallam" and "Mary G. Dallam," q.v. {Ref: Church Records, 1834-1903, p. 296}

DALLAM, John Paca, son of John Paca and Mary G. Dallam. [*Ed. Note:* No date of birth or baptism was given, but the baptism was listed among several others in the register between 1872 and 1876]. {Ref: Church Records, 1834-1903, pp. 40-41}

DALLAM, Mary A., married Joseph H. Christie on 11 Jun 1878. {Ref: Church Records, 1834-1903, p. 148}

DALLAM, Mary G., see "Benjamin R. Dallam" and "Caroline E. B. Dallam" and "John P. Dallam" and "Mary G. Dallam," q.v.

DALLAM, Mary Goldsborough, daughter of John Paca and Mary G. Dallam. [*Ed. Note:* No date of birth or baptism was given, but the baptism was listed among several others in the register between 1872 and 1876]. {Ref: Church Records, 1834-1903, pp. 40-41}

DALLAM, Robert, married Nancy Rice on 2 Jan 1858. {Ref: Church Records, 1834-1903, p. 141}

DALLAM, Robert Lee, son of John Paca and Mary Dallam, born 10 Oct 1863, baptized 21 Jan 1864. {Ref: Church Records, 1834-1903, pp. 34-35}

DALLAM, Sarah C. (colored), married Kane Ranson (colored) on 17 Oct 1867. {Ref: Church Records, 1834-1903, p. 146}

DALLAM, Thomas Jones, born -- Jul 1803, died -- Jun 1868. {Ref: Tombstone inscription}

DASHIELD, Mary Elizabeth (Mrs.), sponsored the baptism of Helen Elizabeth Russell on 12 Apr 1903. {Ref: Church Records, 1834-1903, p. 17}

DAVIDGE, Helen, confirmed 26 Jun 1853. {Ref: Church Records, 1834-1903, p. 296}

DAVIDGE, Mrs. Dr. (mistress), sponsored the baptism of Lewis Richardson (slave) at "The Dairy" on 9 Mar 1836. {Ref: Church Records, 1834-1903, p. 17}

DAVIDGE, Rebecca T., married John L. Dunkel [of Baltimore] on 4 Nov 1847. {Ref: Church Records, 1834-1903, p. 139}

DAVIS FAMILY.
The following family information was entered in the church records under the heading of "Families" circa 1893-1903, but no relationships or ages were indicated, just names. Additional information shown in parenthesis was entered subsequently in the register:
S. Griffith Davis, Mrs. S. G. Davis, Mrs. Fannie Davis (died 18 Nov 1898), Mrs. Mary H. Davis Hopper (removed to Mobile), Miss Fannie C. Davis (married Dr. Wilson), Miss Martha M. Davis (died 7 May 1895), S. G. Davis, Jr. (removed), Septimus Davis, and Boudinot Davis. {Ref: Church Records, 1834-1903, p. 250}

DAVIS, A., see "Alice J. Davis" and "Annie E. G. Davis," q.v.,

DAVIS, Abraham (colored), married Mary L. Lee (colored) on 1 Jun 1867. {Ref: Church Records, 1834-1903, p. 146}

DAVIS, Agnes Jane (adult), daughter of Mr. Davis of Alabama, born ---- [blank], baptized 4 Sep 1859. {Ref: Church Records, 1834-1903, pp. 30-31}

DAVIS, Albert, born 1809, died 1886; sponsored the baptism of Sarah Bias Griffith on 29 Jan 1841; buried 11 Sep 1886; also see "Ellen Richardson," q.v. {Ref: Church Records, 1834-1903, pp. 21, 101; Tombstone inscription}

DAVIS, Alice Jay, daughter of S. G. and A. Davis, born 27 Nov 1871, baptized 5 Jan 1872, died 7 Jan 1872, buried 10 Jan 1872 in S. G. Davis Mausoleum at St. George's. {Ref: Church Records, 1834-1903, pp. 38-39, 96; Cemetery records}

DAVIS, Anna (Miss), buried 2 Feb 1855 in the same grave with Miss Martha Davis. {Ref: Church Records, 1834-1903, p. 92}

DAVIS, Anne (Annie) N. G. (Mrs.), wife of S. Griffith Davis and daughter of W. and M.(?) Hollister of North Carolina, died 21 Apr 1880, buried 23 Apr 1880 in S. G. Davis Mausoleum at St. George's; also see "John H. Davis" and "Kate M. Davis," q.v. {Ref: Church Records, 1834-1903, p. 98; Cemetery records}

DAVIS, Annie, see "Fannie C. Davis" and "John Davis" and "Martha M. Davis" and "John Davis" and "Samuel G. Davis, Jr.," q.v.

DAVIS, Annie Eliza Griffith, daughter of S. G. and A. Davis, born 20 Feb 1863, baptized 26 Sep 1863, married Samuel S. Jay on 11 Nov 1886. {Ref: Church Records, 1834-1903, pp. 32-33, 152-153}

DAVIS, Boudinot, confirmed 11 Dec 1910, later noted as "living in Baltimore" [date not given]; also see "Davis Family," q.v. {Ref: Parish Register, 1903-1958, pp. 88, 110}

DAVIS, Caroline "Carrie" Louisa, daughter of Dr. Davis, born 1811, baptized 1 May 1853 at Belvieu, confirmed 26 Jun 1853, died 30 Mar 1900, age 88, buried 1 Apr 1900; also see "Jay Family," q.v. {Ref: Church Records, 1834-1903, pp. 26-27, 104, 200, 296; Tombstone inscription}

DAVIS, Doctor, see "Caroline L. Davis," q.v.

DAVIS, Edward G., see "Steward G. Davis," q.v.

DAVIS, Elijah and Mary G., buried in S. G. Davis Mausoleum at St. George's; no dates of birth or death indicated, but probably died by 1900. {Ref: Cemetery records}

DAVIS, Eliza, see "Mary G. E. Davis," q.v.

DAVIS, Elizabeth (Mrs.), of Bellevue, died 6 Jan 1852. {Ref: Church Records, 1834-1903, p. 92}

DAVIS, Emma Caroline (adult), daughter of Mr. Davis of Alabama, born ---- [blank], baptized 4 Sep 1859. {Ref: Church Records, 1834-1903, pp. 30-31}

DAVIS, Fannie (Fanny) A. (Mrs.), daughter of Samuel G. and Mary D. Griffith, born 26 Mar 1808, died 18 Nov 1898, age 90, buried 21 Nov 1898 in S. G. Davis

Mausoleum at St. George's. {Ref: Church Records, 1834-1903, pp. 104, 200; Cemetery records}

DAVIS, Fannie Caroline, daughter of Samuel Griffith and Annie Davis, born 2 May 1867, baptized 26 Oct 1868, confirmed 7 Mar 1884; also see "Davis Family," q.v. {Ref: Church Records, 1834-1903, pp. 36-37, 299}

DAVIS, Fanny, see "S. Griffith Davis," q.v.

DAVIS, Frances, confirmed 26 Jun 1853. {Ref: Church Records, 1834-1903, p. 296}

DAVIS, Frances (Miss), sponsored the baptism of Steward Griffith Davis on 28 Jun 1896; also see "Henry B. Wilson," q.v. {Ref: Church Records, 1834-1903, p. 13}

DAVIS, Griffith, see "Davis Family," q.v.

DAVIS, Helen Stocton (Louey or Loney?), member in May, 1914, transferred from Grace Church in Baltimore. {Ref: Parish Register, 1903-1958, p. 110}

DAVIS, James, see "Mary G. E. Davis," q.v.

DAVIS, John Hollister, son of S. Griffith and Anne N. G. Davis, born 3 Dec 18--?, died 20 Dec 1879, buried 23 Dec 1879 in S. G. Davis Mausoleum at St. George's. {Ref: Church Records, 1834-1903, p. 98; Cemetery records}

Davis, Kate Miller, daughter of S. Griffith and Anne N. G. Davis, born and died -- Feb 1866, buried in S. G. Davis Mausoleum at St. George's. {Ref: Cemetery records}

DAVIS, Martha (Miss), buried 1 Feb 1855 in the same grave with Miss Anna Davis. {Ref: Church Records, 1834-1903, p. 92}

DAVIS, Martha Maria, daughter of Samuel Griffith and Annie Davis, born -- Aug 1868, baptized 26 Oct 1868, died 7 May 1895, age 26, buried 10 May 1895 in S. G. Davis Mausoleum at St. George's. {Ref: Church Records, 1834-1903, pp. 36-37, 103, 201; Cemetery records}

DAVIS, Mary G. (Miss), age 89, born 1806, died 1896, buried 4 Feb 1896. {Ref: Church Records, 1834-1903, p. 103; Tombstone inscription}

DAVIS, Mary G. and Elijah, buried in S. G. Davis Mausoleum at St. George's; no dates of birth or death indicated, but probably died by 1900. {Ref: Cemetery records}

DAVIS, Mary Goldsmith Elizabeth, daughter of James G. and Eliza Davis, born 20 Sep 1820, baptized 2 Sep 1846. {Ref: Church Records, 1834-1903, pp. 24-25}

DAVIS, Mary H. (Miss), sponsored the baptism of Henrietta Davis Jay on 28 Sep 1890. {Ref: Church Records, 1834-1903, p. 11}

DAVIS, Mary Hollister, daughter of S. Griffith and Anna Davis, born 18 Feb 1862, baptized 20 Jul 1862, confirmed 19 Feb 1878, married Hardwicke Manning Hooper on 7 Oct 1890 at "Bell Vue" near Havre de Grace. {Ref: Church Records, 1834-1903, pp. 32-33, 156-157, 298}

DAVIS, Martha M. (Miss), confirmed 7 Mar 1884. {Ref: Church Records, 1834-1903, p. 299}

DAVIS, Moses, married Sarah Ann Davy on 18 Mar 1889. {Ref: Church Records, 1834-1903, p. 154}

DAVIS, S. G., sponsored the baptism of Steward Griffith Davis on 28 Jun 1896. {Ref: Church Records, 1834-1903, p. 13}

DAVIS, S. Griffith, son of Septimus and Fanny Davis, born 7 Jan 1835, died 30 Jul 1859, buried in S. G. Davis Mausoleum at St. George's. {Ref: Cemetery records)

DAVIS, Samuel Griffith, son of Dr. Septimus and Frances Davis, born ---- [blank], baptized 22 Sep 1850, died 1913, age 75, buried 23 Apr 1913; also see "Anne N. G. Davis" and "John H. Davis" and "Kate M. Davis" and "Davis Family," q.v. {Ref: Church Records, 1834-1903, pp. 24-25; Parish Register, 1903-1958, p. 159}

DAVIS, Samuel Griffith, Jr., son of Samuel Griffith and Annie Davis, born 24 Jul 1868, baptized 26 Oct 1868, died 6 Dec 1890; also see "Davis Family," q.v. {Ref: Church Records, 1834-1903, pp. 36-37, 202}

DAVIS, Septimus, son of S. Griffith and Anna Davis, born 25 Nov 1860, baptized 14 Jun 1861, confirmed 6 Aug 1879; also see "Davis Family," q.v. {Ref: Church Records, 1834-1903, pp. 30-31, 298}

DAVIS, Septimus, M.D., born 14 Oct 1801, died 8 Jan 1857, buried 10 Jan 1857 ("my father") in S. G. Davis Mausoleum at St. George's (Old Spesutia) Cemetery;

also see "Samuel G. Davis" and "S. Griffith Davis," q.v. {Ref: Church Records, 1834-1903, p. 93; Cemetery records}

DAVIS, Steward Griffith, son of Edward G. and Winifred S. Davis, born 28 Jun 1895, baptized 28 Jun 1896 (sponsors: S. G. Davis, Dr. S. G. Davis, and Miss Frances Davis). {Ref: Church Records, 1834-1903, pp. 12-13}

DAVIS, Winifred S., sponsored the baptism of Martha Davis Jay on 28 Jun 1896; also see "Steward G. Davis," q.v. {Ref: Church Records, 1834-1903, p. 13}

DAVY, Sarah Ann, married Moses Davis on 18 Mar 1889. {Ref: Church Records, 1834-1903, pp. 154-155}

DAWSON, Nannie E., married William M. Wilson on 27 Nov 1889 at Christ Church in Rockville, Maryland. {Ref: Church Records, 1834-1903, pp. 156-157}

DAWSON, Sarah Ann (of Talbott), married Sylvester Mitchell on 24 Oct 1839. {Ref: Church Records, 1834-1903, p. 138}

DEATS, Louisa, married Samuel C. Gerbricks on 15 Jan 1871. {Ref: Church Records, 1834-1903, p. 147}

DEAVER, Ellen, married John Cord on 12 Mar 1857. {Ref: Church Records, 1834-1903, p. 141}

DEAVER, Margaret, married Henry C. Stickney on 12 May 1901. {Ref: Church Records, 1834-1903, pp. 160-161}

DEAVER, Martha, married Alphonzo Matthews on 30 Nov 1871. {Ref: Church Records, 1834-1903, p. 147}

DEBRULER, Mary, married Harry Beck on 19 May 1880. {Ref: Church Records, 1834-1903, p. 149}

DECKMAN FAMILY.
The following family information was entered in the church records under the heading of "Families" circa 1893-1903, but no relationships or ages were indicated, just names:
William Deckman, Mrs. Margaret E. Deckman, Clarence C. Deckman, Rebecca Ann Deckman, Mary Elizabeth Deckman, Jacob Deckman, Martha Susan Deckman, Charles Hilbert Deckman, and Rosa Ambrose Deckman. {Ref: Church Records, 1834-1903, p. 260}

DECKMAN, Charles Hilbert, son of William and Margaret E. Deckman, born 11 Sep 1895, baptized 29 Dec 1900 (sponsors: the parents); also see "Deckman Family," q.v. {Ref: Church Records, 1834-1903, pp. 14-15}

DECKMAN, Clarence Coleman, son of William and Margaret E. Deckman, born 12 Apr 1884, baptized 29 Dec 1900 (sponsors: the parents); also see "William P. Deckman" and "Deckman Family," q.v. {Ref: Church Records, 1834-1903, pp. 14-15}

DECKMAN, Emma, see "William P. Deckman," q.v.

DECKMAN, Jacob, son of William and Margaret E. Deckman, born 8 Mar 1890, baptized 29 Dec 1900 (sponsors: the parents); also see "Deckman Family," q.v. {Ref: Church Records, 1834-1903, pp. 14-15}

DECKMAN, Jesse O'Neal, age 6 months, buried 7 Feb 1904 in Methodist Cemetery. {Ref: Parish Register, 1903-1958, p. 158}

DECKMAN, Margaret, see "Deckman Family," q.v.

DECKMAN, Martha Susan, daughter of William and Margaret E. Deckman, born 16 Sep 1892, baptized 29 Dec 1900 (sponsors: the parents); also see "Deckman Family," q.v. {Ref: Church Records, 1834-1903, pp. 14-15}

DECKMAN, Mary Elizabeth, daughter of William and Margaret E. Deckman, born 10 Sep 1888, baptized 29 Dec 1900 (sponsors: the parents). {Ref: Church Records, 1834-1903, pp. 14-15}

DECKMAN, Rebecca Ann, daughter of William and Margaret E. Deckman, born 1 May 1886, baptized 29 Dec 1900 (sponsors: the parents), confirmed 29 Dec 1901, age 15; also see "Deckman Family," q.v. {Ref: Church Records, 1834-1903, pp. 14-15, 303}

DECKMAN, Rosa Ambrose, daughter of William and Margaret E. Deckman, born 9 Apr 1900, baptized 29 Dec 1900 (sponsors: the parents); also see "Deckman Family," q.v. {Ref: Church Records, 1834-1903, pp. 14-15}

DECKMAN, William, married Margaret E. Hoops on 9 Nov 1882; also see "Deckman Family," q.v. {Ref: Church Records, 1834-1903, p. 150}

DECKMAN, William H., married Dennie McCartney on 26 Feb 1898. {Ref: Church Records, 1834-1903, pp. 160-161}

DECKMAN, William Pusey, son of Clarence Cloman and Emma Agusta Deckman, born 20 Mar 1907, private baptism on 27 Jul 1907 (ill). {Ref: Parish Register, 1903-1958, pp. 30-31}

DEITZ, Catherine, married George F. Gerwig on 24 Nov 1870. {Ref: Church Records, 1834-1903, p. 147}

DELL, Louis Jean, age 40, buried 2 Mar 1894 in Garrettson's Chapel Graveyard. {Ref: Church Records, 1834-1903, p. 102}

DEMONT, John (colored), buried 6 Aug 1882 at the colored church. {Ref: Church Records, 1834-1903, p. 100}

DENHAM FAMILY.
The following family information was entered in the church records under the heading of "Families" circa 1893-1903, but no relationships or ages were indicated, just names:
John Doyle Denham, Mrs. Maggie C. Denham, ---- [blank] Denham, ---- [blank] Denham, ---- [blank] Denham, and Wilford Jennings Bryan Denham. {Ref: Church Records, 1834-1903, p. 261}

DENHAM, Benjamin, see "John D. Denham," q.v.

DENHAM, Caroline, see "John D. Denham," q.v.

DENHAM, Carrie Adele, confirmed 25 Apr 1908, married John Henry Kimble on 17 Apr 1915 [name listed once as "Carry Denham"]. {Ref: Parish Register, 1903-1958, pp. 87, 109, 138-139}

DENHAM, Howard Burney, "age 17, date of birth 29 Jul 1893, Sincerely, Mrs. J. D. Denham" [*Ed. Note:* This information was written on an undated note and inserted into the register]; confirmed 11 Dec 1910, later removed [date not given]. {Ref: Church Records, 1834-1903, p. 307; Parish Register, 1903-1958, pp. 87, 110}

DENHAM, J. D. (Mrs.), see "Howard B. Denham" and "Winfield D. Denham," q.v.

DENHAM, John (Mr. & Mrs.), sponsored the baptism of Robert Linwood Kimble on 1 Oct 1916. {Ref: Parish Register, 1903-1958, pp. 32-33}

DENHAM, John Doyle, son of Benjamin B. and Caroline Denham, born 12 Sep 1869, baptized 16 Nov 1902 (sponsor: Mrs. Maggie C. Denham), confirmed 7 Dec

1902, age 33, no church affiliation, Roman Catholic parents, confirmation at St. George's P. E. Church; also see "Denham Family," q.v. {Ref: Church Records, 1834-1903, pp. 14-15, 303}

DENHAM, John Randolph, son of John Doyle and Margaret Catherine (Waters) Denham, born 2 Jun 1904, baptized 30 Apr 1905 (sponsors: the parents and R. C. Cronin); confirmed 9 Mar 1919; "moved away (Chester)" [date not given]. {Ref: Parish Register, 1903-1958, pp. 30-31, 89, 111}

DENHAM, Maggie C. (Mrs.), sponsored the baptism of John Doyle Denham on 16 Nov 1902; "no church affiliation, Methodist baptism, church influence, confirmed at St. George's P. E. Church" on 7 Dec 1902, age 35; church member in 1903; "moved away" [date not given]; also see "Wilford J. B. Denham" and "Denham Family," q.v. {Ref: Church Records, 1834-1903, pp. 15, 303; Parish Register, 1903-1958, p. 106}

DENHAM, Margaret Evelyn, daughter of John Doyle and Margaret Catherine (Waters) Denham, born 18 Oct 1906, baptized 7 Jul 1907 (sponsors: the parents), confirmed 9 Mar 1919. {Ref: Parish Register, 1903-1958, pp. 30-31, 89, 111}

DENHAM, Wilford Jennings Bryan, son of John D. and Maggie C. Denham, born 5 Nov 1901, baptized 10 Oct 1902 (sponsors: the mother and Mrs. Margaret B. Cullum); confirmed 13 Jun 1915, "moved away" [date not given]; also see "Denham Family," q.v. {Ref: Church Records, 1834-1903, pp. 14-15; Parish Register, 1903-1958, pp. 88, 111}

DENHAM, Winfield Doyle, "age 11, date of birth 10 Jul 1899, Sincerely, Mrs. J. D. Denham." [*Ed. Note:* This information was written on an undated note and inserted into the register]; confirmed 11 Dec 1910, later removed [date not given]. {Ref: Church Records, 1834-1903, p. 307; Parish Register, 1903-1958, pp. 87, 110}

DENIZEN, Isabella, daughter of Charles and Elizabeth Denizen, born ---- [blank], baptized 1 Sep 1878. {Ref: Church Records, 1834-1903, pp. 42-43}

DENIZEN, John Hawer, son of Charles and Elizabeth Denizen, born ---- [blank], baptized 1 Sep 1878. {Ref: Church Records, 1834-1903, pp. 42-43}

DENNISON, Annie Eliza Cornelia (colored), daughter of Milkie Ann Webster and Isaac Dennison, born 20 Nov 1881, private baptism on 15 Jul 1883. {Ref: Church Records, 1834-1903, pp. 2-3}

DENNISON, Dinah, married Calvin Clark on 21 Feb 1861. {Ref: Church Records, 1834-1903, p. 143}

DENNISON, Eliza Jane (colored), married Charles Washington Hoke (colored) on 20 Sep 1888. {Ref: Church Records, 1834-1903, pp. 154-155}

DENNISON, John C. (colored), married Eliza J. Simms (colored) on 3 Oct 1867. {Ref: Church Records, 1834-1903, p. 146}

DENNISON, William T. (colored), married Mitty Ann Harvey (colored) on 13 May 1883 at Colored M. E. Church. {Ref: Church Records, 1834-1903, p. 150}

DEVER, Richard, age 77, buried 6 Apr 1899 in Garrettson's Chapel Graveyard. {Ref: Church Records, 1834-1903, p. 104}

DEVOE, Annie, married Daniel Gallup on 28 Sep 1864. {Ref: Church Records, 1834-1903, p. 145}

DORR, Ann, married Joseph Howard on 15 May 1858. {Ref: Church Records, 1834-1903, p. 142}

DORSEY, Eliza (colored), of Hickory Ridge, buried 23 Mar 1872. {Ref: Church Records, 1834-1903, p. 96}

DORSEY, Frederick (colored), married Mary Jane Morson (colored) on 15 Oct 1893. {Ref: Church Records, 1834-1903, pp. 158-159}

DORSEY, Jane (colored), married Sidney Stump (colored) on 19 Mar 1865. {Ref: Church Records, 1834-1903, p. 146}

DORSEY, Joshua (colored), son of Margaret Bowie Dorsey, born 27 Apr 1864, baptized 5 Feb 1866. {Ref: Church Records, 1834-1903, pp. 36-37}

DORSEY, Margaret, see "Joshua Dorsey," q.v.

DULANEY, George Kennedy, son of Dr. H. K. and Helen R. Dulaney, born 30 Oct 1915, baptized 4 Jun 1916 (sponsors: the parents and Miss M. Dulaney). {Ref: Parish Register, 1903-1958, pp. 32-33}

DULANEY, II. K., sponsored the baptism of Helen Roberts Dulaney on 4 Jun 1916; also see "Henry K. Dulaney" and "Miriam P. Dulaney" and "---- Dulaney," q.v. {Ref: Parish Register, 1903-1958, p. 33}

DULANEY, Helen Roberts, daughter of ---- [blank], born 27 Dec 1884, baptized 4 Jun 1916 (sponsors: Dr. H. K. Dulaney and Miss W. Emmord); Quaker, confirmed 18 Jun 1916. {Ref: Parish Register, 1903-1958, pp. 32-33, 88, 111}

DULANEY, Henry Kennedy (doctor), Methodist, confirmed 18 Jun 1916 [*Ed. Note:* His name was some times given in the records as Harry instead of Henry]. {Ref: Parish Register, 1903-1958, pp. 88, 111}

DULANEY, Henry Stier (Mr. & Mrs.), sponsored the baptism of Henry Stier Dulaney and Josephine Estelle Dulaney on 31 Dec 1914. {Ref: Parish Register, 1903-1958, p. 33}

DULANEY, Henry Stier, son of Dr. Henry K. and Helen R. Dulaney, born 2 May 1913, baptized 31 Dec 1914 at parents' home in Perryman. {Ref: Parish Register, 1903-1958, pp. 32-33}

DULANEY, Josephine Estelle, daughter of Dr. Henry K. and Helen R. Dulaney, born 17 Oct 1914, baptized 31 Dec 1914 at parents' home in Perryman (sponsors: Mr. & Mrs. Henry Stier Dulaney and Dr. & Mrs. J. H. Stier). {Ref: Parish Register, 1903-1958, pp. 32-33}

DULANEY, Miriam (Miss), sponsored the baptisms of George Kennedy Dulaney on 4 Jun 1916 and Miriam Pennington Dulaney on 3 Aug 1919. {Ref: Parish Register, 1903-1958, pp. 33, 35}

DULANEY, Miriam Pennington, daughter of Dr. Harry K. and Helen R. Dulaney, born 25 Mar 1918, baptized 3 Aug 1919 (sponsors: the parents and Miss Miriam Dulaney). {Ref: Parish Register, 1903-1958, pp. 34-35}

DULANEY, ----, infant son of Dr. and Mrs. Harry Dulaney, age 1 hour, buried 29 May 1912. {Ref: Parish Register, 1903-1958, p. 158}

DUNKEL, Catharine, daughter of George Bloucher and Sarah Nichols Dunkel, born 1 Aug 1844, baptized 27 Jun 1846. {Ref: Church Records, 1834-1903, pp. 22-23}

DUNKEL, Earnest Augustus, son of John L. and Rebecca T. Dunkel, born 11 Jul 1849, baptized 16 Jun 1850. {Ref: Church Records, 1834-1903, pp. 24-25}

DUNKEL, Elizabeth Troup, daughter of John L. and Rebecca T. Dunkel, buried 9 Jul 1849. [*Ed. Note:* In another Parish Register, 1696-1851, it indicates she was about 12 months old]. {Ref: Church Records, 1834-1903, p. 91}

DUNKEL, George Augustus, son of George Bloucher and Sarah Nichols Dunkel, born 11 May 1846, baptized 27 Jun 1846. {Ref: Church Records, 1834-1903, pp. 22-23}

DUNKEL, George B., see "Catharine Dunkel" and "George A. Dunkel," q.v.

DUNKEL, John L. [of Baltimore], married Rebecca T. Davidge on 4 Nov 1847; also see "Earnest A. Dunkel" and "Elizabeth T. Dunkel," q.v. {Ref: Church Records, 1834-1903, p. 139}

DUNKEL, Rebecca, see "Earnest A. Dunkel" and "Elizabeth T. Dunkel," q.v.

DUNKEL, Sarah N., see "George A. Dunkel," q.v.

DUVAL, Agnes Jay, see "Jay Family," q.v.

DUVAL, Edmund Bryce, married Agnes Susan Jay on 11 Dec 1889 at Grace Church in Baltimore. {Ref: Church Records, 1834-1903, pp. 156-157}

DUVALL, Elizabeth, confirmed 19 Feb 1874. {Ref: Church Records, 1834-1903, p. 297}

EARLE, Rev. [Edward H.], rector, 1908-1909. {Ref: Parish Register, 1903-1958, p. ii}

EDEN, Anna Louisa, daughter of Charles Henry and Francisco L. C. Eden, born 10 Jan 1895, baptized 20 Oct 1895 at home near Perryman (sponsors: the parents). {Ref: Church Records, 1834-1903, pp. 12-13}

EDEN, Charles Henry, married Francisco Louisa Conrad on 10 Feb 1891. {Ref: Church Records, 1834-1903, pp. 156-157}

EHLERT, Frederick, age 75, buried 15 Jan 1884 at Mr. Lem Matthews' farm. {Ref: Church Records, 1834-1903, p. 100}

ELLIOTT, Annie C., married Jacob C. Hollis on 20 Feb 1878. {Ref: Church Records, 1834-1903, p. 148}

ELLIOTT, Elizabeth (Mrs.), age 79, buried 8 May 1898 in Grove Church Cemetery. {Ref: Church Records, 1834-1903, p. 104}

ELLIOTT, Harriett M., married James T. Sullivan on 8 Feb 1835. {Ref: Church Records, 1834-1903, p. 138}

ELLIOTT, Ione, married Dr. James H. Kennedy on 26 Feb 1878. {Ref: Church Records, 1834-1903, p. 148}

ELLIOTT, William, married Catharine Ann Baron on 13 Dec 1836. {Ref: Church Records, 1834-1903, p. 138}

EMMORD FAMILY.
The following family information was entered in the church records under the heading of "Families" circa 1893-1903, but no relationships or ages were indicated, just names:
Mr. ---- [blank] Emmord, Mrs. ---- [blank] Emmord, Henry O. Emmord, and Laura W. Emmord. {Ref: Church Records, 1834-1903, p. 258}

EMMORD, Eva Grace (Forwood), member in May, 1914, transferred from Grace Chapel, Hickory. {Ref: Parish Register, 1903-1958, p. 110}

EMMORD, Grace, see "Marion J. Emmord" and "Ralph F. Emmord," q.v.

EMMORD, Harry Oscar, age 19, confirmed 30 Apr 1899, married Eva Grace Forwood on 31 Jan 1911 at Perryman; also see "Ralph F. Emmord" and "Emmord Family," q.v. {Ref: Church Records, 1834-1903, p. 302; Parish Register, 1903-1958, pp. 138-139}

EMMORD, J. H., see "Laura W. Emmord," q.v.

EMMORD, Laura Winifred, daughter of J. H. and L. E. Emmord, born 20 Sep 1882, private baptism on 18 Apr 1883, confirmed 30 Apr 1899, age 16; sponsored the baptism of Marion Jeanette Emmord on 31 Dec 1913; also see "Emmord Family," q.v. {Ref: Church Records, 1834-1903, pp. 2-3, 302; Parish Register, 1903-1958, pp. 32-33}

EMMORD, L. E., see "Laura W. Emmord," q.v.

EMMORD, Marion Jeanette, daughter of Harry O. and Grace Emmord, born 2 Mar 1913, baptized 31 Dec 1913 (sponsors: Jay F. Towner, Bessie Forwood and L. Winifred Emmord. {Ref: Parish Register, 1903-1958, pp. 32-33}

EMMORD, Ralph Frederick, son of Harry O. and Grace Emmord, born 21 Feb 1917, baptized 16 Nov 1919. {Ref: Parish Register, 1903-1958, pp. 34-35}

EMMORD, W. (Miss), sponsored the baptism of Helen Roberts Dulaney on 4 Jun 1916. {Ref: Parish Register, 1903-1958, p. 33}

ERGOOD, Anna, wife of Jacob Ergood, died 13 Jul 1863, age 70. {Ref: Tombstone inscription}

ERGOOD, Caroline, wife of Gabriel Sutor Ergood, died 12 Mar 1883, age 64. {Ref: Tombstone inscription}

ERGOOD, Catherine J. (Miss), of Havre de Grace, died 11 Sep 1855, age 25. {Ref: Church Records, 1834-1903, p. 92; Tombstone inscription}

ERGOOD, Gabriel Sutor, husband of Caroline Miller Ergood, born 23 Dec 1823, died 13 Jul 1910. {Ref: Tombstone inscription}

ERGOOD, Jacob, died 28 May 1852, age 55; also see "Anna Ergood," q.v. {Ref: Tombstone inscription}

ERGOOD, Jacob N., died 23 Nov 1846, age 21 years, 1 month and 18 days. {Ref: Tombstone inscription}

ERGOOD, Mary Ann, married John A. Myers on 25 Jan 1855 at Havre de Grace. {Ref: Church Records, 1834-1903, p. 140}

ETHIER, Frederick K., married Maggie R. Lear on 19 Jan 1887. {Ref: Church Records, 1834-1903, pp. 152-153}

EVANS, Amos, buried 12 Sep 1837. {Ref: Church Records, 1834-1903, p. 90}

EWING, Susie, buried 15 Mat 1883, age 20. {Ref: Church Records, 1834-1903, p. 100}

FAMARASS, Austin, married Florence Griffin on 7 Feb 1877. {Ref: Church Records, 1834-1903, p. 148}

FERGUSON, Richard Thomas, married Minerva Ann McClasky on 18 May 1841. {Ref: Church Records, 1834-1903, p. 139}

FINCH, Jane (colored), married Thomas T. Monk (colored) on 12 Oct 1866. {Ref: Church Records, 1834-1903, p. 146}

FINLAY, Catherine, died 12 Apr 1855, age 68. {Ref: Tombstone inscription}

FINLAY, Ellen, born 6 Apr 1830, died 18 Nov 1869. {Ref: Tombstone inscription}

FISHER, Dorsey Idella (colored), child of George and Harriet Fisher, born 19 Apr 1886, private baptism on 21 Jun 1893 at home. {Ref: Church Records, 1834-1903, pp. 10-11}

FISHER, Isabel Lavinia (colored), daughter of George and Harriet Fisher, born 13 Sep 1882, private baptism on 21 Jun 1893 at home. {Ref: Church Records, 1834-1903, pp. 10-11}

FISHER, Joseph Isaiah (colored), son of George and Harriet Fisher, born 15 Jul 1881, private baptism on 21 Jun 1893 at home. {Ref: Church Records, 1834-1903, pp. 10-11}

FISHER, Mary, sponsored the baptism of John Fisher Preston on 4 Jul 1841. {Ref: Church Records, 1834-1903, pp. 20-21}

FISHER, Milford Barron (colored), son of George and Harriet Fisher, born 31 Oct 1887, private baptism on 21 Jun 1893 at home. {Ref: Church Records, 1834-1903, pp. 10-11}

FITZHUGH, Isabella H., married Rev. Edward G. Perryman on 8 May 1862. {Ref: Church Records, 1834-1903, p. 144}

FLINT, Elizabeth, married William Stewart on 11 Apr 1857. {Ref: Church Records, 1834-1903, p. 141}

FLUTKA, Helen Elizabeth, daughter of Charles and Dora Flutka, born 7 Oct 1914, baptized 8 Jan 1915 near Aberdeen (sponsor: Dora Flutka). {Ref: Parish Register, 1903-1958, pp. 32-33}

FLUTKA, Wilbur Herman, son of Charles H. and Dora (Lautner) Flutka, born 10 Jul 1910, baptized 28 Aug 1910 (sponsors: the mother, Herman August Trautner and J. F. Towner). {Ref: Parish Register, 1903-1958, pp. 30-31}

FORD FAMILY.
The following family information was entered in the church records under the heading of "Families" circa 1893-1903, but no relationships or ages were indicated, just names:
George Ford, Mrs. ---- [blank] Ford, Mary Ford, Harry Ford, and Orem Ford. {Ref: Church Records, 1834-1903, p. 261}

FORD, Bertha, born and died in 1871. {Ref: Tombstone inscription}

FORD, Elsie L., born 1881, died 1915. {Ref: Tombstone inscription}

FORD, George, see "Martha L. Ford" and "Ford Family," q.v.

FORD, Harriet, born 1838, died 1879. {Ref: Tombstone inscription}

FORD, Harriett Edna, daughter of James T. and Marion Ford, born and died in 1887. {Ref: Tombstone inscription}

FORD, Harry, see "Ford Family," q.v.

FORD, James T., see "Harriett E. Ford" and "Cornelia Bauer," q.v.

FORD, John, born 1863, died 1866. {Ref: Tombstone inscription}

FORD, Marion, see "Harriett E. Ford" and "Cornelia Bauer," q.v.

FORD, Martha, born 1859, died 1861. {Ref: Tombstone inscription}

FORD, Mary, see "Ford Family," q.v.

FORD, Mary Hall, confirmed 26 Jun 1853. {Ref: Church Records, 1834-1903, p. 296}

FORD, Martha L., wife of George M. Ford, born 26 Feb 1837, died 20 Jan 1908. {Ref: Tombstone inscription}

FORD, Orem, see "Ford Family," q.v.

FORD, Orie Wallace, confirmed 25 Apr 1908, later dropped [date not given]. {Ref: Parish Register, 1903-1958, pp. 87, 109}

FORD, William, born 1830, died 1903. {Ref: Tombstone inscription}

FORD, William, born 1875, died 1890. {Ref: Tombstone inscription}

FORWOOD, Bessie, sponsored the baptism of Marion Jeanette Emmord on 31 Dec 1913. {Ref: Parish Register, 1903-1958, p. 33}

FORWOOD, Eva Grace, married Harry Oscar Emmord on 31 Jan 1911 at Perryman. {Ref: Parish Register, 1903-1958, pp. 138-139}

FORWOOD, Thomas (Mr.), of Spesutia, buried 5 Oct 1839. {Ref: Church Records, 1834-1903, p. 90}

FOX, George W., died 13 Nov 1907, age 72. {Ref: Tombstone inscription}

FRENCH, William, see "Rena Towner," q.v.

FRISBY, Aquila, married Charlott Simms on 14 Feb 1852. {Ref: Church Records, 1834-1903, p. 140}

FRISBY, Eliza, buried 15 May 1860; also see "George N. Frisby" and "Martha M. Frisby," q.v. {Ref: Church Records, 1834-1903, p. 93}

FRISBY, Ella C. D. (colored), married Jacob H. Monk (colored) on 28 Jun 1891. {Ref: Church Records, 1834-1903, pp. 156-157}

FRISBY, George, see "Wilson Frisby," q.v.

FRISBY, George Nathaniel, son of Henry and Eliza Frisby, born ---- [blank] 1859, baptized, 15 Dec 1859. {Ref: Church Records, 1834-1903, pp. 30-31}

FRISBY, Henry, see "Henry Frizby" and "George N. Frisby" and "Mary M. Frisby," q.v.

FRISBY, Jinny, see "Wilson Frisby," q.v.

FRISBY, Joseph, married Mary Ann Clark on 28 Aug 1859. {Ref: Church Records, 1834-1903, p. 142}

FRISBY, Joseph, see "Sarah E. Frisby," q.v.

FRISBY, Louisa, see "Sarah E. Frisby," q.v.

FRISBY, Martha, married Andrew Reed on 4 Jul 1857. {Ref: Church Records, 1834-1903, p. 141}

FRISBY, Mary Martha (colored), daughter of Henry and Eliza Frisby, born 16 Jun(?) 1848, baptized 10 Jul 1848, buried 12 Jul 1848. {Ref: Church Records, 1834-1903, pp. 22-23, 91}

FRISBY, Prene (colored), married James Monk (colored) ---- 1877. [*Ed. Note:* The date was blank, but the marriage was listed between June and December in the register]. {Ref: Church Records, 1834-1903, p. 148}

FRISBY, Sarah Elizabeth (colored), daughter of Joseph and Louisa Frisby, born ---- [blank], baptized 30 Dec 1846. {Ref: Church Records, 1834-1903, pp. 22-23}

FRISBY, Wilson, son of George and Jinny Frisby, born 8 Jun 1850, baptized 16 Jan 1853. {Ref: Church Records, 1834-1903, pp. 24-25}

FRIZBY, George, married Jinny Green on 25 May 1849. {Ref: Church Records, 1834-1903, p. 140}

FRIZBY, Henry, married Eliza Ringgold on 26 May 1848. [*Ed. Note:* In another Parish Register, 1696-1851, it indicates Henry Frizby, a servant man of Mr. G. Henderson, married Eliza Ringgold, a servant woman of Mrs. I. A. Perryman, on 26 May 1847, both "persons of color"]. {Ref: Church Records, 1834-1903, p. 139}

FROST, Albert, son of William and Susan Frost, born 12 Jul 1848, died 4 Aug 1877. {Ref: Church Records, 1834-1903, p. 97; Tombstone inscription}

FROST, Harry, son of William and Susan Frost, born 6 Dec 1850, died 19 Apr 1855. {Ref: Tombstone inscription}

FROST, Harry W., born 3 Oct 1861, died 23 Dec 1917. {Ref: Tombstone inscription}

FROST, Susan, wife of William Frost, born 17 Sep 1821, died 18 Aug 1876. {Ref: Church Records, 1834-1903, p. 97}

FROST, William, born 16 Aug 1806, died 12 Jan 1868 (of Baltimore), buried 14 Jan 1868 in Spesutia Cemetery (St. George's); also see "Susan Frost," q.v. {Ref: Church Records, 1834-1903, p. 95; Tombstone inscription}

FULFORD, Avarilla (Miss), confirmed 9 Jun 1836. {Ref: Church Records, 1834-1903, p. 296}

FULFORD, Catherine, daughter of William and Mary Fulford, died 24 Feb 1915. {Ref: Tombstone inscription}

FYLE FAMILY.

The following family information was entered in the church records under the heading of "Families" circa 1893-1903, but no relationships or ages were indicated, just names. Additional information shown in parenthesis was entered subsequently in the register:
Mr. ---- [blank] Fyle (removed to Havre de Grace), Mrs. E. M. Fyle (removed to Havre de Grace), Ethel D. Fyle (removed to Havre de Grace), Maude Fyle (removed to Havre de Grace), Leon Fyle (at Bush River), Percy Fyle (removed to Havre de Grace), Rissie Fyle (removed to Havre de Grace), and William Fyle (removed to Havre de Grace). A line was drawn diagonally through all the names. {Ref: Church Records, 1834-1903, p. 259}

FYLE, Ethel Dashiell (Miss), confirmed 12 Mar 1896, removed to the Church of the Holy Innocents in Baltimore on 8 Nov 1897; also see "Fyle Family," q.v. {Ref: Church Records, 1834-1903, pp. 204-205, 302}

FYLE, Evelyn (Mrs.), sponsored the baptism of James William Fyle on 8 Aug 1900. {Ref: Church Records, 1834-1903, p. 15}

FYLE, Evelyn Maud, age 18, confirmed 18 Nov 1900. {Ref: Church Records, 1834-1903, p. 303}

FYLE, Evelyn Maude, confirmed 28 Apr 1918; also see "Fyle Family," q.v. {Ref: Parish Register, 1903-1958, pp. 89, 111}

FYLE, George Horace, confirmed 18 Jun 1916, later noted "Dropped - married while first wife yet living, moved away to Carroll County, Maryland." {Ref: Parish Register, 1903-1958, pp. 89, 111}

FYLE, James William, son of Leon and Mary Elizabeth Fyle, born 27 Jul 1900, baptized 8 Aug 1900 at Bush River Station (sponsors: the mother and Mrs. Evelyn Fyle). {Ref: Church Records, 1834-1903, pp. 14-15}

FYLE, Leon, see "James W. Fyle" and "Fyle Family," q.v.

FYLE, Mary Elizabeth, confirmed 19 Aug 1917, "moved away" [date not given]; also see "James W. Fyle," q.v. {Ref: Parish Register, 1903-1958, pp. 89, 111}

FYLE, Maude, see "Fyle Family," q.v.

FYLE, Percy, see "Fyle Family," q.v.

FYLE, Rissie, see "Fyle Family," q.v.

FYLE, William Murdock, age 15, confirmed 18 Nov 1900; also see "Fyle Family," q.v. {Ref: Church Records, 1834-1903, p. 303}

GALLION, Garrett G., born 1839, died 1885. {Ref: Tombstone inscription}

GALLION, Susan Stockham, wife of Garrett G. Gallion, born 1832, died 1920. {Ref: Tombstone inscription}

GALLION, William, married Avarilla Wright ---- 1878. [*Ed. Note:* The date was blank, but the marriage was listed between March and June in the register]. {Ref: Church Records, 1834-1903, p. 148}

GALLOWAY, Sarah H., wife of Moses Galloway, died 28 Oct 1851, age 74. {Ref: Tombstone inscription}

GALLUP FAMILY.

The following family information was entered in the church records under the heading of "Families" circa 1893-1903, but no relationships or ages were indicated, just names. Additional information shown in parenthesis was entered subsequently in the register:

Daniel Gallup (dead, 28 Apr 1895, named lined out), Mrs. Anna E. Gallup, Flora M. Gallup (removed to Roanoke, Virginia, married C. E. Michael, name lined out), Edward D. Gallup, Annie V. Gallup, Emily B. Gallup, and Mrs. Florence Gallup. {Ref: Church Records, 1834-1903, p. 255}

Mrs. Susan Gallup (removed to Baltimore, died 20 Nov 1900), Lawrence J. Gallup (removed to Baltimore), Edward B. Gallup (removed to Baltimore), Joseph N. Gallup (removed to Baltimore), and Eldridge Gallup (removed to Baltimore). {Ref: Church Records, 1834-1903, p. 255}

GALLUP, Alfred Patterson, born 1861, died 1917, age 56, buried 17 Sep 1917. {Ref: Parish Register, 1903-1958, p. 159; Tombstone inscription}

GALLUP, Annie Eliza, wife of Daniel Gallup, born 25 Aug 1836, confirmed 1 May 1892; sponsored the baptism of Virginia Gallup Michael on 11 Nov 1894; died 17 Mar 1907, buried 19 Mar 1907. {Ref: Church Records, 1834-1903, pp. 13, 301; Parish Register, 1903-1958, pp. 106, 158; Tombstone inscription}

GALLUP, Annie Mabel, daughter of Edmund D. and Mary Florence Gallup, born 23 May 1892, private baptism on 6 Aug 1892 at home at "Chelsea" and died 28 Sep 1892, age 4 months, buried 29 Sep 1892. [*Ed. Note:* However, the grave marker indicates Annie E. Gallup, daughter of E. D. and A. E. Gallup, was born

May 23, 1892 and died Sep 28, 1892]. {Ref: Church Records, 1834-1903, pp. 10-11, 102; Tombstone inscription}

GALLUP, Annie Virginia, daughter of Daniel and Annie E. Gallup, born ---- [blank], baptized 13 Jul 1879, confirmed 9 Nov 1890, sponsored the baptism of Lilien Osborn Gallup on 11 Nov 1894; married Samuel S. Sutton on 30 Jun 1906; also see "Annie Virginia Sutton," q.v. {Ref: Church Records, 1834-1903, pp. 13, 42-43, 301; Parish Register, 1903-1958, pp. 106, 138-139}

GALLUP, Annie Virginia, wife of John O. Gallup, died 13 Jul 1894. {Ref: Tombstone inscription}

GALLUP, Catherine (Mrs. Oliver), died 3 Aug 1891, age 85. {Ref: Tombstone inscription}

GALLUP, Charles T., born 28 Aug 1837, died 17 Nov 1889. {Ref: Tombstone inscription}

GALLUP, Daniel, son of Oliver and Catharine Gallup, born 16 Dec 1830, baptized 5 Apr 1836, married Annie Devoe on 28 Sep 1864, confirmed 1 May 1892, died 28 Apr 1895, age 64, buried 30 Apr 1895; also see "Annie E. Gallup" "and Martha L. Gallup" and "Gallup Family," q.v. {Ref: Church Records, 1834-1903, pp. 16-17, 102, 145, 204-205, 301; Tombstone inscription}

GALLUP, E. W. (Mrs.), buried 28 Sep 1889; also see "Fannie A. Taylor," q.v. {Ref: Church Records, 1834-1903, p. 101}

GALLUP, Edmund D., born 1869, died 1920, age 61, buried 11 Jun 1920; also see "Annie M. Gallup" and "Flora M. Gallup" and "Lilien O. Gallup," q.v. {Ref: Parish Register, 1903-1958, p. 160; Tombstone inscription}

GALLUP, Edward B., born 17 Mar 1848, died 27 Aug 1883, buried 28 Aug 1883, age 35. {Ref: Church Records, 1834-1903, p. 100; Tombstone inscription}

GALLUP, Edward Beech, son of Edward B. and Susie S. Gallup, born 18 Feb 1884, private baptism on 30 Apr 1884. {Ref: Church Records, 1834-1903, pp. 4-5}

GALLUP, Eldridge W. (captain), died 5 Sep 1884, age 67; also see "Margaret A. Gallup," q.v. {Ref: Tombstone inscription}

GALLUP, Elizabeth A., married George A. Nelson on 3 Jan 1861. {Ref: Church Records, 1834-1903, p. 143}

GALLUP, Emily Bay, daughter of Daniel and Annie E. Gallup, born ---- [blank], baptized 13 Jul 1879, confirmed 9 Jun 1893, married Robert Lytle Morgan on 15 Nov 1905; also see "Emily Bay Morgan," q.v. {Ref: Church Records, 1834-1903, pp. 42-43, 301; Parish Register, 1903-1958, pp. 106, 138-139}

GALLUP, Flora (Miss), confirmed 9 Oct 1887. {Ref: Church Records, 1834-1903, p. 300}

GALLUP, Flora Michael, daughter of Edmund D. and Mary Florence Gallup, born 24 Feb 1898, baptized 9 Oct 1898 (sponsors: the parents and Mrs. Mary C. Cronin). {Ref: Church Records, 1834-1903, pp. 12-13}

GALLUP, Flora Mitchell, married Charles Edwin Michael on 19 Oct 1893. {Ref: Church Records, 1834-1903, pp. 158-159}

GALLUP, George W., born 16 Jan 1844, died 21 Oct 1900; also see "Mary E. Gallup," q.v. {Ref: Tombstone inscription}

GALLUP, John Oliver, son of Oliver and Catharine Gallup, born 21 Aug 1833, baptized 5 Apr 1836, died 17 May 1873, age 40; also see "Annie V. Gallup," q.v. {Ref: Church Records, 1834-1903, pp. 16-17; Tombstone inscription}

GALLUP, Laura, see "Mary E. Gallup," q.v.

GALLUP, Lawrence Johnson, son of Edward B. and Susie S. Gallup, born 16 Feb 1882, private baptism on 30 Apr 1884. {Ref: Church Records, 1834-1903, pp. 4-5}

GALLUP, Lilien (Lilian) Osborn (Osborne), daughter of Edmund D. and Mary Florence Gallup, born 14 Jan 1894, baptized 11 Nov 1894 (sponsors: the parents and Miss Annie V. Gallup); Methodist, confirmed 21 Nov 1909; "Dropped - Baltimore - married Jacobs" [no date given; note unclear]. {Ref: Church Records, 1834-1903, pp. 12-13; Parish Register, 1903-1958, pp. 87, 109}

GALLUP, M. A., see "Fannie A. Taylor," q.v.

GALLUP, Margaret A., wife of Eldridge W. Gallup, died 26 Sep 1889, age 63. {Ref: Tombstone inscription}

GALLUP, Martha (Mattie) L. (Miss), confirmed 7 Mar 1884; married George Slee on 15 Aug 1888; also see "Martha L. Slee," q.v. {Ref: Church Records, 1834-1903, pp. 154-155, 299}

GALLUP, Martha Laurinda (adult), daughter of Daniel and Annie E. Gallup, born 4 Oct 1867, baptized 20 Jul 1884 (sponsors: Mrs. Buck, Miss F. Michael and Mr. J. H. Michael). {Ref: Church Records, 1834-1903, pp. 4-5}

GALLUP, Mary (Miss), confirmed 27 Nov 1886, removed to Roanoke, Virginia in March, 1890. {Ref: Church Records, 1834-1903, pp. 202, 300}

GALLUP, Mary Ethel, daughter of George W. and Laura Gallup, born 5 Jun 1887, died 10 Jul 1892. {Ref: Tombstone inscription}

GALLUP, Mary L., born 21 Oct 1835, died 17 Nov 1889. {Ref: Tombstone inscription}

GALLUP, Mary Martha, wife of Thomas Gallup, died 14 Jul 1866 of heart disease, age 31; also see "Mary M. Gallup" and "Noble C. Gallup" and "William A. P. Gallup," q.v. {Ref: Church Records, 1834-1903, p. 95; Tombstone inscription}

GALLUP, Mattie L., see "Martha L. Gallup" and "Martha L. Slee," q.v.

GALLUP, Mollie C. (Miss), confirmed 10 Oct 1882, married Clinton Cronin on 8 Jan 1885. {Ref: Church Records, 1834-1903, pp. 152-153, 299}

GALLUP, Noble Canon (or Cannon), son of Thomas Francis and Mary Martha Gallup, born 15 Feb 1859 [tombstone inscription indicates 1860], baptized 12 May 1863, confirmed 27 Jan 1889, removed to Roanoke, Virginia in March, 1890, returned 28 Apr 1892, removed to Baltimore on 24 Oct 1892, died 1918. {Ref: Church Records, 1834-1903, pp. 32-33, 202, 204-205, 257, 300; Tombstone inscription}

GALLUP, Oliver, sponsored the baptism of Rachel Louisa Kirby, Thomas Edward Kirby, and Mary Lucretia Kirby on 24 Oct 1839; died 7 Dec 1861, age 63; also see "Catherine Gallup" and "Daniel Gallup" and "John Oliver Gallup," q.v. {Ref: Church Records, 1834-1903, p. 21; Tombstone inscription}

GALLUP, Sarah E., born 1847, died 1912. {Ref: Tombstone inscription}

GALLUP, Susan (Susie) S. (Mrs.), born 4 Aug 1856, confirmed 27 Nov 1886, removed to Baltimore in April, 1895, died 21 Nov 1900, age 44 years, 3 months and 16 days, buried 23 Nov 1900; also see "Edward B. Gallup" and "Lawrence J. Gallup" and "Gallup Family," q.v. {Ref: Church Records, 1834-1903, pp. 104, 202, 300; Tombstone inscription}

GALLUP, Thomas Francis, "drowned himself at Havre de Grace; church service not read; buried at Spesutia" [St. George's Churchyard] on 2 Jun 1868; also see "Mary M. Gallup" and "Noble C. Gallup" and "William A. P. Gallup," q.v. {Ref: Church Records, 1834-1903, p. 95}

GALLUP, William Alfred Patterson, son of Thomas Francis and Mary Martha Gallup, born 12 Nov 1861, baptized 12 May 1863. {Ref: Church Records, 1834-1903, pp. 32-33}

GALLUP, William H., born 13 Jul 1824, died 4 Dec 1903. {Ref: Tombstone inscription}

GALLUP, William T., buried 12 Jan 1891, age 27. {Ref: Church Records, 1834-1903, p. 102}

GARDNER, Augustus, buried 15 Aug 1872. {Ref: Church Records, 1834-1903, p. 96}

GARDNER, Florence Elizabeth, daughter of James Augustus and Mary A. Gardner, born 22 Jul 1868, baptized 27 Aug 1872. {Ref: Church Records, 1834-1903, pp. 40-41}

GARRETTSON, Alexander (colored), married Martha Christie (colored) on 15 Jan 1891. {Ref: Church Records, 1834-1903, pp. 156-157}

GARRETTSON, Mary, died 3 Mar 1835, age 78, and below her name on the same stone is Elizabeth Barnes, died ---- [illegible, stone partially buried]. {Ref: Tombstone inscription}

GARRISON, Robert (colored), married Rosa Smith (colored) on 12 Aug 1883. {Ref: Church Records, 1834-1903, p. 151}

GARWICK, Christena, buried 13 May 1870, age about 4 years. {Ref: Church Records, 1834-1903, p. 96}

GARWICK, Frederick, born 1 Mar 1847 in Germany, died of typhus fever and buried 12 Mar 1866 in Garrettson's Chapel. {Ref: Church Records, 1834-1903, p. 95}

GARWICK, George F., son of George F. and Christiana Garwick, born 18 Nov 1853, buried 20 Jul 1858. {Ref: Church Records, 1834-1903, p. 94}

GARWICK, Jacobina, daughter of George F. and Christiana Garwick, born 2 May 1862, buried 5 Jan 1864. {Ref: Church Records, 1834-1903, p. 94}

GARWICK, John, son of George F. and Christiana Garwick, born 10 Jun 1858, buried 26 Nov 1858. {Ref: Church Records, 1834-1903, p. 94}

GAY, Septimus Davis, son of John and Mary G. E. Gay, born 21 Aug 1853, baptized 21 Sep 1854. {Ref: Church Records, 1834-1903, pp. 26-27}

GEARY, Sadie O'Neil, daughter of James and Amelia A. Geary, born 27 Mar 1889, private baptism on 25 Jul 1889. {Ref: Church Records, 1834-1903, p. 9}

GENETTS, Margaret, daughter of John and Rebecca Genetts, buried 3 Aug 1868, age 10 months. {Ref: Church Records, 1834-1903, p. 95}

GERBRICKS, Samuel C., married Louisa Deats on 15 Jan 1871. {Ref: Church Records, 1834-1903, p. 147}

GERWIG, George F., married Catherine Deitz on 24 Nov 1870. {Ref: Church Records, 1834-1903, p. 147}

GIBSON, Ellen (colored), married George Williams (colored) on 11 Dec 1892. {Ref: Church Records, 1834-1903, pp. 158-159}

GIBSON, Ellen Louisa (colored), daughter of Howell and Ellen Gibson, born 27 Jul 1875, baptized 21 Sep 1881 (sponsors: the mother and Mrs. Harriett E. Michael). {Ref: Church Records, 1834-1903, pp. 2-3}

GIBSON, Howell, see "Ellen L. Gibson" and "Pearson C. Gibson" and "Walter C. Gibson," q.v.

GIBSON, Lizzie (colored), married John Jiles (colored) on 10 Mar 1892. {Ref: Church Records, 1834-1903, pp. 158-159}

GIBSON, Milley Ann (colored), married Isaac Reed (colored) on 18 Mar 1869. {Ref: Church Records, 1834-1903, p. 147}

GIBSON, Nellie, see "Pearson C. Gibson," q.v.

GIBSON, Pearson Chapman (colored), son of Howell and Nellie Gibson, born 4 Jul 1883, private baptism on 8 Aug 1884. {Ref: Church Records, 1834-1903, pp. 4-5}

GIBSON, Theodore (colored), married Cora Stansbury (colored) on 8 Sep 1892. {Ref: Church Records, 1834-1903, pp. 158-159}

GIBSON, Walter Cook (colored), son of Howell and Ellen Gibson, born 8 Aug 1880, baptized 21 Sep 1881 (sponsors: the mother and Mrs. Harriett E. Michael). {Ref: Church Records, 1834-1903, pp. 2-3}

GILBERT, Abner (Mr.), buried 7 Apr 1851. [*Ed. Note:* In another Parish Register, 1696-1851, it indicates Abner Gilbert was buried 7 Apr 1850]. {Ref: Church Records, 1834-1903, p. 91}

GILBERT, Eliza Jane, daughter of Parker and Elizabeth Gilbert, born ---- [blank], baptized 20 May 1849. [*Ed. Note:* In another Parish Register, 1696-1851, it indicates she was 4 years old]. {Ref: Church Records, 1834-1903, pp. 22-23}

GILBERT, Elizabeth, see "Priscilla Mitchell" and "Eliza J. Gilbert" and "John F. GIlbert" and "Mary C. Gilbert" and "Sarah C. Gilbert," q.v.

GILBERT, Gideon, married Rachel A. Gilbert on 28 Feb 1865. {Ref: Church Records, 1834-1903, p. 146}

GILBERT, Jane (Mrs.), buried 1 Jan 1850. {Ref: Church Records, 1834-1903, p. 91}

GILBERT, Joel (Mrs.), died 22 Dec 1883 in her 76th year. {Ref: Church Records, 1834-1903, p. 100}

GILBERT, Joel Harrison, married Rachel Jane Gilbert on 21 Jan 1841. {Ref: Church Records, 1834-1903, p. 138}

GILBERT, John Franklin, son of Parker and Elizabeth Gilbert, born ---- [blank], baptized 20 May 1849. [*Ed. Note:* In another Parish Register, 1696-1851, it indicates he was 6 years old]. {Ref: Church Records, 1834-1903, pp. 22-23}

GILBERT, Mary (Mrs.), buried 20 May 1849. {Ref: Church Records, 1834-1903, p. 91}

GILBERT, Mary Cassander, daughter of Parker and Elizabeth Gilbert, born 4 (or 5?) Sep 1849, baptized 5 Apr 1851. {Ref: Church Records, 1834-1903, pp. 24-25}

GILBERT, Parker, see "Priscilla Mitchell" and "Eliza J. Gilbert" and "John F. GIlbert" and "Mary C. Gilbert" and "Sarah C. Gilbert," q.v.

GILBERT, Rachel A., married Gideon Gilbert on 28 Feb 1865. {Ref: Church Records, 1834-1903, p. 146}

GILBERT, Rachel Jane, married Joel Harrison Gilbert on 21 Jan 1841. {Ref: Church Records, 1834-1903, p. 138}

GILBERT, Sally, buried 5 Oct 1865. {Ref: Church Records, 1834-1903, p. 94}

GILBERT, Sarah Bennet, confirmed 26 Jun 1853. {Ref: Church Records, 1834-1903, p. 296}

GILBERT, Sarah Cordelia, daughter of Parker and Elizabeth Gilbert, born ---- [blank], baptized 20 May 1849. [Ed. Note: In another Parish Register, 1696-1851, it indicates he was 5 years old]. {Ref: Church Records, 1834-1903, pp. 22-23}

GILES, Amanda (colored), married William Carter (colored) ---- 1878. [Ed. Note: The date was blank, but the marriage was listed between March and June in the register]. {Ref: Church Records, 1834-1903, p. 148}

GILES, Cordelia, widow of Edward Giles and daughter of James Phillips, sponsored the baptism of Martha Phillips Hall on 26 Mar 1840; died 16 Nov 1853, age 68, buried 17 Nov 1853. {Ref: Church Records, 1834-1903, pp. 21, 92; Tombstone inscription}

GILES, Edward, see "Cordelia Giles," q.v.

GILES, Frances, see "Walter J. Giles," q.v.

GILES, Jacob (colored), married Ganowfeen Shepperd (colored) on 1 Jan 1893. {Ref: Church Records, 1834-1903, pp. 158-159}

GILES, Jacob W., born 26 Jun 1776, died 7 Nov 1851, buried 8 Nov 1851. {Ref: Church Records, 1834-1903, p. 92; Tombstone inscription}

GILES, James, see "John T. Giles" and "Wesley Giles," q.v.

GILES, John, see "John Jiles," q.v.

GILES, John Thomas (twin of Wesley), son of James and Millie Giles (colored), born 26 Jul 1886, baptized 19 Nov 1886. {Ref: Church Records, 1834-1903, p. 6}

GILES, Lewis, married Nancy Hughes on 27 Sep 1866. {Ref: Church Records, 1834-1903, p. 146}

GILES, Millie, see "John T. Giles" and "Wesley Giles," q.v.

GILES, Myrtle Isabel (colored), daughter of Sarah Giles and ---- [blank], born ---- [blank] 1888, baptized 4 Feb 1889 "evidently bastard." {Ref: Church Records, 1834-1903, p. 8}

GILES, Nancy (colored), daughter of Nancy Giles and ---- [blank], born ---- [blank], baptized 4 Feb 1889 "evidently bastard." {Ref: Church Records, 1834-1903, p. 8}

GILES, Sarah, see "Myrtle I. Giles," q.v.

GILES, Sidney, see "Sidney Jiles," q.v.

GILES, Solomon (colored), married Amelia Brown (colored) on 26 Jun 1879. {Ref: Church Records, 1834-1903, p. 149}

GILES, Walter Jefferson (colored), son of Frances Giles and Walter Jefferson, born ---- [blank], baptized 4 Feb 1889 "evidently bastard." {Ref: Church Records, 1834-1903, p. 8}

GILES, Wesley (twin of John), son of James and Millie Giles (colored), born 26 Jul 1886, baptized 19 Nov 1886. {Ref: Church Records, 1834-1903, p. 6}

GITHENS, Horace G., married Georgie Stockham on 5 Jun 1895. {Ref: Church Records, 1834-1903, pp. 160-161}

GLASS, Avarilla W., born 1830, died 1904. {Ref: Tombstone inscription}

GLASS, Sarah Elizabeth, daughter of Thomas and Avarilla Glass, born 24 Jun 1863, baptized 24 Dec 1863. {Ref: Church Records, 1834-1903, pp. 34-35}

GLASS, Thomas, born 1827, died 1864, buried 4 Apr 1864. {Ref: Church Records, 1834-1903, p. 94; Tombstone inscription}

GLASS, Thomas, born 1860, died 1863, buried 24 Dec 1863, "age about 5 years." {Ref: Church Records, 1834-1903, p. 94; Tombstone inscription}

GLASS, Thomas Wildey, son of Thomas and Avarilla Glass, born 14 Nov 1864, baptized 27 Aug 1865 at house of Joseph M. Clay. {Ref: Church Records, 1834-1903, pp. 36-37}

GLASS, William Henry, son of Thomas and Avarilla Glass, born 6 Sep 1861, baptized 24 Dec 1863. {Ref: Church Records, 1834-1903, pp. 34-35}

GLOVER, Hester (colored), married Edward Johnson (colored) on 13 May 1877. {Ref: Church Records, 1834-1903, p. 148}

GLOVER, Hester Jane, married Robert Monk on 29 Aug 1858. {Ref: Church Records, 1834-1903, p. 142}

GODWIN, Amanda M., born 8 Oct 1838, died 21 Feb 1909. {Ref: Tombstone inscription}

GODWIN, Minnie B. Taylor, wife of Daniel N. Godwin, born 12 Sep 1869, died 27 Sep 1914. {Ref: Tombstone inscription}

GODWIN, Thomas, born 10 Dec 1818, died 29 Aug 1900. {Ref: Tombstone inscription}

GOODWIN, Thomas, confirmed 6 Aug 1879. {Ref: Church Records, 1834-1903, p. 298}

GORDY, Paul Dulaney, son of ---- [blank] and Nettie M. Gordy, born 17 Sep 1914, baptized 21 Jan 1915 in the church rectory (sponsor: Amanda Lynch). {Ref: Parish Register, 1903-1958, pp. 32-33}

GORRELL, J. L. (Mrs.), buried 1 Aug 1889 in Baltimore. {Ref: Church Records, 1834-1903, p. 101}

GOUGH, William, born 1801, died 1872. {Ref: Tombstone inscription}

GOVER, Agnes Courtney Langdon, daughter of Philip and Sallie R. Gover, born 28 Mar 1864, baptized 16 Aug 1868. {Ref: Church Records, 1834-1903, pp. 36-37}

GOVER, Ann (Mrs.), confirmed 9 Feb 1873. {Ref: Church Records, 1834-1903, p. 297}

GOVER, Ella, confirmed 19 Feb 1874. {Ref: Church Records, 1834-1903, p. 297}

GOVER, Mrs., see "Sarah Ann Johnson," q.v.

GOVER, Nathaniel G., see "Sarah Gover," q.v.

GOVER, Philip, buried 13 Mar 1872 at Rock Spring Church; also see "Agnes C. L. Gover," q.v. {Ref: Church Records, 1834-1903, p. 96}

GOVER, Sarah, wife of Nathaniel Giles Gover, died 14 Feb 1860, age 80. {Ref: Church Records, 1834-1903, p. 93; Tombstone inscription}

GRAFTON, Alta McVail, daughter of Jacob Alexander and Emma Virginia Grafton, born 20 Mar 1893, baptized 31 Oct 1909 (sponsors: C. W. Michael and Mabel Hyde); Methodist *[sic]*, confirmed 21 Nov 1909, transferred to St. Michael, All Angels, Baltimore, on 26 Oct 1914. {Ref: Parish Register, 1903-1958, pp. 30-31; Parish Register, 1903-1958, pp. 31, 87, 109}

GRAHAM, Matilda, sponsored the baptism of James Bias Hammond and John Barrett Hammond on 31 Oct 1840. {Ref: Church Records, 1834-1903, pp. 20-21}

GREEN, Ariel Street (Miss), removed to 140 Beacon Street in Boston, Massachusetts ---- (blank). [*Ed. Note:* There was no date given, but it was some time after 10 Oct 1882 which was when she was confirmed in Maryland]. {Ref: Church Records, 1834-1903, pp. 201, 299}

GREEN, Isaac (colored servant of Miss Adaline Hall), born 31 Oct 1845, baptized 22 Sep 1863, buried 5 Jan 1870. {Ref: Church Records, 1834-1903, pp. 32-33, 96}

GREEN, Jinny, married George Frizby on 25 May 1849. {Ref: Church Records, 1834-1903, p. 140}

GREENE, Fannie, see "Kennedy Family," q.v.

GREENLEE, Margaret, buried 15 Apr 1872. {Ref: Church Records, 1834-1903, p. 96}

GREENWAY, Sarah B., married Joseph Henriques on 22 Oct 1863. {Ref: Church Records, 1834-1903, p. 145}

GREENWAY, Wilton, sponsored the baptism of Hugh Douglas Stier on 30 Jul 1893. {Ref: Church Records, 1834-1903, p. 13}

GRICE, Sarah Elizabeth, age 59, buried 23 Apr 1913 in Calvary M. E. Churchyard. {Ref: Parish Register, 1903-1958, p. 159}

GRIEZ (GUEZ?), George Frederick, son of Jacob and Christiana Griez (Guez?), born 24 Sep 1867 at "Chelsea" and baptized 18 Jan 1868. {Ref: Church Records, 1834-1903, pp. 36-37}

GRIFFIN, Florence, married Austin Famarass on 7 Feb 1877. {Ref: Church Records, 1834-1903, p. 148}

GRIFFIN, Hester, died 6 Mar 1867 at the h-i-n? [illegible], about 80, and buried at Mr. Osborn's. {Ref: Church Records, 1834-1903, p. 95}

GRIFFIN, James, married Delia Tilden on 26 Jan 1859. {Ref: Church Records, 1834-1903, p. 142}

GRIFFIN, Robert, married Eliza Stansbury on 26 Feb 1880. {Ref: Church Records, 1834-1903, p. 149}

GRIFFITH, Delia, married William Henry Stansbury on 16 Aug 1860. {Ref: Church Records, 1834-1903, p. 142}

GRIFFITH, E., see "Frederick H. Stewart" and "Stepney York" and "Lottie Taylor" and "Milly York" and "George ----" and "Margaret ----" and "Isaac William ----" and "John York," q.v.

GRIFFITH, Edward, in his 89th year, died 4 Jul 1867 at his residence and was interred in Greenmount Cemetery in Baltimore. {Ref: Church Records, 1834-1903, p. 95}

GRIFFITH, Edward, see "Charles Jones" and "Harriet Stewart" and "Rachel Stewart" and "Charles Stewart" and "Samuel Ramsay" and "Philip Ramsay" and "John Henry York," q.v.

GRIFFITH, Elizabeth, consort of Samuel Griffith, born 25 Mar 1772, died 4 Jan 1852. {Ref: Tombstone inscription}

GRIFFITH, Emily, wife of George Griffith, died 13 Aug 1821 (1824?) in her 28th year. {Ref: Tombstone inscription}

GRIFFITH, George (colored), married Hattie Reid (colored) on 11 Oct 1883. {Ref: Church Records, 1834-1903, p. 151}

GRIFFITH, George, see "Emily Griffith," q.v.

GRIFFITH, Goldsborough S., Jr., married Ella Michael on 14 Jun 1864. {Ref: Church Records, 1834-1903, p. 145}

GRIFFITH, John L., born 5 Feb 1810, died 1 May 1865, buried 3 May 1865; also see "Priscilla S. Griffith," q.v. {Ref: Church Records, 1834-1903, p. 94; Tombstone inscription}

GRIFFITH, Lawrence, sponsored the baptism of Garbiel Ellis Porter on 12 Jul 1891. {Ref: Church Records, 1834-1903, p. 11}

GRIFFITH, Luke, see "Virginia Griffith," q.v.

GRIFFITH, Mary, see "Charles Jones" and "Harriet Stewart" and "Rachel Stewart" and "Charles Stewart" and "Samuel Ramsay" and "Philip Ramsay," q.v.

GRIFFITH, Mary Ann (Mrs.), buried 6 Nov 1856, in her 58th year. {Ref: Church Records, 1834-1903, p. 92}

GRIFFITH, Mary D., see "Fannie A. Davis," q.v.

GRIFFITH, Mary L., of Palmer's Point, daughter of John L. and P. Griffith, age 2, died 27 Jan 1841, buried 29 Jan 1841. {Ref: Church Records, 1834-1903, p. 90; Tombstone inscription}

GRIFFITH, Milche (colored), married Richard Moore (colored) on 28 Nov 1868. {Ref: Church Records, 1834-1903, p. 147}

GRIFFITH, Priscilla Stump, wife of John L. Griffith, born 14 Oct 1817, died 18 Aug 1907, age 89, buried 21 Aug 1907. {Ref: Parish Register, 1903-1958, p. 158; Tombstone inscription}

GRIFFITH, Samuel, see "Elizabeth Griffith," q.v.

GRIFFITH, Samuel G., see "Fannie A. Davis," q.v.

GRIFFITH, Sarah (Sally) Bias, daughter of John L. and Priscilla Griffith, born 9 Dec 1840, baptized 29 Jan 1841 (sponsors: Sarah Stump, Fanny J. Hammond and Albert Davis), confirmed 14 May 1865 married Otho S. Lee on 14 Mar 1867. {Ref: Church Records, 1834-1903, pp. 20-21, 146, 294}

GRIFFITH, Virginia (adult), daughter of Luke Griffith, born ---- [blank], baptized 27 May 1855, married Gen. Thomas F. Bowie on 24 Jul 1855. {Ref: Church Records, 1834-1903, pp. 26-27 140}

GRILL, Caroline Christiana, daughter of Frank and Catharine Grill, born 28 May 1867, baptized 15 Sep 1867. {Ref: Church Records, 1834-1903, pp. 36-37}

GRILL, Charles Earnest, son of Frank and Catharine Grill, born 26 May 1863, baptized 24 Mar 1864. {Ref: Church Records, 1834-1903, pp. 34-35}

GRILL, John Christian, son of Frank and Catharine Grill, born 7 Jun 1868, baptized 25 Dec 1868. {Ref: Church Records, 1834-1903, pp. 36-37}

GRILL, Michael, son of Frank and Catherine Grill, born 28 Nov 1870, baptized 7 Nov 1871, buried 12 Nov 1871. {Ref: Church Records, 1834-1903, pp. 38-39, 96}

GRILL, Randolph Frederick, son of Frank and Catharine Grill, born 25 Sep 1861, baptized 1 Jan 1862. {Ref: Church Records, 1834-1903, pp. 32-33}

GUERNEY, Mary Adeline, member in 1904, transferred to St. Paul's Chapel, Severn Parish, on 4 Apr 1905; also see "Palmer Family," q.v. {Ref: Parish Register, 1903-1958, p. 109}

GUHL, Frederick, married Mary B. Mohr on 30 Mar 1880. {Ref: Church Records, 1834-1903, p. 149}

GUILFORD, E. Gassaway, see "Alice Mary Jay," q.v.

HAINES, Blanche Franklin, daughter of Rev. C. R. and Corrie G. Haines, born 12 Sep 1859, baptized 3 Nov 1859. {Ref: Church Records, 1834-1903, pp. 30-31}

HAINES, Claudius R. (reverend), married Cordelia Giles Hall on 5 Oct 1858. {Ref: Church Records, 1834-1903, p. 142}

HALL FAMILY.
The following family information was entered in the church records under the heading of "Families" circa 1893-1903, but no relationships or ages were indicated, just names. Additional information shown in parenthesis was entered subsequently in the register:
Andrew Hall (dead), Mrs. Martha P. Hall (dead), Phillips M. Hall, Mrs. William Hall (name lined out), Claudius H. Hall, Martha P. Hall, John Botts

(named lined out), Mrs. Botts (name lined out), and Mrs. Matilda C. Hall (Mrs. Phillips M. Hall). {Ref: Church Records, 1834-1903, p. 251}

HALL, Adaline, see "Elizabeth Pinion" and "Isaac Green" and "Louis Nelson" and "Harriet Amanda ----" and "Laura Frances ----" and "Permela Ann ----" and "Ann Rebecca ----" and "May Jane ----" and "---- Peyton," q.v.

HALL, Adaline B., born 19 Apr 1797, died 9 Feb 1872, buried 12 Feb 1872 at Cranberry Farm. {Ref: Church Records, 1834-1903, p. 96; Tombstone inscription}

HALL, Albert, see "Alice C. Hall," q.v.

HALL, Alice Cornelia (colored), daughter of Albert and Sarah Hall, born 18 Nov 1889, private baptism on 12 Sep 1892 (sick) at home. {Ref: Church Records, 1834-1903, pp. 10-11}

HALL, Andrew, see "Ann J. Hall" and "Hall Family," q.v.

HALL, Andrew, died 9 Jul 1857, buried 10 Jul 1857. {Ref: Church Records, 1834-1903, p. 93; Tombstone inscription}

HALL, Andrew, married Martha P. Hall on 4 Nov 1857. {Ref: Church Records, 1834-1903, p. 141}

HALL, Andrew, son of Andrew and Martha P. Hall, born 6 Feb 1864, baptized 2 Apr 1864, buried 12 Apr 1864. {Ref: Church Records, 1834-1903, pp. 34-35, 94}

HALL, Andrew, son of Andrew and Martha P. Hall, born 20 Sep 1867 at "Belvidere," baptized 21 Sep 1867. {Ref: Church Records, 1834-1903, pp. 36-37}

HALL, Andrew, confirmed 14 May 1865. {Ref: Church Records, 1834-1903, p. 294}

HALL, Andrew, died 15 Apr 1896, age 73, buried 17 Apr 1896, age 71 *[sic]*. {Ref: Church Records, 1834-1903, pp. 103, 200; Tombstone inscription}

HALL, Andrew (Mrs.), wife of Andrew Hall, Jr., buried 15 Oct 1849. [*Ed. Note:* In another Parish Register, 1696-1851, it indicates the wife of Andrew Hall, Jr. died in Chicago, Illinois and was buried in Baltimore County]. {Ref: Church Records, 1834-1903, p. 91}

HALL, Andrew G., see "Claudius H. Hall" and "Edward L. Hall," q.v.

HALL, Ann J., wife of Andrew Hall, died 26 Aug 1873 in her 78th year. {Ref: Tombstone inscription}

HALL, Anna (Annie) Maria, daughter of John Sidney and Martha P. Hall, born 28 Jul 1843, baptized 12 Feb 1853, confirmed 27 Apr 1856, died 25 Feb 1864, age 21. {Ref: Church Records, 1834-1903, pp. 24-25, 94, 297; Tombstone inscription}

HALL, Annie, daughter of Andrew and Martha (Mattie) P. Hall, born 16 May 1865, baptized 3 Jun 1865, died 6 Jul 1865 of cholera infantum, age 2 months and 10 days *[sic]*. {Ref: Church Records, 1834-1903, pp. 34-35, 95}

HALL, Annie, daughter of Andrew and Martha P. Hall, born 28 Jun 1866, baptized 17 Aug 1866 at Belvidere, died 1 Feb 1872 at Belvidier *[sic]*. {Ref: Church Records, 1834-1903, pp. 36-37, 96}

HALL, Avarilla Jane, daughter of Josias and Martha Hall, died 2 Sep 1852, age 58 years, 3 months and 14 days. {Ref: Tombstone inscription}

HALL, Charles P., died 9 Aug 1850, age 9. {Ref: Tombstone inscription}

HALL, Claudius Haines (twin of Edward), son of Andrew G. and Martha P. Hall, born 9 Jan 1869, baptized 24 Jan 1869; also see "Hall Family," q.v. {Ref: Church Records, 1834-1903, pp. 36-37}

HALL, Cordelia Giles, daughter of John Sidney and Martha H. Hall, born ---- [blank], baptized 26 Jul 1835 at "The Dairy" (sponsors: the parents and Mr. W. T. Hall). {Ref: Church Records, 1834-1903, pp. 16-17}

HALL, Cordelia Giles, daughter of John Sidney and Martha P. Hall, born 12 Apr 1835, baptized 12 Feb 1853. {Ref: Church Records, 1834-1903, pp. 24-25}

HALL, Cordelia Giles, married Rev. Claudius R. Haines on 5 Oct 1858. {Ref: Church Records, 1834-1903, p. 142}

HALL, Corrie Giles, confirmed 22 Aug 1854. {Ref: Church Records, 1834-1903, p. 296}

HALL, Edward B., buried 3 Apr 1837. {Ref: Church Records, 1834-1903, p. 90}

HALL, Edward Leeds (twin of Claudius), son of Andrew G. and Martha P. Hall, born 9 Jan 1869, baptized 24 Jan 1869, died 29 Apr 1869. {Ref: Church Records, 1834-1903, pp. 36-37, 96}

HALL, Eliza (colored), married James Wheeler (colored) on 25 Feb 1872. {Ref: Church Records, 1834-1903, p. 147}

HALL, Elizabeth, born 18 Dec 1762, died 11 Nov 1840. {Ref: Tombstone inscription}

HALL, Emeline Cordelia, daughter of Josias and Martha Hall, died 26 Apr 1820, age 16 years, 3 months and 8 days. {Ref: Tombstone inscription}

HALL, George Josias Ontario, son of Josias and Martha Hall, died 2 Apr 1845, age 42 years and 4 days. {Ref: Tombstone inscription}

HALL, George Washington, of Havre de Grace, buried 21 Oct 1853. {Ref: Church Records, 1834-1903, p. 92}

HALL, Henry, son of Walter T. and C. W. Hall, age 11, died 9 Mar 1859, buried 10 Mar 1859. {Ref: Church Records, 1834-1903, p. 93; Tombstone inscription}

HALL, Isabel, wife of Thomas Hall, died -- Oct 1827, age 53. {Ref: Tombstone inscription}

HALL, J. Sidney, see "Prina E. James" and "Araminta James" and "Priscilla H. Hall," q.v.

HALL, James H. (colored), married Harriet Moore (colored) on 12 Apr 1894. {Ref: Church Records, 1834-1903, pp. 158-159}

HALL, Jane (Miss), of Hickory Ridge, died 4 Sep 1852. {Ref: Church Records, 1834-1903, p. 92}

HALL, John Carvil Cranberry, son of Josias and Martha Hall, died 26 Jan 1855, age 59 years, 8 months and 20 days. {Ref: Church Records, 1834-1903, p. 92; Tombstone inscription}

HALL, John Sidney, married Priscilla C. Christie on 19 Feb 1856. {Ref: Church Records, 1834-1903, p. 140}

HALL, John Sidney, age 61, died 2 Jul 1864; also see "Martha P. Hall," q.v. {Ref: Church Records, 1834-1903, p. 94; Tombstone inscription}

HALL, John Sidney (Mr.), confirmed 27 Aug 1846. {Ref: Church Records, 1834-1903, p. 296}

HALL, Joseph (colored), married Hester Wilmer (colored) on 24 Jul 1892. {Ref: Church Records, 1834-1903, pp. 158-159}

HALL, Josias, died 31 Aug 1832, age 80 years and 5 months; also see "Avarilla J. Hall" and "Emeline C. Hall" and "George J. O. Hall" and "John C. C. Hall" and "Louisa E. Hall" and "Mary C. Hall," q.v. {Ref: Tombstone inscription}

HALL, Louisa Elizabeth, daughter of Josias and Martha Hall, died 26 Jan 1855, age 64 years, 9 months and 1 day. {Ref: Church Records, 1834-1903, p. 92; Tombstone inscription}

HALL, Martha, see "Claudius H. Hall" and "Edward L. Hall" and "Avarilla J. Hall" and "Emeline C. Hall" and "George J. O. Hall" and "John C. C. Hall" and "Louisa E. Hall" and "Mary C. Hall" and "Sidney Hall," q.v.

HALL, Martha P. (Miss), sponsored the baptism of Lily Isabel Cullum and Mary Edith Cullum on 8 Sep 1901. {Ref: Church Records, 1834-1903, p. 15}

HALL, Martha P. (Mrs.), sponsored the baptism of Nannie Moore Smith on 10 Jul 1892 and Ellen Moore Smith on 23 Aug 1903. {Ref: Church Records, 1834-1903, pp. 11, 17}

HALL, Martha Phillips, daughter of J. Syd. and M. P. Hall, born 25 Mar 1840, private baptism on 26 Mar 1840 (sponsors: Susan Hall and Cordelia Giles). {Ref: Church Records, 1834-1903, pp. 20-21}

HALL, Martha Phillips, daughter of John Sidney and Martha P. Hall, born 15 Mar 1840, baptized 12 Feb 1853, confirmed 3 Oct 1858. {Ref: Church Records, 1834-1903, pp. 24-25, 294}

HALL, Martha Phillips, wife of John Sidney Hall, died 20 Nov 1854, age 50, buried 21 Nov 1854. {Ref: Church Records, 1834-1903, p. 92; Tombstone inscription}

HALL, Martha Phillips, married Andrew Hall on 4 Nov 1857, died 2 Mar 1895, age 55, buried 4 Mar 1895. {Ref: Church Records, 1834-1903, pp. 102, 141, 200; Tombstone inscription}

HALL, Martha Phillips, daughter of Andrew and Martha P. Hall, born ---- [blank], baptized 1 Sep 1878, confirmed 9 Jun 1893, church member in 1903, married in the Philippines to Harold North, a British subject [date not given]; also see "Hall

Family," q.v. {Ref: Church Records, 1834-1903, pp. 42-43, 301; Parish Register, 1930-1958, p. 106}

HALL, Mary, born 30 Apr 1760, died 20 Feb 1845. {Ref: Tombstone inscription}

HALL, Mary (colored), age 18, died 29 Sep 1867 at Woodlawn and was interred in cemetery at colored people's meeting house. {Ref: Church Records, 1834-1903, p. 95}

HALL, Mary Clarissa, daughter of Josias and Martha Hall, died 14 Oct 1851, age 60 years and 6 days, buried 16 Oct 1851. {Ref: Church Records, 1834-1903, p. 92; Tombstone inscription}

HALL, Mary Moore, married Robert H. Smith on 12 Dec 1861. {Ref: Church Records, 1834-1903, p. 143}

HALL, Matilda C. (Mrs. Phillips M.), received from St. Mark's Church in Washington & Frederick Counties on 11 Sep 1901; sponsored the baptism of Edward Alfred Cullum and Edna Matilda Cullum on 26 Apr 1903; also see "---- Hall" and "Hall Family," q.v. {Ref: Church Records, 1834-1903, pp. 17, 206}

HALL, Mrs. A., see "Effie Thompson" and "Margaretta Wallace," q.v.

HALL, Nannie, married Edward Leeds Kerr on 16 Sep 1868. {Ref: Church Records, 1834-1903, p. 147}

HALL, Nannie, daughter of Sidney and Martha P. Hall, born 28 Jun 1866, died -- Feb 1871. {Ref: Tombstone inscription}

HALL, P. M. (Mrs.), sponsored the baptisms of Naomi Matilda Thompson on 19 May 1914 and Rosa Margarite Thompson on 29 Mar 1916. {Ref: Parish Register, 1903-1958, p. 33}

HALL, Philip Moore, died 13 Oct 1843 in his 23rd year. {Ref: Tombstone inscription}

HALL, Phillips Moore, son of Andrew and Martha P. Hall, born 3 Jul 1858, baptized 13 Jul 1858, confirmed 30 Sep 1876; sponsored the baptisms of Edward Alfred Cullum and Edna Matilda Cullum on 26 Apr 1903, Ellen Moore Smith on 23 Aug 1903 and Chapman Stuart Clark on 11 Sep 1910; also see "Matilda C. Hall" and "Hall Family," q.v. {Ref: Church Records, 1834-1903, pp. 17, 28-29, 298; Parish Register, 1903-1958, p. 31}

HALL, Priscilla C., confirmed 14 May 1865. {Ref: Church Records, 1834-1903, p. 294}

HALL, Priscilla H., wife of J. Sidney Hall, born 9 Oct 1810, died 24 Oct 1897. {Ref: Tombstone inscription}

HALL, Sarah, died 21 Dec 1827, age 65. {Ref: Tombstone inscription}

HALL, Sarah, see "Alice C. Hall," q.v.

HALL, Sidney, son of J. Sidney and Martha P. Hall, born 2 Sep 1832, baptized 23 Aug 1838. {Ref: Church Records, 1834-1903, pp. 18-19}

HALL, Sidney, son of John Sidney and Martha P. Hall, born 2 Sep 1837, baptized 12 Feb 1853, died 30 Oct 1859, age 23 [sic], buried 1 Nov 1859. {Ref: Church Records, 1834-1903, pp. 24-25, 93; Tombstone inscription}

HALL, Sidney, infant son of Andrew and Martha P. Hall, born 22 Nov 1860, baptized 31 May 1861. {Ref: Church Records, 1834-1903, pp. 30-31}

HALL, Silas Marine, died 27 Feb 1856 at Nice, Italy, had gone for health. {Ref: Church Records, 1834-1903, p. 92}

HALL, Sophia, relict of William Hall, died 18 Apr 1853, age 86 years, 1 month and 5 days. {Ref: Church Records, 1834-1903, p. 92; Tombstone inscription}

HALL, Sophia S., died 10 Feb 1873. {Ref: Tombstone inscription}

HALL, Susan, sponsored the baptism of Martha Phillips Hall on 26 Mar 1840; died [probably 18 Mar 1866] and buried 20 Mar 1866. {Ref: Church Records, 1834-1903, pp. 21, 94}

HALL, Thomas, died 9 Aug 1804, age 53; also see "Isabel Hall," q.v. {Ref: Tombstone inscription}

HALL, William, see "Sophia Hall," q.v.

HALL, William Henry (colored), son of Andrew and Mary Hall, born -- Jun 1845, baptized 10 Jul 1848, buried 4 Apr 1850. [*Ed. Note:* In another Parish Register, 1696-1851, it indicates Mary Hall was a servant woman of Mrs. Perryman]; also see "Hall Family," q.v. {Ref: Church Records, 1834-1903, pp. 22-23, 91}

HALL, W. T. (Mrs.), sponsored the baptism of Cordelia Giles Hall on 26 Jul 1835. {Ref: Church Records, 1834-1903, p. 17}

HALL, ---- (unnamed), daughter of P. M. and Matilda C. Hall, buried 17 May 1902, age 5 hours. {Ref: Church Records, 1834-1903, p. 104}

HALLON, ---- [blank], daughter of William and Harriett Hallon (colored), born ---- [blank] 1888, baptized 24 Aug 1888. {Ref: Church Records, 1834-1903, p. 7}

HAMILTON, William (orphan), born ---- [blank], baptized 5 Apr 1836. {Ref: Church Records, 1834-1903, pp. 16-17}

HAMILTON, Sarah E. (mother), wife of William T. Hamilton, born 9 Aug 1833, died 2 Jan 1907. {Ref: Tombstone inscription}

HAMILTON, William T. (father), born 3 Apr 1814, died 19 Mar 1879. {Ref: Tombstone inscription}

HAMMEL, Nellie May, daughter of William J. and Bertha E. Hammel, born 28(?) Apr 1919. {Ref: Parish Register, 1903-1958, pp. 34-35}

HAMMEL, Lillian Melba, daughter of William J. and Bertha E. Hammel, born 1 Dec 1920. {Ref: Parish Register, 1903-1958, pp. 34-35}

HAMMOND, Anna Hoke, daughter of Henry and Fanny Hammond, born 9 Jun 1839, baptized 24 Jun 1839. {Ref: Church Records, 1834-1903, pp. 18-19}

HAMMOND, Fanny J., sponsored the baptism of Sarah Bias Griffith on 29 Jan 1841. {Ref: Church Records, 1834-1903, pp. 20-21}

HAMMOND, Hannah Jane Allander, daughter of Henry and Fanny Hammond, born ---- [blank], baptized 27 Dec 1847, age about 3 years. {Ref: Church Records, 1834-1903, pp. 22-23}

HAMMOND, Henry, son of Henry and Fanny Hammond, born 2 Feb 1838, baptized 24 Jun 1839. {Ref: Church Records, 1834-1903, pp. 18-19}

HAMMOND, James Bias (twin of John), son of Henry and Fanny Jackson Hammond, born 17 Jun 1840, baptized 31 Oct 1840 (sponsor: Matilda Graham). {Ref: Church Records, 1834-1903, pp. 20-21}

HAMMOND, John Barrett (twin of James), son of Henry and Fanny Jackson Hammond, born 17 Jun 1840, baptized 31 Oct 1840 (sponsor: Matilda Graham). {Ref: Church Records, 1834-1903, pp. 20-21}

HAMMOND, Mildred, daughter of Henry and Fanny Hammond, born 5 Mar 1849, baptized 2 Apr 1849. {Ref: Church Records, 1834-1903, pp. 22-23}

HAMMOND, Sally, daughter of Henry and Fanny Hammond, buried 2 Oct 1846. [*Ed. Note:* In another Parish Register, 1696-1851, it indicates she was about 3 years old]. {Ref: Church Records, 1834-1903, p. 91}

HANSON, Raymond F., married Sarah E. Smith on 29 Jul 1916. {Ref: Parish Register, 1903-1958, pp. 138-139}

HANWAY, Thomas, confirmed 30 Sep 1876. {Ref: Church Records, 1834-1903, p. 298}

HANWAY, Thomas Howard (Mrs.), confirmed 10 Oct 1882. {Ref: Church Records, 1834-1903, p. 299}

HARLAN, David, M.D. (Medical Director, U. S. Navy), born 30 Nov 1809, baptized 8 May 1852, confirmed 27 Apr 1856, died 12 Jul 1893; also see "Margaret Harlan," q.v. {Ref: Church Records, 1834-1903, pp. 24-25, 297; Tombstone inscription}

HARLAN, H., M.D., sponsored the baptism of Herbert Harlan Michael on 11 Sep 1881. {Ref: Church Records, 1834-1903, p. 3}

HARLAN, James B., see "Mary Ann Harlan," q.v.

HARLAN, Margaret Rebecca, wife of Dr. David Harlan, born 15 Jun 1826, died 20 Jul 1903. {Ref: Tombstone inscription}

HARLAN, Mary Ann (mother), of Churchville, consort of James B. Harlan, born 30 Oct 1800, died 3 Feb 1869 "by second marriage M. A. Smith," buried 5 Feb 1869. {Ref: Church Records, 1834-1903, p. 95; Tombstone inscription}

HARLAN, Oleita Herbert, daughter of David and Margaret R. Harlan, died 23 Aug 1866, age 18. {Ref: Tombstone inscription}

HARRIS, Annie (colored), married Harrison Williams (colored) on 6 Jan 1870. {Ref: Church Records, 1834-1903, p. 147}

HARRIS, Catherine (colored), married Charles W. Tilson (colored) on 12 Aug 1869. {Ref: Church Records, 1834-1903, p. 147}

HARRIS, Fannie, married Zacharia Paine on 4 Jun 1864. {Ref: Church Records, 1834-1903, p. 145}

HARRIS, Fannie Cordelia (colored), daughter of Stephen and Harriet Harris, born ---- [blank], baptized -- Sep 1879. {Ref: Church Records, 1834-1903, pp. 42-43}

HARRIS, Frances (colored), married John W. Pitt (colored) on 16 Apr 1865. {Ref: Church Records, 1834-1903, p. 146}

HARRIS, Harriet (colored), married Caleb Reed (colored) on 3 Mar 1871. {Ref: Church Records, 1834-1903, p. 147}

HARRIS, Martha (Mrs.), buried 24 Dec 1847. {Ref: Church Records, 1834-1903, p. 91}

HARRIS, Mary Ella (colored), daughter of Stephen and Harriett Harris, born 27 Apr 1886, baptized 24 May 1887. {Ref: Church Records, 1834-1903, p. 6}

HARRIS, Stephen, see "Fannie C. Harris," q.v.

HARRIS, Susan (colored), daughter of Steve and Harriett Harris, born 13 Jan 1881, private baptism on 14 Mar 1882. {Ref: Church Records, 1834-1903, pp. 2-3}

HARRIS, Wesley (colored), married Frances Reed (colored) ---- 1877. [*Ed. Note:* The date was blank, but the marriage was listed between June and December in the register]. {Ref: Church Records, 1834-1903, p. 148}

HARRISON, Margaret F., married William C. Chase on 24 Dec 1885. {Ref: Church Records, 1834-1903, pp. 152-153}

HARTEAUFT, John, see "Marion Stockham," q.v.

HARVEY, Mary Elizabeth, daughter of ---- [blank], born ---- [blank], baptized 26 Sep 1880. {Ref: Church Records, 1834-1903, pp. 42-43}

HARVEY, Mitty Ann (colored), married William T. Dennison (colored) on 13 May 1883 at Colored M. E. Church. {Ref: Church Records, 1834-1903, p. 150}

HASKY, Antoine, son of Antoine and Margaret Haskey, born 18 Jan 1888, baptized 3 Jun 1888. {Ref: Church Records, 1834-1903, p. 7}

HAWKINS, Ann (Miss), confirmed 9 Jun 1836. {Ref: Church Records, 1834-1903, p. 296}

HAWKINS, Annie Jolley, married William Jolley Wallis [of Baltimore] on 15 Jan 1846. {Ref: Church Records, 1834-1903, p. 139}

HAWKINS, John, died 15 May 1831 age 31. {Ref: Tombstone inscription}

HAWKINS, Martha, buried 2 May 1866. {Ref: Church Records, 1834-1903, p. 94}

HAWKINS, Matthew, died 17 Feb 1831, age 36. {Ref: Tombstone inscription}

HAWKINS, Sarah, died 27 Apr 1803 in her 36th year. {Ref: Tombstone inscription}

HAYCOCK, Thomas Henry (colored), married Mary Eliza Pinion (colored) on 12 Mar 1891. {Ref: Church Records, 1834-1903, pp. 156-157}

HAYN, John W., married Theresa M. Rehren on 1 Oct 1881. {Ref: Church Records, 1834-1903, p. 150}

HEATH, Charles, married Caroline Ringgold on 20 Sep 1856. {Ref: Church Records, 1834-1903, p. 140}

HEMLESS, Margaret, married John Whitman on 7 Sep 1869. {Ref: Church Records, 1834-1903, p. 147}

HENDERSON, George, died 3 Oct 1847, age 74; also see "John H. Chauncey" and "Sarah Henderson," q.v. {Ref: Church Records, 1834-1903, p. 91; Tombstone inscription}

HENDERSON, John Munro, married Emily Cowan Nelson on 24 Jun 1914. {Ref: Parish Register, 1903-1958, pp. 138-139}

HENDERSON, Mary Alice, daughter of J. Munro and Emily C. Henderson, born 6 Mar 1916, baptized 11 Jun 1916 (sponsors: Dr. & Mrs. H. H. Street and Mrs. G. W. Thomas). {Ref: Parish Register, 1903-1958, pp. 32-33}

HENDERSON, Mary Amanda Henderson, married John Henry Chauncey on 12 May 1835. {Ref: Church Records, 1834-1903, p. 138}

HENDERSON, Priscilla Ann (of Spesutia), married John Cowen on 16 Jan 1840. {Ref: Church Records, 1834-1903, p. 138}

HENDERSON, Sarah, wife of George Henderson, sponsored the baptism of Sarah Elizabeth Cowan and George Anna Nelson on 1 Aug 1841; died 13 Sep 1857, age 73. {Ref: Church Records, 1834-1903, pp. 20-21, 93; Tombstone inscription}

HENDRICKSON, George Griffith, son of Col. Thomas and Elizabeth A. Hendrickson, born 27 Dec 1855, private baptism -- Feb 1856 (sponsors: the parents). [*Ed. Note:* This baptism was listed out of order in the register among the baptisms recorded in 1885-1886]. {Ref: Church Records, 1834-1903, pp. 4-5}

HENDRICKSON, Thomas (colonel, U. S. Army), married Elizabeth A. Perryman at Fort Smith, Arkansas by Rev. Washburn, on 25 Apr 1853. [*Ed. Note:* The foregoing information was entered in the register at St. George's in 1885]. Also, indicated he died 24 Oct 1878, age 79, and was buried in St. Louis, Missouri. {Ref: Church Records, 1834-1903, pp. 101, 152-153}

HENNING, Anna M., married Christian Linlop on 9 Jul 1850. {Ref: Church Records, 1834-1903, p. 140}

HENRIQUES, Joseph, born 18 Jun 1825, married Sarah B. Greenway on 22 Oct 1863, died 7 Apr 1900. {Ref: Church Records, 1834-1903, p. 145; Tombstone inscription}

HENRIQUES, Peter Hoke, son of Joseph and Sarah B. Henriques, born 31 Jul 1864, baptized 28 Sep 1864, died 24 Nov 1873. {Ref: Church Records, 1834-1903, pp. 34-35; Tombstone inscription}

HENRIQUES, Sarah Biays, wife of Joseph Henriques and daughter of Jacob and Ann Hoke, born 1 Feb 1829, died 22 Dec 1910, age 82 *[sic]*, buried 24 Dec 1910. {Ref: Parish Register, 1903-1958, p. 158; Tombstone inscription}

HERBERT, Elizabeth (Miss), age 70, born 4 Jul 1819, died 19 Sep 1899, buried 21 Sep 1899. {Ref: Church Records, 1834-1903, p. 104; Tombstone inscription}

HERBERT, James B., died 16 Jul 1830, age 36 years, 9 months and 1 day. {Ref: Tombstone inscription}

HERBERT, John (captain), died 12 Mar 1825, age 52 years, 8 months and 12 days. {Ref: Tombstone inscription}

HERBERT, Margaret, wife of Capt. John Herbert and mother of James B. Herbert and William P. Herbert, died 19 Jun 1849, age 98. {Ref: Tombstone inscription}

HERBERT, William P., M.D., died 16 Aug 1821, age 24 years, 5 months and 18 days. {Ref: Tombstone inscription}

HESS, Mary Catherine, daughter of Henry and Lizzie Hess, born 9 Nov 1870, baptized 13 Aug 1871. {Ref: Church Records, 1834-1903, pp. 38-39}

HIGBEE (HIGBIE), Edward Young (reverend), born 1808; rector of St. John's at Havre de Grace and St. George's at Perryman, 1829-1845; died 10 Dec 1871, age 63, buried in church yard. {Ref: Directory of Ministers and the Maryland Churches They Served, 1634-1990, Vol. I, p. 320; Historical Sketch of St. George's Parish (1953), pp. 9-10, 13}

HIGBEE, Mary Sophia Thomas, wife of Rev. Edward Young Higbee and daughter of Abraham Jarrett and Mary S. Thomas, born 25 Aug 1815, died 1 Jul 1836. {Ref: Tombstone inscription}

HINCHMAN FAMILY.
The following family information was entered in the church records under the heading of "Families" circa 1893-1903, but no relationships or ages were indicated, just names:
Wilfred Hinchman, Mrs. ---- [blank] Hinchman, and Ethel Hinchman. {Ref: Church Records, 1834-1903, p. 259}

HINSON, John Henry (colored), married Mary L. Carry (colored) on 17 Jun 1894 at "Medford" near Perryman. {Ref: Church Records, 1834-1903, pp. 158-159}

HITCHCOCK, Florence Viola, age 18 months, buried 23 Apr 1913. {Ref: Parish Register, 1903-1958, p. 159}

HOFFMAN, Allan, married Minerva J. Taylor on 21 Jun 1865. {Ref: Church Records, 1834-1903, p. 146}

HOKE, Ann, see "Sarah B. Henriques," q.v.

HOKE, Ann B., wife of Jacob Hoke and daughter of Col. James Biays, confirmed 14 May 1865, died 27 Oct 1875. {Ref: Church Records, 1834-1903, p. 294; Tombstone inscription}

HOKE, Charles Washington (colored), married Eliza Jane Dennison (colored) on 20 Sep 1888. {Ref: Church Records, 1834-1903, p. 154}

HOKE, Fannie, born 16 Jun 1832, died 23 Mar 1895. {Ref: Tombstone inscription}

HOKE, Jacob, born 7 Apr 1799, died 6 Jan 1876; also see "Ann B. Hoke" and "Mary J. Hoke" and "Peter Hoke," q.v. {Ref: Tombstone inscription}

HOKE, James, son of Semelia A. Hoke, born ---- [blank], baptized 7 Jul 1878. {Ref: Church Records, 1834-1903, pp. 42-43}

HOKE, Mary Jane, daughter of Jacob and Ann Hoke, died 12 May 1838, age 13 years, 8 months and 2 days, buried 13 May 1838. {Ref: Church Records, 1834-1903, p. 90; Tombstone inscription}

HOKE, Peter, of Havre de Grace, only son of Jacob and Ann Hoke, born 31 Jan 1831, died 13 Oct 1855, buried 15 Oct 1855. {Ref: Church Records, 1834-1903, p. 92; Tombstone inscription}

HOKE, Semelia, see "James Hoke," q.v.

HOKE, Virginia (colored), married George H. Matthews (colored) on 7 Feb 1866. {Ref: Church Records, 1834-1903, p. 146}

HOLLAND, Henry V. (colored), married Charlotte R. Stewart (colored) on 8 May 1884. {Ref: Church Records, 1834-1903, p. 151}

HOLLAND, John Isaiah, married Mary Elizabeth Williams on 10 Oct 1861. {Ref: Church Records, 1834-1903, p. 143}

HOLLAND, Sophia, married Henry Lisby on 11 Jun 1863. {Ref: Church Records, 1834-1903, p. 144}

HOLLAND, Susan, married Philip Monk on 27 Dec 1860. {Ref: Church Records, 1834-1903, p. 143}

HOLLINGSWORTH, Susan Ellen (servant of Mrs. Chauncey of "Primrose"), daughter of ---- [blank], born 11 Sep 1833, baptized 30 Jun 1837. {Ref: Church Records, 1834-1903, pp. 18-19}

HOLLIS FAMILY.
The following family information was entered in the church records under the heading of "Families" circa 1893-1903, but no relationships or ages were indicated, just names. Additional information shown in parenthesis was entered subsequently in the register:
Jacob Hollis (paralyzed 1909, dead, name lined out), Mrs. Ann C. Hollis, Kate E. Cooley (Mrs. B. Keen Michael), Ella Hollis, and Elliott F. Hollis. {Ref: Church Records, 1834-1903, p. 256}

HOLLIS, Anna Catherine, wife of Jacob C. Hollis, born 2 Dec 1842; sponsored the baptism of Mary Catharine Michael on 10 Dec 1899; confirmed 7 Dec 1902, age 60, Methodist affiliation, at the residence of Mr. Matthews; died 22 Dec 1915, age about 75, buried 24 Dec 1915; also see "Ella Hollis" and "Elliott F. Hollis" and "Hollis Family," q.v. {Ref: Church Records, 1834-1903, pp. 15, 303; Parish Register, 1903-1958, pp. 106, 159; Tombstone inscription}

HOLLIS, Benjamin, see "Mary R. Hollis," q.v.

HOLLIS, Ella, daughter of Jacob C. and Annie C. Hollis, born 15 Dec 1881, baptized 23 Jul 1882 (sponsors: the parents); received from the Church of the Ascension in Baltimore on 6 Sep 1901, married John Fletcher Hopkins on 28 Aug 1907; also see "Hollis Family," q.v. {Ref: Church Records, 1834-1903, pp. 2-3, 206; Parish Register, 1903-1958, pp. 106, 138-139}

HOLLIS, Ella, married Lewis D. Michael on 12 Jan 1864. {Ref: Church Records, 1834-1903, p. 145}

HOLLIS, Elliott Fernandis, son of Jacob and Annie C. Hollis, born ---- [blank], baptized 17 Sep 1879; also see "Hollis Family," q.v. {Ref: Church Records, 1834-1903, pp. 42-43}

HOLLIS, Jacob C., born 1 May 1835, married Annie C. Elliott on 20 Feb 1878, died 22 Aug 1910, age 76 [sic], buried 24 Aug 1910; also see "Ella Hollis" and "Elliott F. Hollis" and "Hollis Family," q.v. {Ref: Church Records, 1834-1903, p. 148; Parish Register, 1903-1958, p. 158; Tombstone inscription}

HOLLIS, Mary R., wife of Benjamin O. Hollis, died 20 Jan 1872, age 71. {Ref: Tombstone inscription}

83

HOLLISTER, W., see "Anne N. G. Davis," q.v.

HOLLOWAY, Charles C., born 26 Sep 1829, died 18 Sep 1900. {Ref: Tombstone inscription}

HOLLOWAY, Eleanor H., daughter of Carl and Ethel Holloway, born 24 Nov 1908, died 4 Dec 1908. {Ref: Tombstone inscription}

HOLLOWAY, Frank, sponsored the baptism of Sophia Louise Smithson on 20 Apr 1919. {Ref: Parish Register, 1903-1958, p. 35}

HOLLOWAY, George W., died 21 Jul 1904, age 73. {Ref: Tombstone inscription}

HOLLOWAY, H. S. (Mrs.), sponsored the baptism of Marshall William Baldwin on 16 Sep 1913. {Ref: Parish Register, 1903-1958, p. 33}

HOLMES, Charles (colored), married Harriett Smith (colored) on 22 Dec 1887. {Ref: Church Records, 1834-1903, p. 154}

HOLMES, Charles Wilton (colored), son of Rosina Holmes, born 31 Mar 1867 at Mr. John Martin's, baptized 11 Aug 1867. {Ref: Church Records, 1834-1903, pp. 36-37}

HOLMES, Rosina, see "Charles W. Holmes," q.v.

HONES (HOMES?), Charles (colored man), buried 6 May 1871. {Ref: Church Records, 1834-1903, p. 96}

HOOPES, Florence C., born 1884, died 1897. {Ref: Tombstone inscription}

HOOPES, Frank and Maggie, born 1896, died 1899. {Ref: Tombstone inscription}

HOOPES, Margaret Allen, daughter of James D. and Mary A. Hoopes, born 23 Nov 1891, private baptism (sick) on 10 Dec 1891 at home. {Ref: Church Records, 1834-1903, pp. 10-11}

HOOPMAN, C. Augustus, born 1834, died 1881. {Ref: Tombstone inscription}

HOOPMAN, Laura V., born 1838, died 1883. {Ref: Tombstone inscription}

HOOPMAN, Samuel C., born 1863, died 1881. {Ref: Tombstone inscription}

HOOPMAN, Walter W., born 1861, died 1882, buried 18 Jul 1882. {Ref: Church Records, 1834-1903, p. 100; Tombstone inscription}

HOOPS, Margaret E., married William Deckman on 9 Nov 1882. {Ref: Church Records, 1834-1903, p. 150}

HOPKINS, Carroll C., married Laura M. E. Baldwin on 1 Jan 1914 at the residence of the bride's father (also noted "See Register of Deer Creek Parish"). {Ref: Parish Register, 1903-1958, pp. 138-139}

HOPKINS, Edgar H., born 20 Aug 1902, died 8 Jul 1903. {Ref: Tombstone inscription}

HOPKINS, Ella Hollis, member in 1906, later removed [date not given]; also see "John F. Hopkins," q.v. {Ref: Parish Register, 1903-1958, p. 109}

HOPKINS, Frances, married Henry Allender (Alender) on 28 Oct 1860. {Ref: Church Records, 1834-1903, p. 143}

HOPKINS, George H., son of John H. and Mary M. Hopkins, died 1 Aug 1879, age 8 months. {Ref: Tombstone inscription}

HOPKINS, Henrietta (colored), married Lewis Pinion (colored) on 26 Jan 1867. {Ref: Church Records, 1834-1903, p. 146}

HOPKINS, Hetty, married Frank Maxfield on 23 May 1861. {Ref: Church Records, 1834-1903, p. 143}

HOPKINS, Jacob H., died 24 Jul 1870, age 12. {Ref: Tombstone inscription}

HOPKINS, John Fletcher, married Ella Hollis on 28 Aug 1907. {Ref: Parish Register, 1903-1958, pp. 138-139}

HOPKINS, John H., born 15 Nov 1834, died 29 Nov 1885; also see "Mary M. Hopkins" and "Oscar Hopkins," q.v. {Ref: Tombstone inscription}

HOPKINS, Margaret, married Richard M. Taylor on 16 May 1861. {Ref: Church Records, 1834-1903, p. 143}

HOPKINS, Martha A., sponsored the baptism of Annie Taylor on 24 Jun 1883. {Ref: Church Records, 1834-1903, p. 3}

HOPKINS, Mary Martha, wife of John H. Hopkins, born 29 Nov 1839, died 5 Oct 1910; also see "Oscar Hopkins," q.v. {Ref: Tombstone inscription}

HOPKINS, Oscar, son of John H. and Mary M. Hopkins, died 20 Oct 1885, age 12. {Ref: Tombstone inscription}

HOPPER, Hardwicke Manning, married Mary Hollister Davis on 7 Oct 1890 at "Bell Vue" near Havre de Grace. {Ref: Church Records, 1834-1903, pp. 156-157}

HOPPER, Mary H., see "Davis Family," q.v.

HORSEY, John (colored), married Elmira Christie (colored) on 25 Dec 1864. {Ref: Church Records, 1834-1903, p. 145}

HORTON, Lewis, buried 22 Feb 1864. {Ref: Church Records, 1834-1903, p. 94}

HOUSE, Samuel A., married Mary E. Sullivan on 10 Oct 1861. {Ref: Church Records, 1834-1903, p. 143}

HOWARD, Elizabeth, wife of Nathan Howard, died 19 Jan 1854, age 59. {Ref: Tombstone inscription}

HOWARD, Joseph, married Ann Dorr on 15 May 1858. {Ref: Church Records, 1834-1903, p. 142}

HOWARD, Leonard M., age 62, died 17 May 1851, buried 18 May 1851. [*Ed. Note:* In another Parish Register, 1696-1851, it indicates Mr. Leonard Howard, about 62 years old, died very suddenly and was buried 18 May 1850]. {Ref: Church Records, 1834-1903, p. 91; Tombstone inscription}

HOWARD, Nathan, see "Elizabeth Howard," q.v.

HOWE, James, died 3 Mar 1858 in his 18th year. {Ref: Tombstone inscription}

HUFF, Bertha M., born and died in 1904. {Ref: Tombstone inscription}

HUFF, Marjorie W., born and died in 1911. {Ref: Tombstone inscription}

HUGGINS, Hugh Thompson, son of Henry S. and Margaret Huggins, born 29 Sep 1853, baptized 23 Apr 1854. {Ref: Church Records, 1834-1903, pp. 26-27}

HUGGINS, John Robert Henry, son of Henry S. and Margaret Huggins, born 19 Jul 1857, baptized 10 Jan 1858. {Ref: Church Records, 1834-1903, pp. 28-29}

HUGHES, Benjamin F., born 22 Mar 1879, died 17 Jul 1910. {Ref: Tombstone inscription}

HUGHES, Joseph Lee, Presbyterian, confirmed 9 Mar 1919. {Ref: Parish Register, 1903-1958, pp. 89, 111}

HUGHES, Nancy, married Lewis Giles on 27 Sep 1866. {Ref: Church Records, 1834-1903, p. 146}

HUGHES, P. (mother), born 26 Jan 1854, died 22 Oct 1893. {Ref: Tombstone inscription}

HUGHES, W. Walter, born 18 Feb 1878, died 29 Jan 1916. {Ref: Tombstone inscription}

HUME, Evelyn Caldwell, daughter of Dr. R. C. and Sara C. Hume, born 10 Mar 1915, baptized 14 Nov 1916 at Adamstown, Maryland (sponsors: Mr. & Mrs. James Rogers and Mrs. George W. Thomas). {Ref: Parish Register, 1903-1958, pp. 32-33}

HUNTER, Mary, age 41, buried 17 Aug 1913 in Methodist Graveyard. {Ref: Parish Register, 1903-1958, p. 159}

HYDE, Annie M., wife of Harry S. Hyde, died 25 Sep 1886, age 30. {Ref: Tombstone inscription}

HYDE, Annie Mabel, Methodist, member in April, 1905, confirmed 22 Oct 1905, married James Herbert Owens on 1 Aug 1914. {Ref: Parish Register, 1903-1958, pp. 138-139; Parish Register, 1903-1958, p. 87, 109}

HYDE, Harry S., born 18 Oct 1850, died 23 Nov 1907; also see "Annie M. Hyde," q.v. {Ref: Tombstone inscription}

HYDE, Mabel, sponsored the baptisms of Henry Tarring on 19 Jul 1908, Alta McVail Grafton on 31 Oct 1909 and Malcolm Yarnall Tarring on 1 Jun 1913. {Ref: Parish Register, 1903-1958, pp. 31, 33}

ISER, Frank (colored), buried 23 Aug 1869. {Ref: Church Records, 1834-1903, p. 95}

ISER, Milcah Ann, daughter of Frank and Mary Iser (servants of Dr. Lemmon), born ---- [blank], baptized 8 Apr 1855. {Ref: Church Records, 1834-1903, pp. 26-27}

ISER, Sarah Ann, daughter of Frank and Mary Iser (servants of Dr. Lemmon), born ---- [blank], baptized 8 Apr 1855. {Ref: Church Records, 1834-1903, pp. 26-27}

ISER, Wilks Stansbury, son of Frank and Mary Iser (servants of Dr. Lemmon), born ---- [blank], baptized 8 Apr 1855. {Ref: Church Records, 1834-1903, pp. 26-27}

IVANS, Samuel B., married Sarah Ary on 20 Oct 1859. {Ref: Church Records, 1834-1903, p. 142}

IZER, Eliza, married Israel Robertson on 13 Mar 1848. {Ref: Church Records, 1834-1903, p. 139}

JACKSON, Alice D., daughter of William E. and A. A. Jackson, died 4 Mar 1884, age 10. {Ref: Tombstone inscription}

JACKSON, Henry, married Emaline Maxwell on 12 Apr 1857. {Ref: Church Records, 1834-1903, p. 141}

JACOBS, ----, see "Lilien Gallup," q.v.

JAEGER, Esther (neé Silver), born 20 Nov 1906. {Ref: Parish Register, 1903-1958, p. 42}

JAMES, Henry Manderson, church member in 1903, "removed-divorced-married" [dates not given]. {Ref: Parish Register, 1903-1958, pp 108-109}

JAMES, Henry Richardson, Presbyterian, confirmed 10 Apr 1904. {Ref: Parish Register, 1903-1958, p. 87}

JAMES, Prina Elizabeth (slave of J. Sidney Hall), daughter of ---- [blank], born -- Mar 1836, baptized 23 Aug 1838. {Ref: Church Records, 1834-1903, pp. 18-19}

JARRET, Charles (colored), married Harriet Ellen Curtis (colored) on 26 Apr 1867. {Ref: Church Records, 1834-1903, p. 146}

JAY FAMILY.

The following family information was entered in the church records under the heading of "Families" circa 1893-1903, but no relationships or ages were indicated, just names. Additional information shown in parenthesis was entered subsequently in the register:

    John Jay (dead), Mrs. ---- Jay, and Agnes Jay Duval (removed to Baltimore). {Ref: Church Records, 1834-1903, p. 250}

    Samuel S. Jay, Mrs. Annie E. Jay, Alice Mary Jay, Henrietta Davis Jay, Martha Davis Jay, and Miss Carrie Davis (died 30 Mar 1900). {Ref: Church Records, 1834-1903, p. 250}

JAY, Agnes S., confirmed 6 Aug 1879. {Ref: Church Records, 1834-1903, p. 298}

JAY, Agnes Susan, daughter of John G. and Mary G. E. Jay, born 30 Nov 1862, baptized 12 Sep 1863, married Edmund Bryce Duval on 11 Dec 1889 at Grace Church in Baltimore. {Ref: Church Records, 1834-1903, pp. 32-33. 156-157}

JAY, Alice Mary, daughter of John G. and M. G. E. Jay, born 4 Nov 1845, baptized 2 Sep 1846, confirmed 14 May 1865, died 15 Oct 1870, buried 17 Oct 1870 in John Jay Mausoleum at St. George's. {Ref: Church Records, 1834-1903, pp. 24-25, 96, 294; Cemetery records}

JAY, Alice Mary, daughter of Samuel S. and Annie E. Jay, born 18 Mar 1888, baptized 1 Jul 1888, confirmed 21 Nov 1909, married John Merryman Black on 28 May 1918 at Mr. & Mrs. E. Gassaway Guilford's home. [*Ed. Note:* The birth date was entered in the church records in a different handwriting from the baptism date]; also see "Jay Family," q.v. {Ref: Church Records, 1834-1903, p. 7; Parish Register, 1903-1958, pp. 87, 109, 138-139}

JAY, Annie E. (Mrs.), confirmed 9 Oct 1887; also see "Henrietta D. Jay" and "Martha D. Jay" and "Jay Family," q.v. {Ref: Church Records, 1834-1903, p. 300}

JAY, Edward Griffith, son of John G. and M. G. E. Jay, born 13 Jul 1850, baptized 26 Sep 1853(?) *[sic]*, confirmed 9 Aug 1867. {Ref: Church Records, 1834-1903, pp. 24-25, 297}

JAY, Henrietta Davis, daughter of Samuel S. and Annie E. Jay, born 29 Mar 1890, baptized 28 Sep 1890 (sponsors: the parents and Miss Mary H. Davis), confirmed 21 Nov 1909; also see "Jay Family," q.v. {Ref: Church Records, 1834-1903, pp. 10-11; Parish Register, 1903-1958, pp. 87, 109}

JAY, Henry, buried 4 Jan 1892, age 30(?). [*Ed. Note:* His age was written in the register as such, but in a different handwriting]. {Ref: Church Records, 1834-1903, p. 102}

JAY, Henry Davis, son of John and Mary G. E. Jay, born 12 Jun 1852, baptized 18 Sep 1852, confirmed 9 Aug 1867, died 27 Feb 1891 in Pallbrook, buried in John Jay Mausoleum at St. George's. [*Ed. Note:* The register indicates he was born 12 Jan 1852]. {Ref: Church Records, 1834-1903, pp. 24-25, 297; Cemetery records}

JAY, John, born 20 Feb 1817, died 24 Apr 1892, age 75, buried 26 Apr 1892 in John Jay Mausoleum at St. George's; also see "Mary G. E. Jay" and "Jay Family," q.v. {Ref: Church Records, 1834-1903, p. 102; Cemetery records}

JAY, John Goldsmith, son of John G. and M. G. E. Jay, born 26 Jun 1848, baptized 26 Sep 1853(?) *[sic]*, confirmed 14 May 1865. {Ref: Church Records, 1834-1903, pp. 24-25, 294}

JAY, John O., M.D., born 27 Jun 1848, died 10 Apr 1921, buried in John Jay Mausoleum at St. George's. {Ref: Cemetery records}

JAY, Martha (Mrs.), buried 4 Aug 1847. [*Ed. Note:* In another Parish Register, 1696-1851, it indicates she was 76 years old]. {Ref: Church Records, 1834-1903, p. 91}

JAY, Martha Davis, daughter of Samuel S. and Annie Jay, born 23 Feb 1893, baptized 28 Jun 1896 (sponsors: the parents and Mrs. Winifred S. Davis); member in 1910, later noted as "(Transferred) Living at Reading" [date not given]; also see "Jay Family," q.v. {Ref: Church Records, 1834-1903, pp. 12-13; Parish Register, 1903-1958, p. 110}

JAY, Mary G. E., wife of John Jay, born -- Sep 1821, died 8 May 1912, age 91, buried 11 May 1912 in John Jay Mausoleum at St. George's (her name was listed in register as Mrs. Mary G. E. D. Jay). {Ref: Parish Register, 1903-1958, p. 158; Cemetery records}

JAY, Samuel, see "Martha Smith," q.v.

JAY, Samuel Smith, son of John G. and M. G. E. Jay, born 10 May 1847, baptized 26 Sep 1853(?) *[sic]*, confirmed 14 May 1865, married Annie E. G. Davis on 11 Nov 1886; also see "Henrietta D. Jay" and "Martha D. Jay" and "Jay Family," q.v. {Ref: Church Records, 1834-1903, pp. 24-25, 152-153, 294}

JAY, Septimus D., M.D., son of John and Mary G. E. Jay, born 21 Apr 1858, died 15 Feb 1885, age 30, buried 18 Feb 1885 in John Jay Mausoleum at St. George's. {Ref: Church Records, 1834-1903, p. 100; Cemetery records}

JEFFERSON, Walter, see "Walter Giles," q.v.

JILES, John (colored), married Lizzie Gibson (colored) on 10 Mar 1892. {Ref: Church Records, 1834-1903, pp. 158-159}

JILES, Sidney (colored), married Crumwell Johnson (colored) on 10 Mar 1892. {Ref: Church Records, 1834-1903, pp. 158-159}

JOHNES, Henrietta (colored), married Solomon Stansbury (colored) on 15 Aug 1878. {Ref: Church Records, 1834-1903, p. 148}

JOHNSON FAMILY.
The following family information was entered in the church records under the heading of "Families" circa 1893-1903, but no relationships or ages were indicated, just names. Additional information shown in parenthesis was entered subsequently in the register:
Arthur E. Johnson, Mrs. Lucy Gertrude Johnson, Elwood Herbert Johnson (dead), and Helen Irene Johnson (dead). {Ref: Church Records, 1834-1903, p. 262}
Frank Johnson, Mrs. Gertrude Johnson (died, name lined out), Otis N. Johnson, and Alice Lear (dead). {Ref: Church Records, 1834-1903, p. 257}

JOHNSON, Abbie Marie, buried 17 Feb 1897, age 3 months. {Ref: Church Records, 1834-1903, p. 103}

JOHNSON, Albert, buried 19 Oct 1886, age 34. {Ref: Church Records, 1834-1903, p. 101}

JOHNSON, Alvin Maurice, son of Arthur and Lucy Johnson, born 3 Jan 1913, private baptism on 4 Jan 1913 at Perryman (ill), died 6 Jan 1913, age 3 days, buried 7 Jan 1913. {Ref: Parish Register, 1903-1958, pp. 30-31, 158}

JOHNSON, Anna (Mrs.), buried 27 Nov 1899, age 69. {Ref: Church Records, 1834-1903, p. 104}

JOHNSON, Arthur, see "Alvin M. Johnson" and "Elwood H. Johnson" and "Helen I. Johnson" and "Johnson Family," q.v.

JOHNSON, Benjamin Franklin, born 2 Sep 1861, married Gertrude E. Abrams on 20 Feb 1889 at the Church of the Epiphany in Philadelphia, died 12 Feb 1913, age 74 *[sic]*, buried 15 Feb 1913; also see "Gertrude E. Johnson," q.v. {Ref: Church Records, 1834-1903, p. 154; Parish Register, 1903-1958, p. 158; Tombstone inscription}

JOHNSON, Benjamin Frederick, son of Benjamin Franklin and Gertrude Etta (Abrams) Johnson, born 13 Dec 1907, baptized 13 Dec 1907 at Perryman (sponsors: W. B. Johnson, Charles H. Johnson and Stella Johnson). {Ref: Parish Register, 1903-1958, pp. 30-31}

JOHNSON, Benjamin S. (colored), married Olivia J. Stansbury (colored) on 14 Jan 1879. {Ref: Church Records, 1834-1903, p. 148}

JOHNSON, Caroline, see "William W. Johnson," q.v.

JOHNSON, Charles H., sponsored the baptism of Benjamin Frederick Johnson on 13 Dec 1907. {Ref: Parish Register, 1903-1958, p. 31}

JOHNSON, Crumwell (colored), married Sidney Jiles (colored) on 10 Mar 1892. {Ref: Church Records, 1834-1903, pp. 158-159}

JOHNSON, Edward (colored), married Hester Glover (colored) on 13 May 1877. {Ref: Church Records, 1834-1903, p. 148}

JOHNSON, Ella Keen, daughter of Otho N. and Ella (Keen) Johnson, born 3 Apr 1910, baptized on 11 Apr 1910 at home at "Wayside" (sponsors: the parents and Miss Elizabeth P. Porter). {Ref: Parish Register, 1903-1958, pp. 30-31}

JOHNSON, Ella Keen (neé Porter), church member in 1905, "(married in Darlington)" *[sic]*. {Ref: Parish Register, 1903-1958, p. 109}

JOHNSON, Elwood Herbert, son of Arthur E. and Lucy Gertrude Johnson, born 14 Jul 1900, private baptism on 21 Jul 1900 (very sick) in a house at the Flat Iron, buried 23 Jul 1900, age 8 days; also see "Johnson Family," q.v. {Ref: Church Records, 1834-1903, pp. 14-15, 104}

JOHNSON, Frank, married Sarah Christie on 28 Dec 1861; also see "Johnson Family," q.v. {Ref: Church Records, 1834-1903, p. 144}

JOHNSON, Gertrude Etta, wife of Benjamin F. Johnson, born 24 Apr 1866, confirmed 9 Jun 1893, died 13 Dec 1907, buried 16 Dec 1907; also see "Benjamin

F. Johnson" and "Elwood H. Johnson" and "Helen I. Gertrude" and "Johnson Family," q.v. {Ref: Church Records, 1834-1903, p. 301; Parish Register, 1903-1958, pp. 107, 158; Tombstone inscription}

JOHNSON, Harriet (slave of Dr. J. A. Preston), born -- Aug 1834, baptized 12 Aug 1838. {Ref: Church Records, 1834-1903, pp. 18-19}

JOHNSON, Helen Irene, daughter of Arthur E. and Lucy Gertrude Johnson, born 15 Mar 1902, private baptism on 16 Mar 1902 (sick) at "The Park Farm" and died 17 Mar 1902, age 2¼ days; buried 19 Mar 1902; also see "Johnson Family," q.v. {Ref: Church Records, 1834-1903, pp. 14-15, 104}

JOHNSON, James, buried 8 Oct 1895, age 55. {Ref: Church Records, 1834-1903, p. 103}

JOHNSON, James W., see "Lydia Johnson," q.v.

JOHNSON, Lucy, see "Alvin M. Johnson" and "Elwood H. Johnson" and "Helen I. Johnson" and "Johnson Family," q.v.

JOHNSON, Lydia A. W., wife of James W. Johnson, age 24, died 7 Jan 1854. {Ref: Tombstone inscription}

JOHNSON, Mary, married Charles Ringgold on 26 Dec 1857. {Ref: Church Records, 1834-1903, p. 141}

JOHNSON, May, age not indicated, buried 17 Sep 1918. {Ref: Parish Register, 1903-1958, p. 159}

JOHNSON, Otho, see "Ella K. Johnson" and "Willie W. Johnson" and "Keen Family," q.v.

JOHNSON, Otis N., see "Johnson Family," q.v.

JOHNSON, Samuel, see "William W. Johnson," q.v.

JOHNSON, Sarah Ann (slave of Mrs. Gover), born -- Sep 1838, baptized 29 Sep 1839. {Ref: Church Records, 1834-1903, pp. 20-21}

JOHNSON, Stella, sponsored the baptism of Benjamin Frederick Johnson on 13 Dec 1907. {Ref: Parish Register, 1903-1958, p. 31}

JOHNSON, W. B., sponsored the baptism of Benjamin Frederick Johnson on 13 Dec 1907. {Ref: Parish Register, 1903-1958, p. 31}

JOHNSON, William Warburton, son of Samuel W. and Caroline Johnson, born 28 Jan 1878; baptized 25 Aug 1907 at Perryman. [*Ed. Note:* "(Hypothetical)" is written in the "Sponsors" column; also sponsored the baptism of Willie Warburton Johnson on that same day. {Ref: Parish Register, 1903-1958, pp. 30-31}

JOHNSON, Willie, see "Porter Family," q.v.

JOHNSON, Willie? (Mrs.), sponsored the baptism of Ella Keen Steel on 1 Aug 1920. {Ref: Parish Register, 1903-1958, p. 35}

JOHNSON, Willie Warburton, son of Otho Nowland and Ella (Keen) Johnson, born 22 Nov 1906, baptized 25 Aug 1907 at Perryman (sponsors: the mother, W. W. Johnson and (by proxy) Mamie K. Rischel), confirmed 14 Mar 1920. {Ref: Parish Register, 1903-1958, pp. 30-31, 89, 111}

JONES, Charles (slave of Edward and Mary Griffith), son of ---- [blank], born 1822, baptized 14 Oct 1838. {Ref: Church Records, 1834-1903, pp. 18-19}

JONES, Charles, married Harriet ---- [blank] on 28 Nov 1847. {Ref: Church Records, 1834-1903, p. 139}

KEEN FAMILY.
The following family information was entered in the church records under the heading of "Families" circa 1893-1903, but no relationships or ages were indicated, just names. Additional information shown in parenthesis was entered subsequently in the register:
Benedict H. Keen (dead, name lined out), Mrs. Mary C. Keen, B. Frank Keen (removed to Philadelphia), Mrs. Nellie Keen, Mrs. ---- [blank] Keen (dead, name lined out, Mrs. Otho Johnson), and Mrs. Ella Keen Porter. {Ref: Church Records, 1834-1903, p. 252}

KEEN, Benedict Francis, son of Benedict H. and Mary C. Keen, born 28 Dec 1861, baptized, 20 Jul 1862; also see "Keen Family," q.v. {Ref: Church Records, 1834-1903, pp. 32-33}

KEEN, Benedict Hall, born 20 Nov 1823; he and wife sponsored the baptism of Warren Keen Rishel on 25 Sep 1881; died 14 Oct 1892, buried 16 Oct 1892, age 69; also see "Benedict F. Keen" and "Ella Keen" and "George P. Keen" and "Mary Keen" and "Keen Family," q.v. {Ref: Church Records, 1834-1903, pp. 3, 102, 200}

KEEN, Elizabeth, see "Joseph T. W. Keen," q.v.

KEEN, Ella, daughter of Benedict H. and Mary C. Keen, born 5 Feb 1866, baptized 23 Sep 1866 at New Market, married Dr. Alexander S. Porter on 10 Jun 1890; also see "Ella Keen Johnson" and "Willie W. Johnson," q.v. {Ref: Church Records, 1834-1903, pp. 36-37, 156-157}

KEEN, Frank, age 40+ years, buried -- May 1910. {Ref: Parish Register, 1903-1958, p. 158}

KEEN, George Bartol(?), buried 7 May 1866. [*Ed. Note:* His middle name was written in the register with a question mark after it.]; also see "Sarah Keen," q.v. {Ref: Church Records, 1834-1903, p. 94}

KEEN, George Percival, son of B. H. and Mary C. Keen, born 17 Apr 1871, died 2 Jul 1875. [*Ed. Note:* No date of baptism was given, but his baptism was listed among several others in the register between 1872 and 1875]. {Ref: Church Records, 1834-1903, pp. 40-41, 97; Tombstone inscription}

KEEN, Henry, see "Joseph T. W. Keen," q.v.

KEEN, James, see "Sarah G. Keen," q.v.

KEEN, John R., sponsored the baptism of William Henry Taylor on 26 Apr 1908; also see "John R. Keen, III" and "Norval B. Keen" and "William H. T. Keen" and "Laura B. Taylor," q.v. {Ref: Parish Register, 1903-1958, p. 31}

KEEN, John Robert, III, son of John Robert Jr. and Laura B. Keen, born 4 Dec 1910, baptized 1 Apr 1916 at the home of Mr. W. H. Taylor (sponsors: Mrs. William H. Taylor, Mrs. Byrd and Lawrence M. Taylor). {Ref: Parish Register, 1903-1958, pp. 32-33}

KEEN, Joseph T. Webster, son of Henry and Elizabeth Keen, born 19 Feb 1870, baptized 5 Apr 1870. {Ref: Church Records, 1834-1903, pp. 38-39}

KEEN, Laura, see "John R. Keen, III" and "Norval B. Keen" and "William H. T. Keen" and "Laura B. Taylor," q.v.

KEEN, Lizzie, married James Michael on 12 Feb 1863. {Ref: Church Records, 1834-1903, p. 144}

KEEN, Mary, daughter of Benedict and Mary C. Keen, born 29 Mar 1856, baptized 6 Jun 1857, confirmed 9 Feb 1873, married Abia Clark Reishel on 17 Jan 1878. {Ref: Church Records, 1834-1903, pp. 28-29, 148, 297}

KEEN, Mary, see "Sarah G. Keen," q.v.

KEEN, Mary, confirmed 9 Aug 1867, married Dr. Thomas P. Temple on 29 Sep 1870. {Ref: Church Records, 1834-1903, pp. 28-29, 147}

KEEN, Mary C. (Mrs.), sponsored the baptism of Katharine Keen Porter on 2 Jul 1893 at St. George's Church; removed in February, 1900, then received from St. Michael's and All Angels' Church in Baltimore on 17 Sep 1901; also see "Benedict F. Keen" and "Ella Keen" and "George P. Keen" and "Mary Keen" and "Keen Family," q.v. {Ref: Church Records, 1834-1903, pp. 13, 200, 206}

KEEN, Mister, see "Aminta ----," q.v.

KEEN, Mollie, see "Sarah Keen," q.v.

KEEN, Mrs., see "Taylor Family," q.v.

KEEN, Nathaniel B., died 14 Jul 1876, age 61. {Ref: Church Records, 1834-1903, p. 97; Tombstone inscription}

KEEN, Nellie, see "Keen Family," q.v.

KEEN, Norval Byrd, son of J. Robert Jr. and Laura B. Keen, born 21 May 1917. {Ref: Parish Register, 1903-1958, pp. 38-39}

KEEN, Robert, buried 17 Sep 1872. {Ref: Church Records, 1834-1903, p. 97}

KEEN, Robert, Jr., see "Laura B. Taylor," q.v.

KEEN, Roderick Dorsey, son of B. Franklin and Henrietta S. Keen, born 24 Aug 1889, baptized 1 Dec 1889, died 27 Jul 1890, age 11 months and 3 days, buried 28 Jul 1890. {Ref: Church Records, 1834-1903, pp. 9, 101; Tombstone inscription}

KEEN, Sarah, daughter of George B. and Mollie Keen, born 26 Feb 1864, baptized 19 Jun 1864. {Ref: Church Records, 1834-1903, pp. 34-35}

KEEN, Sarah Gaskins, daughter of James T. and Mary Keen, age 15 months, buried 2 Jul 1867 at Perrymanville. {Ref: Church Records, 1834-1903, p. 95}

KEEN, Sarah S. (Mrs.), buried -- Apr 1879. {Ref: Church Records, 1834-1903, p. 97}

KEEN, Susan, died 4 Apr 1852. {Ref: Tombstone inscription}

KEEN, William Henry Taylor, son of J. R. Jr. and Laura T. Keen, born 19 Jan 1908, baptized 26 Apr 1908. {Ref: Parish Register, 1903-1958, pp. 30-31}

KELL, Florence Elizabeth, infant daughter of Robert and Sally Kell, born ---- [blank], baptized 14 Apr 1860. {Ref: Church Records, 1834-1903, pp. 30-31}

KELL, Robert, married Sally Thompson on 31 May 1857. {Ref: Church Records, 1834-1903, p. 141}

KELL, Robert Alexander, son of Robert A. and Sally Kell, born -- Dec 1863, baptized 28 Jul 1864. {Ref: Church Records, 1834-1903, pp. 34-35}

KEMP, Perrin, married Louise R. Smith on 8 Nov 1866. {Ref: Church Records, 1834-1903, p. 146}

KENLEY, Elizabeth, see "William Kenley," q.v.

KENLEY, James Frank, Jr., married Mavourneen Williams on 15 Sep 1914 at A. K. Williams' residence in Ijamsville, Maryland. {Ref: Parish Register, 1903-1958, pp. 138-139}

KENLEY, Sarah (colored), age about 90, died 2 Jan 1867 at Woodlawn and was buried in the cemetery at colored people's meeting house. {Ref: Church Records, 1834-1903, p. 95}

KENLEY, William, son of Richard and Elizabeth M. Kenley, born 9 May 1858, baptized 12 Jun 1858. {Ref: Church Records, 1834-1903, pp. 28-29}

KENLY, B. Frank, born 1834, died 1893. {Ref: Tombstone inscription}

KENLY, Carryal Brides, daughter of William and Lena Rebecca Kenly, born ---- [blank], baptized -- Jul 1878. {Ref: Church Records, 1834-1903, pp. 40-41}

KENLY, John (colored), married Annie Williams (colored) on 15 Dec 1881. {Ref: Church Records, 1834-1903, p. 150}

KENLY, Lena, see "Semelia Kenly" and "Sarah R. Kenly" and "Carryal B. Kenly," q.v.

KENLY, Mary F., born 1836, died 1914. {Ref: Tombstone inscription}

KENLY, Richard, see "William Kenley," q.v.

KENLY, Sarah Rebecca, daughter of William and Lena Rebecca Kenly, born ---- [blank], baptized -- Jul 1878. {Ref: Church Records, 1834-1903, pp. 40-41}

KENLY, Semelia, daughter of William and Lena Rebecca Kenly, born ---- [blank], baptized -- Jul 1878. {Ref: Church Records, 1834-1903, pp. 40-41}

KENLY, William, see "William Kenley" and "Semelia Kenly" and "Sarah R. Kenly" and "Carryal B. Kenly," q.v.

KENNEDY FAMILY.

The following family information was entered in the church records under the heading of "Families" circa 1893-1903, but no relationships or ages were indicated, just names. Additional information shown in parenthesis was entered subsequently in the register:
Dr. James H. Kennedy, Mrs. Ione E. Kennedy, Elise Kennedy, Ethel Kennedy (Mrs. Howard H. Mitchell), Douglas E. Kennedy, and Miss Fannie Greene (removed). {Ref: Church Records, 1834-1903, p. 254}

KENNEDY, Douglas (Mr. & Mrs.), sponsored the baptism of John Sappington Mitchell and Nancy Carrol Mitchell on 24 Aug 1919. {Ref: Parish Register, 1903-1958, pp. 34-35}

KENNEDY, Douglas Elliott, son of James H. and Ione E. Kennedy, born 17 Apr 1886, baptized 23 Jun 1893 at home in Aberdeen (sponsor: the mother), confirmed 21 Nov 1909, married Sarah Elizabeth Cole on 13 Jun 1914; also see "Kennedy Family," q.v. {Ref: Church Records, 1834-1903, pp. 12-13; Parish Register, 1903-1958, pp. 87, 109, 138-139}

KENNEDY, Douglas Elliott, Jr., son of Douglas E. and Sarah E. Kennedy, born 29 May 1917, baptized 2 Sep 1917 at Dr. Kennedy's residence (sponsors: Cornelius Cole, Dr. J. H. Kennedy and Ethel Mitchell). {Ref: Parish Register, 1903-1958, pp. 32-33}

KENNEDY, Elise, daughter of Dr. James H. and Ione Kennedy, born ---- [blank], baptized 30 Jun 1879, confirmed 30 Apr 1899, age 20, died 21 Oct 1918, age not indicated, buried 23 Oct 1918 in Grove Churchyard; also see "Kennedy Family," q.v. {Ref: Church Records, 1834-1903, pp. 42-42, 302; Parish Register, 1903-1958, pp. 106, 159}

KENNEDY, Ethel, daughter of James H. and Ione E. Kennedy, born 2 Dec 1880, baptized 9 Jul 1893 (sponsor: the mother), confirmed 30 Apr 1899, age 18, married Howard Holmes Mitchell on 18 Jun 1902 at "Litchfield" in Aberdeen; also see "Kennedy Family," q.v. {Ref: Church Records, 1834-1903, pp. 12-13, 162-163, 203}

KENNEDY, Ione, see "Douglas E. Kennedy" and "Elise Kennedy" and "Ethel Kennedy" and "Kennedy Family," q.v.

KENNEDY, James H. (doctor), married Ione Elliott on 26 Feb 1878; sponsored the baptism of Douglas Elliott Kennedy, Jr. on 2 Sep 1917; also see "Douglas E. Kennedy" and "Elise Kennedy" and "Ethel Kennedy" and "Kennedy Family," q.v. {Ref: Church Records, 1834-1903, p. 148; Parish Register, 1903-1958, p. 33}

KENNEDY, Sarah, see "Douglas E. Kennedy, Jr.," q.v.

KERR, Edward Leeds, married Nannie Hall on 16 Sep 1868. {Ref: Church Records, 1834-1903, p. 147}

KERR, Nannie Hall (wife of E. Leeds Kerr), age 85, buried 11 May 1907. [*Ed. Note:* Her name was entered as "Mammie" instead of "Nannie" in the church record]. {Ref: Parish Register, 1903-1958, p. 158}

KEYSER, George Washington, born 1864, died 1919, age 35, buried 2 Apr 1919. {Ref: Parish Register, 1903-1958, p. 159; Tombstone inscription}

KEYSER, Mary Claypoole, born 1 Mar 1839, died 3 Jun 1895. {Ref: Tombstone inscription}

KIMBALL, Eliza, see "Botts Family," q.v.

KIMBALL, Hannah (Miss), buried 25 Mar 1887. {Ref: Church Records, 1834-1903, p. 101}

KIMBALL, Howard Stanly, buried 11 May 1895, age 14 months. {Ref: Church Records, 1834-1903, p. 103}

KIMBLE FAMILY.
The following family information was entered in the church records under the heading of "Families" circa 1893-1903, but no relationships or ages were indicated, just names:

Mr. Frank Kimble, Mrs. ---- [blank] Kimble, Ethel Belle Kimble, George Kimble, and Annie Kimble. {Ref: Church Records, 1834-1903, p. 260}

KIMBLE, Annie, see "Kimble Family," q.v.

KIMBLE, Carrie, see "John H. Kimble" and "Robert L. Kimble," q.v.

KIMBLE, Clay, "killed by the cars" and buried 1 Aug 1872. {Ref: Church Records, 1834-1903, p. 96}

KIMBLE, Eliza E., wife of Henry Kimble, born 22 Apr 1826, died 8 Apr 1899, buried 11 Apr 1899a; also see "Elizabeth J. Kimble," q.v. {Ref: Church Records, 1834-1903, p. 104; Tombstone inscription}

KIMBLE, Eliza Hattie (Miss), confirmed 1 May 1892, married Joseph Steele ---- 1900 [exact date not given]; also see "Eliza H. Steele," q.v. {Ref: Church Records, 1834-1903, pp. 204-205, 301}

KIMBLE, Elizabeth J., daughter of Henry and Eliza E. Kimble, born 15 Jan 1849, died 15 Jul 1850. {Ref: Tombstone inscription}

KIMBLE, Ethel, see "Kimble Family," q.v.

KIMBLE, Frances S., married James H. Rollason on 9 Apr 1868. {Ref: Church Records, 1834-1903, p. 146}

KIMBLE, Frank, see "Howard S. Kimble" and "Sarah C. Kimble" and "Kimble Family," q.v.

KIMBLE, George, see "Kimble Family," q.v.

KIMBLE, H. Clay, born 4 Dec 1848, died 2 Jul 1852. {Ref: Tombstone inscription}

KIMBLE, Hannah, see "John H. Kimble" and "Samuel Z. Kimble" and "Hannah Kimball," q.v.

KIMBLE, Henry, born 15 Sep 1813, died 30 Jan 1879; also see "Eliza E. Kimble" and "Elizabeth J. Kimble," q.v. {Ref: Tombstone inscription}

KIMBLE, Howard S., son of Frank C. and Sarah R. Kimble, born 1894, died 1895. {Ref: Tombstone inscription}

KIMBLE, John Henry, son of Samuel Z. and Hannah C. Kimble, born 17 Nov 1889, married Carrie Adele Denham on 17 Apr 1915, died 6 Nov 1916; also see "Robert L. Kimble," q.v. {Ref: Parish Register, 1903-1958, pp. 138-139; Tombstone inscription}

KIMBLE, Mary Susan, married John Henry Bradfield on 10 Aug 1869. {Ref: Church Records, 1834-1903, p. 147}

KIMBLE, Robert Linwood, son of John H. and Carrie Adele Kimble, born 16 Apr 1916, baptized 1 Oct 1916 at Perryman (sponsors: Mr. Kimble and Mr. & Mrs. John Denham). {Ref: Parish Register, 1903-1958, pp. 32-33}

KIMBLE, Samuel Z., husband of Hannah C. Kimble, born 4 Sep 1854, died 17 Mar 1919; also see "John H. Kimble," q.v. {Ref: Tombstone inscription}

KIMBLE, Sarah, married Charles Nelson ---- 1879. [*Ed. Note:* The date was blank, but the marriage was listed between January and April in the register]. {Ref: Church Records, 1834-1903, p. 148}

KIMBLE, Sarah Cordelia, daughter of Frank C. and Sarah R. Kimble, born 2 Feb 1902, died 25 Dec 1906, age 4, buried 27 Dec 1906. {Ref: Parish Register, 1903-1958, p. 158; Tombstone inscription}

KIMBLE, Sarah Naomi (adult), daughter of ---- [blank], born ---- [blank], baptized 12 Mar 1870, confirmed 14 Mar 1871. {Ref: Church Records, 1834-1903, pp. 38-39, 297}

KIMBLE, Sarah R., see "Howard S. Kimble" and "Sarah C. Kimble" and "Kimble Family," q.v.

KIMBLE, Zecharia, buried 27 Dec 1865. {Ref: Church Records, 1834-1903, p. 94}

KING, Benjamin (servant of Septimus D. Sewell), born 1845, baptized 26 Mar 1853. {Ref: Church Records, 1834-1903, pp. 26-27}

KING, William R. (major), age about 55, buried 19 Jul 1918 in Brooklyn, New York. {Ref: Parish Register, 1903-1958, p. 159}

KINSOLVING, Annie Laurie Pitt, member in 1911, transferred from Fort Collins, Colorado, later removed [date not given]. {Ref: Parish Register, 1903-1958, p. 110}

KINSOLVING, Wythe L. (reverend), rector from 1909 to 1912. {Ref: Parish Register, 1903-1958, p. ii}

KIRBY, Evelyn Elizabeth, daughter of Harry and Mary Kirby, born 5 Dec 1903, baptized 23 Apr 1918 in the church rectory (sponsor: the mother), confirmed 28 Apr 1918. {Ref: Parish Register, 1903-1958, pp. 34-35, 89, 111}

KIRBY, Gladys Marie, daughter of Henry and Mary Kirby, born 18 Feb 1900, baptized 23 Apr 1914 in the church rectory (sponsor: G. W. Thomas), confirmed 17 May 1914. {Ref: Parish Register, 1903-1958, pp. 32-33, 88, 110}

KIRBY, Harry (Henry), see "Evelyn E. Kirby" and "Gladys M. Kirby" and "Helen V. Kirby," q.v.

KIRBY, Harry Mason, confirmed 17 May 1914. {Ref: Parish Register, 1903-1958, pp. 88, 110}

KIRBY, Helen Virginia, daughter of Harry and Mary Kirby, born 3 May 1909. {Ref: Parish Register, 1903-1958, pp. 36-37}

KIRBY, Louisa, see "Mary L. Kirby" and "Rachel L. Kirby" and "Thomas E. Kirby," q.v.

KIRBY, Mary, see "Evelyn E. Kirby" and "Gladys M. Kirby" and "Helen V. Kirby," q.v.

KIRBY, Mary Lucretia, daughter of Zebulon and Louisa Kirby, born 17 Sep 1839, baptized 24 Oct 1839 (sponsors: George Nelson, Oliver Gallup, Sylvester Mitchell and Sarah A. Mitchell). {Ref: Church Records, 1834-1903, pp. 20-21}

KIRBY, Rachel Louisa, daughter of Zebulon and Louisa Kirby, born 25 Jan 1837, baptized 24 Oct 1839 (sponsors: George Nelson, Oliver Gallup, Sylvester Mitchell and Sarah A. Mitchell). {Ref: Church Records, 1834-1903, pp. 20-21}

KIRBY, Thomas Edward, son of Zebulon and Louisa Kirby, born 5 May 1838, baptized 24 Oct 1839 (sponsors: George Nelson, Oliver Gallup, Sylvester Mitchell and Sarah A. Mitchell). {Ref: Church Records, 1834-1903, pp. 20-21}

KIRBY, Zebulon, see "Mary L. Kirby" and "Rachel L. Kirby" and "Thomas E. Kirby," q.v.

KIRK, Hannah, consort of John Kirk, died 30 Oct 1826, age 52 years, 4 months and 19 days. {Ref: Tombstone inscription}

KIRK, John, died 5 Jan 1821 in his 50th (59th?) year. {Ref: Tombstone inscription}

KLOMAN FAMILY.
The following family information was entered in the church records under the heading of "Families" circa 1893-1903, but no relationships or ages were indicated, just names:
Mr. Edward K. Kloman, Mrs. Bessie Lee Kloman, and Ellen Lee Kloman. {Ref: Church Records, 1834-1903, p. 261}

KLOMAN, Bessie Lee, see "Edward N. Kloman" and "Ellen L. Kloman" and "Kloman Family," q.v.

KLOMAN, Agnes P., sponsored the baptism of Edward Nelson Kloman on 17 Jul 1903. {Ref: Church Records, 1834-1903, p. 17}

KLOMAN, Edward K., see "Edward N. Kloman" and "Ellen L. Kloman" and "Kloman Family," q.v.

KLOMAN, Edward Nelson, son of Edward K. and Bessie Lee Kloman, born 12 Jan 1903, baptized 17 Jul 1903 (sponsors: the parents, Rev. H. F. Kloman and Agnes P. Kloman). {Ref: Church Records, 1834-1903, pp. 16-17}

KLOMAN, Ellen Lee, daughter of Edward K. and Bessie Lee Kloman, born 1 Nov 1901, baptized 13 Apr 1902 (sponsors: the parents and Mrs. M. Alleine Pentz); also see "Kloman Family," q.v. {Ref: Church Records, 1834-1903, pp. 14-15}

KLOMAN, H. F. (reverend), sponsored the baptism of Edward Nelson Kloman on 17 Jul 1903. {Ref: Church Records, 1834-1903, p. 17}

KLOMAN, Nettie, Methodist, confirmed 11 Dec 1910, later removed [date not given]. {Ref: Parish Register, 1903-1958, pp. 88, 110}

KNIGHT, Annie E., born 15 Apr 1809, died 14 Jun 1898. {Ref: Tombstone inscription}

KNIGHT, Harriet Newell, daughter of Henry and Eliza Knight, born 28 May 1845, died 10 (18?) Sep 1848. {Ref: Church Records, 1834-1903, p. 91; Tombstone inscription}

KNIGHT, Henry, see "Harriet N. Knight," q.v.

KNIGHT, Joshua, buried 14 Apr 1885, age 68. {Ref: Church Records, 1834-1903, p. 101}

KNIGHT, Thomas (Mr.), buried 27 Jul 1848. {Ref: Church Records, 1834-1903, p. 91}

KNIGHT, William Amos, born 28 Nov 1841, died 7 Aug 1842. {Ref: Tombstone inscription}

KRIETE, Charles H., M.D., sponsored the baptism of Marcus K. Morgan and Miriam P. Morgan on 13 Dec 1898. {Ref: Church Records, 1834-1903, p. 15}

LACONEY, Joseph, son of Joseph W. and ---- [blank], born 14 Jun 1877, private baptism on 22 Jun 1884. [*Ed. Note:* No last name was given in the register for his parents, so Laconey could have been Joseph's middle name rather than his last name]. {Ref: Church Records, 1834-1903, pp. 4-5}

LAMDIN, Annie, married William L. Bartie on 25 Feb 1868. {Ref: Church Records, 1834-1903, p. 146}

LAMDIN, Eliza P., married Henry G. Brookings on 4 Dec 1867. {Ref: Church Records, 1834-1903, p. 146}

LANSDALE, Eliza, wife of William Lansdale, died 1 Sep 1877 in her 88th year. {Ref: Tombstone inscription}

LANSDALE, William Moylen, died 16 Feb 1831, age 47. {Ref: Tombstone inscription}

LARKIN, Mary Grace Minnie, daughter of John and Mary Larkin, born 14 Oct 1876, baptized 17 May 1885 (sponsors: Mary Larkin and Mary Bond). {Ref: Church Records, 1834-1903, pp. 4-5}

LARKINS, Thomas, confirmed 15 Nov 1885. {Ref: Church Records, 1834-1903, p. 299}

LAUTNER, Dora, see "Wilbur H. Flutka," q.v.

LAWDER FAMILY.
The following family information was entered in the church records under the heading of "Families" circa 1893-1903, but no relationships or ages were indicated, just names. Additional information shown in parenthesis was entered subsequently in the register:
Mr. ---- [blank] Lawder (near Boothby Hill), Mrs. ---- [blank] Lawder, Nellie A. Lawder, Verna V. Lawder, Samuel Lawder, and Raymond R. Lawder. {Ref: Church Records, 1834-1903, p. 260}

LAWDER, Nellie Aldora, age 16, confirmed 29 Dec 1901, church member in 1903; also see "Lawder Family," q.v. {Ref: Church Records, 1834-1903, p. 303; Parish Register, 1903-1958, p. 106}

LAWDER, Raymond Rickie, confirmed 11 Dec 1910, later removed [date not given]; also see "Lawder Family," q.v. {Ref: Parish Register, 1903-1958, pp. 88, 110}

LAWDER, Samuel, see "Lawder Family," q.v.

LAWDER, Verna Venora, age 14, confirmed 7 Dec 1902, church member in 1903; also see "Lawder Family," q.v. {Ref: Church Records, 1834-1903, p. 303; Parish Register, 1903-1958, p. 106}

LAY, Annie, see "Jacob A. Lay," q.v.

LAY, Catherine (Mrs.), died in 1875 or 1876 [exact date not given]; also see "Charles Lay" and "Godfred Lay" and "Jacob F. Lay," q.v. {Ref: Church Records, 1834-1903, p. 97}

LAY, Charles, son of Randolph and Catherine Lay, born 24 Nov 1865, baptized 27 Jul 1866 at Swamp Quarter. {Ref: Church Records, 1834-1903, pp. 36-37}

LAY, Christian, married Maggie Sheep ---- 1877. [*Ed. Note:* The date was blank, but the marriage was listed between June and December in the register]; also see "---- Lay," q.v. {Ref: Church Records, 1834-1903, p. 148}

LAY, Ernest Carroll, born 24 Aug 1910, died 16 Oct 1910, buried 17 Oct 1910. {Ref: Parish Register, 1903-1958, p. 158}

LAY, Godfred, son of Randolph and Catherine Lay, born 22 Jan 1864, baptized 24 Mar 1864, died 1 Jul 1866 of summer complaint. {Ref: Church Records, 1834-1903, pp. 34-35, 96}

LAY, Jacob August, son of Michael and Annie Lay, born 25 Jul 1868, baptized 25 Dec 1868. {Ref: Church Records, 1834-1903, pp. 36-37}

LAY, Jacob Francis, son of Randolph and Catherine Lay, born 5 Sep 1860, baptized 1 Jan 1862. {Ref: Church Records, 1834-1903, pp. 32-33}

LAY, Maggie, see "---- Lay," q.v.

LAY, Michael, see "Jacob A. Lay," q.v.

LAY, Michael (infant), buried -- Aug 1879. {Ref: Church Records, 1834-1903, p. 98}

LAY, Randolph, see "Charles Lay" and "Godfred Lay" and "Jacob F. Lay," q.v.

LAY, ---- [blank], infant of Christian and Maggie Lay, born ---- [blank], baptized 21 Apr 1878. {Ref: Church Records, 1834-1903, pp. 40-41}

LEANEDDLE(?), Eliza (Mrs.), died in 1875 or 1876 [exact date not given] [*Ed. Note:* Her name was written as such in the register with a question mark after it]. {Ref: Church Records, 1834-1903, p. 97}

LEAR, Alice, daughter of George W. and Mary C. Lear, born 26 Jul 1869, confirmed 1 May 1892, died 31 Jan 1896, buried 2 Feb 1896; also see "Johnson Family," q.v. {Ref: Church Records, 1834-1903, pp. 103, 204-205, 301; Tombstone inscription}

LEAR, Dorothy, daughter of John T. and Mary M. Lear, born 21 Sep 1903, private baptism at home on 28 Sep 1903 and died the same day. {Ref: Church Records, 1834-1903, pp. 16-17; Tombstone inscription}

LEAR, Emma M., daughter of George W. and Mary C. Lear, born 2 May 1877, died 11 Jul 1878. {Ref: Tombstone inscription}

LEAR, George W., born 11 Dec 1842, died 4 Feb 1920; also see "Alice Lear" and "Emma M. Lear" and "George W. Lear" and "James B. Lear" and "Morris W. Lear," q.v. {Ref: Tombstone inscription}

LEAR, George Wesley, son of George Wesley and Mary C. Lear, born 29 Oct 1874, baptized 22 Apr 1880, died 7 Mar 1884, buried 9 Mar 1884. {Ref: Church Records, 1834-1903, pp. 42-43, 100; Tombstone inscription}

LEAR, James Bennett, son of George Wesley and Mary C. Lear, born ---- [blank], baptized 22 Apr 1880. {Ref: Church Records, 1834-1903, pp. 42-43}

LEAR, John, see "Dorothy Lear" and "M. Susie Lear" and "Sylvia Lear" and "Nelson Family," q.v.

LEAR, John Walter, son of John and Mary Lear, born 9 Dec 1907, baptized 5 May 1907 (sponsors: the parents and, by proxy, Walter C. Michael), confirmed 14 Mar 1920. {Ref: Parish Register, 1903-1958, pp. 30-31, 89, 111}

LEAR, M. Susie, wife of John T. Lear, born 7 Nov 1859, died 12 Jun 1893. {Ref: Tombstone inscription}

LEAR, Maggie R., married Frederick K. Ethier on 19 Jan 1887. {Ref: Church Records, 1834-1903, pp. 152-153}

LEAR, Mary C., see "Alice Lear" and "George W. Lear" and "James B. Lear" and "Morris W. Lear," q.v.

LEAR, Mary M. (Mrs.), sponsored the baptism of Mary Catharine Michael on 10 Dec 1899; church member in 1903; also see "Dorothy Lear" and "Sylvia Lear," q.v. {Ref: Church Records, 1834-1903, p. 15; Parish Register, 1903-1958, p. 106}

LEAR, Morris W., son of George W. and Mary C. Lear, born 22 Apr 1872, died 23 Jan 1884, buried 25 Jan 1884, age 13 [sic]. {Ref: Church Records, 1834-1903, p. 100; Tombstone inscription}

LEAR, Sylvia, daughter of John T. and Mary M. Lear, born 15 Feb 1900, baptized Easter Sunday, 15 Apr 1900 (sponsors: the parents and Isabel Nelson), confirmed 17 May 1914; also see "Nelson Family," q.v. {Ref: Church Records, 1834-1903, pp. 14-15, 88, 110}

LEAR, ---- [blank], infant child of Mr. and Mrs. Lear, buried -- Jul 1878. {Ref: Church Records, 1834-1903, p. 97}

LEE, Charles W., born 1843, died 5 Jul 1906; also see "Clarence C. Lee" and "Elizabeth E. Lee" and "Emily A. Lee" and "Robert E. Lee" and "William T. Lee," q.v. {Ref: Tombstone inscription}

107

LEE, Clarence C., son of Charles W. and Emily A. Lee, died 7 Apr 1903, age 29. {Ref: Tombstone inscription}

LEE, Elizabeth E., daughter of Charles and Emily Lee, died 18 Nov 1902, age 31 years, 5 months and 1 day. {Ref: Tombstone inscription}

LEE, Ellen (colored), married Clayborn McDow on 24 Oct 1868. {Ref: Church Records, 1834-1903, p. 146}

LEE, Emily A., wife of Charles W. Lee, died 15 Oct 1893, age 39; also see "Clarence C. Lee" and "Elizabeth E. Lee" and "Emily A. Lee" and "Robert E. Lee" and "William T. Lee," q.v. {Ref: Tombstone inscription}

LEE, Harriet, see "Mary L. W. Lee," q.v.

LEE, Ida May, married Benjamin A. Ross on 4 Nov 1897. {Ref: Church Records, 1834-1903, pp. 160-161}

LEE, Joseph, married Rosanna Towson on 16 Jan 1851. {Ref: Church Records, 1834-1903, p. 140}

LEE, Mary L. (colored), married Abraham Davis (colored) on 1 Jun 1867. {Ref: Church Records, 1834-1903, p. 146}

LEE, Mary Louisa Williams (colored), daughter of Harriet Lee, born 11 Mar 1868, baptized 5 Dec 1868. {Ref: Church Records, 1834-1903, pp. 36-37}

LEE, Otho S., married Sally B. Griffith on 14 Mar 1867. {Ref: Church Records, 1834-1903, p. 146}

LEE, Robert E., son of C. W. and E. A. Lee, born 5 Aug 1872, died 12 Aug 1900. {Ref: Tombstone inscription}

LEE, William (colored), married Lucy Ringgold (colored) on 5 Dec 1867. {Ref: Church Records, 1834-1903, p. 146}

LEE, William T., son of Charles W. and Emily A. Lee, born 27 Feb 1904, age 24. {Ref: Tombstone inscription}

LEMMON, Doctor, see "Milcah Ann Iser" and "Sarah Ann Iser" and "Wilks Stansbury Iser," q.v.

LEMON, Matilda, buried 27 Jan 1855. {Ref: Church Records, 1834-1903, p. 92}

LEN(?), Henry, sponsored the baptism of Thomas Hartley Marshall, Jr. on 26 Dec 1914. {Ref: Parish Register, 1903-1958, p. 33}

LEWIS, Ann, see "Eliza Lewis" and "John Lewis" and "Josias W. Lee" and "Julia Lewis" and "Maria A. Lewis" and "Mary M. Lewis" and "Susan Lewis," q.v.

LEWIS, Eliza (colored), daughter of John and Ann Lewis (servants of Miss Milcha Budd), born 22 Mar 1839, baptized 22 Jun 1840. {Ref: Church Records, 1834-1903, pp. 20-21}

LEWIS, Eliza A. (colored), married Emory Ringgold (colored) on 7 Jul 1867. {Ref: Church Records, 1834-1903, p. 146}

LEWIS, John (colored), son of John and Ann Lewis (servants of Miss Milcah Budd), born 1836, baptized 22 Jun 1840; also see "Eliza Lewis" and "Josias W. Lee" and "Julia Lewis" and "Maria A. Lewis" and "Mary M. Lewis" and "Susan Lewis," q.v. {Ref: Church Records, 1834-1903, pp. 20-21}

LEWIS, John, married Emily Ramsy on 7 Jun 1862. {Ref: Church Records, 1834-1903, p. 144}

LEWIS, Josias William (colored), son of John and Ann Lewis (servants of Miss Milcah Budd), born -- Jan 1838, baptized 22 Jun 1840. {Ref: Church Records, 1834-1903, pp. 20-21}

LEWIS, Julia (colored), daughter of John and Ann Lewis (servants of Miss Milcah Budd), born 1833, baptized 22 Jun 1840. {Ref: Church Records, 1834-1903, pp. 20-21}

LEWIS, Maria Ann (colored), daughter of John and Ann Lewis (servants of Miss Milcah Budd), born 1828, baptized 22 Jun 1840. {Ref: Church Records, 1834-1903, pp. 20-21}

LEWIS, Mary Jane, married Solomon Williams on 1 Mar 1862. {Ref: Church Records, 1834-1903, p. 144}

LEWIS, Mary Minerva Monk, wife of William T. Lewis, died 7 Dec 1857, age 29. The following was inscribed on the monument: "Sacred to the memory of Mary Minerva Monk, wife of William T. Lewis of the city of New Orleans, Louisiana, who departed this life in that city 1837, aged 27 years. Her bereaved consort wanted in his presence inscribed on this monument an unfading sketch of her character as they now stand forth fresh and beautiful in his memory. For it would be impossible even for him who knew her best to tell with what perfect propriety, refinement and affection she acted her part in the various relations and social life. Her most intimate acquaintances whose eyes were permitted early to pursue the unsullied page of her life agree that in her character was realized a purity so high, so lovely, so divine, few could sufficiently admire and none could adequately describe it. Her heart was an unspotted mirror. No impure spirit dared to look into it or breathe upon, and through this she enjoyed sweet communion with her heavenly Father. The future world she contemplated with a degree of satisfaction and interest, which nothing but the high Christian faith can produce. Death was in her view, but the entrance, the gateway not dark, but lighted by rays of sun of righteousness and to come to a better world above where happiness shall reign unalloyed and immortal where the dear ties of love and friendship never be sundered, whose bright and undeeming realities will receive for over inaccessible to the evil sin, sorrow and death." {Ref: Tombstone inscription}

LEWIS, Mary Miranda (colored), daughter of John and Ann Lewis (servants of Miss Milcah Budd), born 1823, baptized 22 Jun 1840. {Ref: Church Records, 1834-1903, pp. 20-21}

LEWIS, Sarah, married James Wilmer on 13 May 1866. {Ref: Church Records, 1834-1903, p. 146}

LEWIS, Susan (colored), daughter of John and Ann Lewis (servants of Miss Milcah Budd), born 1837, baptized 22 Jun 1840. {Ref: Church Records, 1834-1903, pp. 20-21}

LEWIS, William E., married Theresa Wachsmuth on 17 Sep 1899. {Ref: Church Records, 1834-1903, pp. 160-161}

LEWIS, William T., see "Mary M. M. Lewis," q.v.

LINDSAY, Florence, sponsored the baptism of Emily McCay Morgan on 19 Sep 1910. {Ref: Parish Register, 1903-1958, p. 31}

LINDSAY, John Henry, sponsored the baptism of Emily McCay Morgan on 19 Sep 1910. {Ref: Parish Register, 1903-1958, p. 31}

LINGAN, John Henry, married Frank Ann Norton on 28 Apr 1863. {Ref: Church Records, 1834-1903, p. 144}

LINLOP, Christian, married Anna M. Henning on 9 Jul 1850. {Ref: Church Records, 1834-1903, p. 140}

LISBURY, Elizabeth (colored), married Abram Stansbury (colored) on 26 Dec 1882. {Ref: Church Records, 1834-1903, p. 150}

LISBY, Elizabeth, married James Amos Pitts on 14 Feb 1861. {Ref: Church Records, 1834-1903, p. 143}

LISBY, Harriet, married Isaac Welch on 5 Nov 1863. {Ref: Church Records, 1834-1903, p. 145}

LISBY, Henry, married Sophia Holland on 11 Jun 1863. {Ref: Church Records, 1834-1903, p. 144}

LITTLEFIELD, Dorothy Flora (neé Sholler), born 24 Mar 1918. {Ref: Parish Register, 1903-1958, p. 40}

LIZBY, Amanda M., married Andrew Harrison Williams on 6 Feb 1862. {Ref: Church Records, 1834-1903, p. 144}

LIZBY, Eliza Jane, married George Henry Bowser on 26 Dec 1861. {Ref: Church Records, 1834-1903, p. 143}

LIZLY, Jacob Theodore (colored), son of Jacob and Semelia Lizly, born 9 Jul 1854, baptized 26 Oct 1869. {Ref: Church Records, 1834-1903, pp. 38-39}

LIZLY, Joseph (colored), son of Jacob and Semelia Lizly, born -- Aug 1857, baptized 26 Oct 1869. {Ref: Church Records, 1834-1903, pp. 38-39}

LIZLY, Peter (colored), son of Jacob and Semelia Lizly, born 1 Jul 1849, baptized 26 Oct 1869. {Ref: Church Records, 1834-1903, pp. 38-39}

LIZLY, Robert Alexander (colored), son of Jacob and Semelia Lizly, born 4 Feb 1852, baptized 26 Oct 1869. {Ref: Church Records, 1834-1903, pp. 38-39}

LOANE, Mary Minnie, daughter of Edwin D. and Mary E. Loane, born 27 May 1865, baptized 25 Aug 1872. {Ref: Church Records, 1834-1903, pp. 40-41}

LOCKWOOD, Hattie, daughter of Robert and Bettie Lockwood, born 1 Oct 1858, buried 26 Jun 1867, buried in Baltimore. {Ref: Church Records, 1834-1903, p. 95}

LOEHNING, John, age 17, confirmed 29 Dec 1901, church member in 1903, later removed [date not given]; also see "Palmer Family," q.v. {Ref: Church Records, 1834-1903, p. 303; Parish Register, 1903-1958, p. 106}

LOEHNING, Louise, daughter of Anumiel and Annie Loehning, born 25 Dec 1882, confirmed 18 Nov 1900, age 18, removed to Church of the Messiah in Baltimore in 1901. {Ref: Church Records, 1834-1903, pp. 14-15, 303, 206-207}

LOVETT, Beulah, died 13 Mar 1854. {Ref: Tombstone inscription}

LOVETT, Joshua P., born 15 Mar 1803, died 21 May 1888. {Ref: Tombstone inscription}

LOVETT, Phoebe, died 21 Jun 1848. {Ref: Tombstone inscription}

LOW, Lizzie, married William C. Burton on 15 Jan 1889. {Ref: Church Records, 1834-1903, pp. 154-155}

LUCAS(?), Maude Nellie, sponsored the baptism of Lawrence Matthew Taylor on 26 Apr 1908. {Ref: Parish Register, 1903-1958, p. 31}

LYNCH, Amanda, sponsored the baptism of Paul Dulaney Gordy on 21 Jan 1915. {Ref: Parish Register, 1903-1958, p. 33}

LYNCH, Irvin Benjamin, son of William B. and Amanda S. Lynch, born 21 Jul 1912, private baptism on 16 Aug 1912 (ill) near Michaelsville. {Ref: Parish Register, 1903-1958, pp. 30-31}

LYNCH, William B., born 1866, died 1912. {Ref: Tombstone inscription}

MACRACKIN (McCRAGHEN), David, age 82, died 3 Feb 1851, buried 4 Feb 1851. [*Ed. Note:* In another Parish Register, 1696-1851, it indicates Mr. David Macrackin, age about 80 years, was buried 4 Feb 1850]. {Ref: Church Records, 1834-1903, p. 91; Tombstone inscription}

MALCOLM FAMILY.
The following family information was entered in the church records under the heading of "Families" circa 1893-1903, but no relationships or ages were indicated, just names. Additional information shown in parenthesis was entered subsequently in the register:
James W. Malcolm, Mrs. Mary E. Malcolm, Helen E. Malcolm, James E. Malcolm, Hugh Bush Malcolm (dead), Miss Anna Sarah Michael (removed to

Roanoke, Virginia), Charles Buck Malcolm, William Bush Malcolm, and Mrs. Sarah N. Nelson. {Ref: Church Records, 1834-1903, p. 252}

Mrs. ---- [blank] Malcolm (name lined out), Miss Georgie Malcolm (name lined out, followed by Mrs. Numbers), and Marion Malcolm (name lined out, but followed by the same name again, Marion Malcolm). {Ref: Church Records, 1834-1903, p. 256}

MALCOLM, Abbie Geneva, wife of Frank B. Malcolm, born 13 Feb 1848, died 5 Jan 1910, age 62, buried 8 Jan 1910. {Ref: Parish Register, 1903-1958, p. 158; Tombstone inscription}

MALCOLM, Charles Buck, son of James W. and Mary E. Malcolm, born 15 Nov 1892, baptized 25 Dec 1892 (sponsors: the parents and F. Willis Michael); also see "Malcolm Family," q.v. {Ref: Church Records, 1834-1903, pp. 10-11}

MALCOLM, Elizabeth A. (Mrs.), age 64, buried 7 May 1895 in Grove Church Cemetery. {Ref: Church Records, 1834-1903, p. 103}

MALCOLM, Frank, son of Oathman and Mary P. Malcolm, died 13 Jan 1890, buried 15 Jan 1890, "age circa 22." {Ref: Church Records, 1834-1903, p. 101; Tombstone inscription}

MALCOLM, Frank B., born 20 Aug 1840, died 15 Jun 1912, age 72, buried 18 Jun 1912; also see "Abbie G. Malcolm," q.v. {Ref: Parish Register, 1903-1958, p. 158; Tombstone inscription}

MALCOLM, Georgie K. (Miss), sponsored the baptism of Robert Bruce Yarnall and Harriet Ellen Yarnall on 2 Nov 1890; also see "Malcolm Family," q.v. {Ref: Church Records, 1834-1903, p. 11}

MALCOLM, Hattie E., married Jacob P. Yarnall on 15 Jan 1884. {Ref: Church Records, 1834-1903, p. 151}

MALCOLM, Helen Elizabeth, daughter of James W. and Mary E. Malcolm, born 16 Nov 1884, private baptism on 10 Feb 1885, confirmed 30 Apr 1899, age 14; church member in 1903 (her name was listed once as "Hellen Elizabeth Malcombe"); sponsored the baptism of Helen Elizabeth Russell on 12 Apr 1903; also see "Malcolm Family," q.v. {Ref: Church Records, 1834-1903, pp. 4-5, 17, 302; Parish Register, 1903-1958, p. 107}

MALCOLM, Hugh Bush, son of James W. and Mary E. Malcolm, born 11 Nov 1889, private baptism (sick) on 5 Jan 1890 (sponsors: the parents, F. Willis Michael and W. A. Alrich), buried 1 Sep 1891, age 1 year and 9 months. {Ref: Church Records, 1834-1903, pp. 9, 102}

MALCOLM, James, died 25 Jan 1853, age 25; also see "Malcolm Family," q.v. {Ref: Tombstone inscription}

MALCOLM, James Emory, son of James W. and Mary Ella Malcolm, born 20 Aug 1887, baptized 30 Oct 1887, confirmed 29 Dec 1901, age 14, church member in 1903. {Ref: Church Records, 1834-1903, pp. 6, 303; Parish Register, 1903-1958, p. 107}

MALCOLM, James W., married M. Ella Michael on 24 Jan 1884; confirmed 27 Nov 1886; sponsored the baptisms of Robert Bruce Yarnall and Harriet Ellen Yarnall on 2 Nov 1890 and John Edward Chase on 7 Oct 1900 and Lily Isabel Cullum and Mary Edith Cullum on 8 Sep 1901 and Helen Elizabeth Russell on 12 Apr 1903; also see "Charles B. Malcolm" and "Helen E. Malcolm" and "Hugh B. Malcolm" and "James E. Malcolm" and "William S. B. Malcolm" and "Malcolm Family," q.v. {Ref: Church Records, 1834-1903, pp. 11, 15, 17, 151, 300}

MALCOLM, John (captain), buried 8 May 1888. {Ref: Church Records, 1834-1903, p. 101}

MALCOLM, John R., son of Oathman and Mary P. Malcolm, died 6 May 1888, age 36. {Ref: Tombstone inscription}

MALCOLM, Marion, see "Oathman A. Malcolm" and "Malcolm Family," q.v.

MALCOLM, Mary, see "Frank Malcolm" and "John R. Malcolm" and "Mary E. Malcolm," q.v.

MALCOLM, Mary E., daughter of Oathman and Mary Malcolm, born 21 Sep 1861, died 28 Jul 1862. {Ref: Tombstone inscription}

MALCOLM, Mary Ella, church member in 1903, removed November, 1907(?); also see "Charles B. Malcolm" and "Helen E. Malcolm" and "Hugh B. Malcolm" and "James E. Malcolm" and "William S. B. Malcolm" and "Malcolm Family," q.v. {Ref: Parish Register, 1903-1958, p. 107}

MALCOLM, Mary P., wife of Oathman Malcolm, born 8 Feb 1826, died 2 Jan 1881. {Ref: Tombstone inscription}

MALCOLM, Oathman, born 13 May 1824, died 30 Oct 1890, buried 1 Nov 1890; also see "Frank Malcolm" and "John R. Malcolm" and "Mary E. Malcolm" and "Mary P. Malcolm," q.v. {Ref: Church Records, 1834-1903, p. 101; Tombstone inscription}

MALCOLM, Oathman Allen, son of Marion and ---- [blank] Malcolm, born 5 May 1894, baptized 24 Jul 1894 (sick) at St. George's Rectory. {Ref: Church Records, 1834-1903, pp. 12-13}

MALCOLM, Otho (Mrs.), buried 4 Jan 1881. {Ref: Church Records, 1834-1903, p. 98}

MALCOLM, Walter (Mrs.), buried -- Jan 1889. {Ref: Church Records, 1834-1903, p. 101}

MALCOLM, William B., see "Malcolm Family," q.v.

MALCOLM, William Edward, buried 9 Jul 1896, age 42. {Ref: Church Records, 1834-1903, p. 103}

MALCOLM, William Sharp Bush, son of James W. and Mary Ellen Malcolm, born 1 Nov 1897, baptized 12 Dec 1897 (sponsors: the parents and Charles W. Michael), died -- Aug 1920, age 23, buried 28 Aug 1920. {Ref: Church Records, 1834-1903, pp. 12-13; Parish Register, 1903-1958, p. 160}

MALCOLM, ---- [blank], buried 26 Feb 1883. {Ref: Church Records, 1834-1903, p. 100}

MARINE, Ellender, see "Ellen Morean," q.v.

MARKEL, Elizabeth, daughter of Adam and Catherine Markel, of "The Cottage," died 3 Aug 1865 of billious dysentery. {Ref: Church Records, 1834-1903, p. 95}

MARSHALL, Louise Trezevant Wigfall, daughter of Thomas Hartley and Margaritta T. Marshall, born 28 Jan 1916, baptized 12 Sep 1916 in the church rectory (sponsors: Judge Daniel G. Wright, Mrs. Mary Frances Taylor and Mrs. Frances P. Clarke). {Ref: Parish Register, 1903-1958, pp. 32-33}

MARSHALL, Thomas Hartley, Jr. son of Thomas and Margaretta T. Marshall, born 3 Sep 1912, baptized 26 Dec 1914 at parents' home at Glebe Farm (sponsors: Henry Len(?) and Frances T. Clarke). {Ref: Parish Register, 1903-1958, pp. 32-33}

MARTIN, A. Maria (Mrs. John), died in 1876. [*Ed. Note:* The exact date was not given in register, but her grave marker indicates she was born 16 Mar 1806 and died 17 Jun 1876]; also "Ann E. Martin" and "Anna M. Martin" and "Elizaebth A. Martin" and "John T. Martin" and "William G. Martin," q.v. {Ref: Church Records, 1834-1903, p. 97; Tombstone inscription}

MARTIN, Ann Elizabeth, wife of John Martin, died 28 Sep 1828, age 50. {Ref: Tombstone inscription}

MARTIN, Anna Mary, daughter of John and Ann E. Martin, died 22 Jun 1839 in her 22nd year. {Ref: Tombstone inscription}

MARTIN, Cornelia S., born 1849, died 1920. {Ref: Tombstone inscription}

MARTIN, Daniel, born 3 Oct 1804, died 3 Dec 1867; also see "Priscilla Martin" and "Daniel E. Martin" and "William S. Martin," q.v. {Ref: Tombstone inscription}

MARTIN, Daniel Edwin, son of Daniel and Priscilla Martin, born 3 Aug 1831, died 1 Jul 1867. {Ref: Tombstone inscription}

MARTIN, E. Jennie, daughter of Henry and Susanna Martin, born 9 Jan 1842, died 4 Jun 1915. {Ref: Tombstone inscription}

MARTIN, Elizabeth, see "Elizabeth McClure," q.v.

MARTIN, Elizabeth Ann, daughter of John and A. Maria Martin, born 1837, died 1851. {Ref: Tombstone inscription}

MARTIN, Elizabeth Streett, wife of Louis Martin, born 3 Nov 1824, died 14 Mar 1873. {Ref: Tombstone inscription}

MARTIN, Fanny Alverta, daughter of John and A. Maria Martin, born 14 Apr 1843, died 17 Jul 1844. {Ref: Tombstone inscription}

MARTIN, Henry, died 21 May 1855, age 47; also see "E. Jennie Martin" q.v. {Ref: Tombstone inscription}

MARTIN, Henry T., married Sarah E. Birckhead on 4 Jun 1868. {Ref: Church Records, 1834-1903, p. 146}

MARTIN, India (Mrs.), sponsored the baptism of Carrie Naudine Simmons on 6 Nov 1892. {Ref: Church Records, 1834-1903, p. 11}

MARTIN, John, see "Charles W. Holmes" and "Elizabeth McClure" and "A. Maria Martin" and "Ann E. Martin" and "Anna M. Martin" and "Elizaebth A. Martin" and "John T. Martin" and "William G. Martin," q.v.

MARTIN, John, died 26 Sep 1841, age 66. {Ref: Tombstone inscription}

MARTIN, John, confirmed 22 Aug 1854. {Ref: Church Records, 1834-1903, p. 296}

MARTIN, John (Mr.), age 63, died in 1876. [*Ed. Note:* The exact date was not given in church register, but his grave marker indicates he was born 9 Apr 1812 and died 2 Jan 1876]. {Ref: Church Records, 1834-1903, p. 97; Tombstone inscription}

MARTIN, J. N. (doctor), born 14 May 1834, died 20 Aug 1903. {Ref: Tombstone inscription}

MARTIN, John Thomas, son of John and A. Maria Martin, born 11 Dec 1846, died 25 Apr 1849. {Ref: Tombstone inscription}

MARTIN, L. C. (reverend), born 16 Sep 1839, died 22 Feb 1907; also see "Susie D. C. Martin," q.v. {Ref: Tombstone inscription}

MARTIN, Lewis, age 68, died 25 Apr 1887, buried 27 Apr 1887. {Ref: Church Records, 1834-1903, p. 101; Tombstone inscription}

MARTIN, Louis, see "Elizabeth S. Martin," q.v.

MARTIN, Maria, confirmed 22 Aug 1854. {Ref: Church Records, 1834-1903, p. 296}

MARTIN, Mary, see "Elizabeth McClure," q.v.

MARTIN, Priscilla, wife of Daniel Martin, born 26 Jan 1808, died 27 Apr 1882; also see "Daniel E. Martin" and "William S. Martin," q.v. {Ref: Tombstone inscription}

MARTIN, Susanna, see "E. Jennie Martin," q.v.

MARTIN, Susie D. Cole, wife of Rev. L. C. Martin, born 25 Nov 1844, died 16 May 1918. {Ref: Tombstone inscription}

MARTIN, Thomas Bay, born 5 Nov 1846, died 1 Jul 1848. {Ref: Tombstone inscription}

MARTIN, William G., son of John and A. Maria Martin, born 26 Oct 1844, died 17 Oct 1883, buried 19 Oct 1883. {Ref: Church Records, 1834-1903, p. 100; Tombstone inscription}

MARTIN, William S., son of Daniel and Priscilla Martin, born 22 Apr 1845, died 25 Oct 1868. {Ref: Tombstone inscription}

MARTIN, --?-- (Miss), sponsored the baptism of Mary Virginia Taylor on 26 Nov 1914. {Ref: Parish Register, 1903-1958, p. 33}

MASSON, James Henry, born 4 Jan 1844, died 8 Sep 1907. {Ref: Tombstone inscription}

MATTHEWS FAMILY.

The following family information was entered in the church records under the heading of "Families" circa 1893-1903, but no relationships or ages were indicated, just names. Additional information shown in parenthesis was entered subsequently in the register:

Lemuel E. Matthews (died 18 Mar 1903, name lined out), Mrs. Ella Matthews, Mrs. ---- [blank] Ruff, Hollis Matthews, and Mrs. Grace N. Matthews. {Ref: Church Records, 1834-1903, p. 256}

MATTHEWS, Alfonso (Alphonzo), born 1850, married Martha Deaver on 30 Nov 1871, died 1913; also see "Mary M. Matthews," q.v. {Ref: Church Records, 1834-1903, p. 147}

MATTHEWS, Alford, age 65, buried 9 Sep 1913. {Ref: Parish Register, 1903-1958, p. 159}

MATTHEWS, Ella, see "Matthews Family," q.v.

MATTHEWS, George H. (colored), married Virginia Hoke (colored) on 7 Feb 1866. {Ref: Church Records, 1834-1903, p. 146}

MATTHEWS, George H., married Sarah J. Reed on 29 Aug 1872. {Ref: Church Records, 1834-1903, p. 147}

MATTHEWS, Grace, see "Matthews Family," q.v.

MATTHEWS, Hollis, see "Matthews Family," q.v.

MATTHEWS, James, married Mary Butler on 17 Oct 1863. {Ref: Church Records, 1834-1903, p. 145}

MATTHEWS, Lemuel (Lem), see "Frederick Ehlert" and "Anna C. Hollis" and "Matthews Family," q.v.

MATTHEWS, Lemuel Ervin, born 6 Feb 1844, Methodist affiliation, age 59, confirmed 7 Dec 1902 (at the residence of Mr. Matthews), died 18 Mar 1903, age 59 years, 1 month and 13 days, buried 21 Mar 1903. {Ref: Church Records, 1834-1903, pp. 104, 208-209, 303}

MATTHEWS, Mary M., wife of Alfonso Matthews, born 1850, died 1919, age 68 years and 11 months, buried 3 Mar 1919. {Ref: Parish Register, 1903-1958, p. 159; Tombstone inscription}

MAXFIELD, Frank, married Hetty Hopkins on 23 May 1861. {Ref: Church Records, 1834-1903, p. 143}

MAXWELL, Emaline, married Henry Jackson on 12 Apr 1857. {Ref: Church Records, 1834-1903, p. 141}

MAYNADIER, J. Murray, married Hermione Rockwell on 24 Jul 1872. {Ref: Church Records, 1834-1903, p. 147}

McCARTNEY, Dennie, married William H. Deckman on 26 Feb 1898. {Ref: Church Records, 1834-1903, pp. 160-161}

McCLASKY, Minerva Ann, married Richard Thomas Ferguson on 18 May 1841. {Ref: Church Records, 1834-1903, p. 139}

McCLAY, Henry S. J., married Margaret Christie on 31 Aug 1854. {Ref: Church Records, 1834-1903, p. 140}

McCLURE, Elizabeth, buried 8 Mar 1851. [*Ed. Note:* In another Parish Register, 1696-1851, it indicates Elizabeth McClure, daughter of John and Ann Martin, was buried 8 Mar 1850]. {Ref: Church Records, 1834-1903, p. 91}

McCLURE, Martha, confirmed 14 May 1865. {Ref: Church Records, 1834-1903, p. 294}

McCOMAS, Caleb (colored), married Rebecca Brown (colored) ---- 1877. [*Ed. Note:* The date was blank, but the marriage was listed between June and December in the register]. {Ref: Church Records, 1834-1903, p. 148}

McCOMAS, Semelia Ann (colored), married Barney Smith (colored) on 30 Jan 1868. {Ref: Church Records, 1834-1903, p. 146}

McCOMMONS, Joseph T., born 1 Apr 1842, died 27 June 1916. {Ref: Tombstone inscription}

McCRAGHEN, David, see "David Macrackin," q.v.

McCRORY, Ruth, see "Ruth Roberta Rice," q.v.

McDOW, Clayborn (colored), married Ellen Lee (colored) on 24 Oct 1868. {Ref: Church Records, 1834-1903, p. 146}

McGAW, Alphonso N., married Nannie Sanders on 15 Dec 1885. {Ref: Church Records, 1834-1903, pp. 152-153}

McGAW, Mary (Mrs.), of Spesutia Island, buried 5 May 1854. {Ref: Church Records, 1834-1903, p. 92}

McGILL, Eliza (Mrs.), sponsored the baptism of Edward Asels Wells on 10 Aug 1884. {Ref: Church Records, 1834-1903, p. 5}

McGRAW, Caroline, died 11 Mar 1856 in her 70th year. {Ref: Tombstone inscription}

McLAUGHLIN, Patrick, age 53, died 23 Jul 1829. {Ref: Tombstone inscription}

McNEILLY, Vance Hill, born 13 Sep 1917. {Ref: Parish Register, 1903-1958, p. 40}

MEYERS, Charles Henry, son of C. H. and M. A. D. Meyers, born 3 Nov 1851, baptized 2 Aug 1852. {Ref: Church Records, 1834-1903, pp. 24-25}

MEYERS, Isabella, daughter of C. H. and M. A. D. Meyers, born ---- [blank], baptized 1 Dec 1850. {Ref: Church Records, 1834-1903, pp. 24-25}

MEYERS, John, see "Kate E. Meyers" and "Winfield C. Meyers," q.v.

MEYERS, Kate Estella, daughter of John A. and Mary Ann Meyers, born 8 Dec 1855, baptized 9 Mar 1856. {Ref: Church Records, 1834-1903, pp. 26-27}

MEYERS, Mary Ann D., confirmed 26 Jun 1853; also see "Mary Myers," q.v. {Ref: Church Records, 1834-1903, p. 296}

MEYERS, Samuel Dodson, son of C. H. and M. A. D. Meyers, born 23 May 1847, baptized 2 Aug 1852. {Ref: Church Records, 1834-1903, pp. 24-25}

MEYERS, Stephen Grimes, son of C. H. and M. A. D. Meyers, born ---- [blank], baptized 1 Dec 1850. {Ref: Church Records, 1834-1903, pp. 24-25}

MEYERS, Winfield Crampton, son of John A. and Mary Ann Meyers, born 25 Oct 1857, baptized 27 Dec 1857. {Ref: Church Records, 1834-1903, pp. 28-29}

MICHAEL FAMILY.
The following family information was entered in the church records under the heading of "Families" circa 1893-1903, but no relationships or ages were indicated, just names. Additional information shown in parenthesis was entered subsequently in the register:

B. Keen Michael (removed to Baltimore), Mrs. Kate E. Michael (removed to Baltimore), Cornelia Michael (removed to Baltimore), and Mary Catherine Michael (removed to Baltimore). {Ref: Church Records, 1834-1903, p. 260}

Charles W. Michael, Mrs. Susan R. Michael, Jacob Edmund Michael, Susanna Rebecca Michael, Fanny Cordelia Michael, Herbert Harlan Michael, Charles W. Michael, Jr., and William Howard Michael. {Ref: Church Records, 1834-1903, p. 259}

J. Jackson Michael (dead, name lined out), Mrs. Susan Michael (dead, name lined out), Charles W. Michael, Miss Fannie C. Michael (Mrs. Chapman, dead, name lined out), and F. Willis Michael (removed to Roanoke, Virginia). {Ref: Church Records, 1834-1903, p. 253}

Louis T. Michael (dead, name lined out), Mrs. Honora Michael, Miss Martha B. Michael (removed to Baltimore), Nora (lined out) Honora B. Michael, Edwin Bonn Michael, Mary Ellen Michael, and Louis Taylor Michael. {Ref: Church Records, 1834-1903, p. 253}

MICHAEL, Anna, see "Malcolm Family," q.v.

MICHAEL, Archer Lee, infant son of William B. and Rachel E. Michael. [*Ed. Note:* No date of birth or baptism was given, but the baptism was listed among several others in the register between 1872 and 1876]; died in 1875 or 1876 [exact date not given]. {Ref: Church Records, 1834-1903, pp. 40-41, 97}

MICHAEL, Benedict Keen, son of James H. and Elizabeth Michael, born 16 Jun 1869, baptized 5 Jun 1870, married Catharine Elliott Cooley on 6 Jun 1894; also see "Mary C. Michael" and "Michael Family" and "Hollis Family," q.v. {Ref: Church Records, 1834-1903, pp. 38-39, 158-159}

MICHAEL, Blanch Eugenia, sponsored the baptism of Blanch Eugenia Baldwin on 27 Oct 1895. {Ref: Church Recods, 1834-1903, p. 13}

MICHAEL, Catharine, daughter of Ethan and Catharine Michael, born ---- [blank], baptized 27 Dec 1838 at Michaelsville (sponsors: the parents); also see "Benedict K. Michael" and "Lewis D. Michael" and "Mary C. Michael" and "William B. Michael," q.v. {Ref: Church Records, 1834-1903, pp. 18-19}

MICHAEL, Charles Edwin, son of William B. and Rachel E. Michael. [*Ed. Note:* No date of birth or baptism was given, but the baptism was listed among several others in the register between 1872 and 1876]; sponsored the baptism of Edwin Bonn Michael on 8 Feb 1891; married Flora Mitchell Gallup on 19 Oct 1893; also see "Virginia G. Michael" and "Gallup Family," q.v. {Ref: Church Records, 1834-1903, pp. 11, 40-41, 158-159}

MICHAEL, Charles Wesley, son of J. J. and Susan Michael, born 26 Apr 1850, confirmed 14 Mar 1871; sponsored the baptisms of Harry Herbert Buck on 16 Nov 1882, Walter Cochran Osborn on 29 Jun 1884, Charles Wesley Michael, Jr. on 6 Jul 1884, William Sharp Bush Malcolm on 12 Dec 1897, Paul Nettleton Richards on 10 May 1903, Elmer Thomas Smith on 26 Apr 1908, and Alta McVail Grafton on 31 Oct 1909; died 23 Jan 1915, age 64 years and 9 months, buried 26 Jan 1915; also see "Michael Family," q.v. {Ref: Church Records, 1834-1903, pp. 13, 17, 297; Parish Register, 1903-1958, pp. 31, 107, 159; Tombstone inscription}

MICHAEL, Charles Wesley, Jr., son of Dr. J. E. and S. R. Michael, born 9 Jan 1884, baptized 6 Jul 1884 (sponsors: Mrs. Michael, CHarles W. Michael and C. Cole), confirmed 30 Apr 1899, age 15; church member in 1903, transferred to Emmanuel Church in Bel Air, Maryland [date not given]. {Ref: Church Records, 1834-1903, pp. 4-5, 302; Parish Register, 1903-1958, p. 107}

MICHAEL, Cordelia, see "Walter C. Michael," q.v.

MICHAEL, Cornelia, see "Michael Family," q.v.

MICHAEL, D., see "Mary Michael," q.v.

MICHAEL, E. K., sponsored the baptism of Elizabeth Keen Nelson on 12 Jul 1885. {Ref: Church Records, 1834-1903, p. 5}

MICHAEL, Edwin Bonn, son of Louis T. and Honora Michael, born 15 Nov 1890, baptized 8 Feb 1891 (sponsors: Charles Edwin Michael, Samuel G. Bonn and Martha B. Michael), confirmed 22 Oct 1905, transferred to Trinity Church in Wilmington, Delaware in 1913; also see "Michael Family," q.v. {Ref: Church Records, 1834-1903, pp. 10-11; Parish Register, 1903-1958, pp. 87, 109}

MICHAEL, Effie Elizabeth, daughter of James H. and Virginia M. Michael, born 21 Aug 1893, baptized 8 Oct 1893 (sponsors: the parents). {Ref: Church Records, 1834-1903, pp. 12-13}

MICHAEL, Elizabeth, see "Benedict K. Michael," q.v.

MICHAEL, Ella, married Goldsborough S. Griffith, Jr. on 14 Jun 1864 and married James W. Malcolm on 24 Jan 1884. {Ref: Church Records, 1834-1903, pp. 145, 151}

MICHAEL, Emily, see "Frank P. Michael" and "Robert L. Michael," q.v.

MICHAEL, Emily Augusta (adult), born 10 Feb 1853, baptized 17 Jun 1884 (witness: Mrs. Charles E. Buck). {Ref: Church Records, 1834-1903, pp. 4-5}

MICHAEL, Emory, confirmed 30 Sep 1876. {Ref: Church Records, 1834-1903, p. 298}

MICHAEL, Ethan, died 10 Sep 1868 in his 69th year, buried 12 Sep 1868; also see "Catharine Michael" and "Martha Michael" and "Martha E. Michael" and "William B. Michael," q.v. {Ref: Church Records, 1834-1903, p. 95; Tombstone inscription}

MICHAEL, Ethan, son of Ethan and Martha Michael, born 16 Feb 1844, died 11 Feb 1845. {Ref: Tombstone inscription}

MICHAEL, Eugene Bush, buried 31 Mar 1869, about 18 months old. {Ref: Church Records, 1834-1903, p. 95}

MICHAEL, F. (Mrs.), sponsored the baptism of Martha Laurinda Gallup (adult) on 20 Jul 1884. {Ref: Church Records, 1834-1903, p. 5}

MICHAEL, F. Willis, sponsored the baptism of Hugh Bush Malcolm on 5 Jan 1890 at St. George's Church; received from Roanoke, Virginia on 28 Apr 1892;

sponsored the baptism of Charles Buck Malcolm on 25 Dec 1892; returned to Virginia [no date given]; also see "Michael Family," q.v. {Ref: Church Records, 1834-1903, pp. 9, 11, 204-205}

MICHAEL, Fannie (Fanny) Cordelia, daughter of Dr. J. Edwin and Susie R. Michael, born ---- [blank], baptized 4 Jul 1880, married Dr. Pearson Chapman on 16 Oct 1895; also see "Michael Family," q.v. {Ref: Church Records, 1834-1903, pp. 42-43, 160-161}

MICHAEL, Fanny Cordelia, received from Grace Church in Baltimore on 10 Apr 1897. {Ref: Church Records, 1834-1903, p. 206}

MICHAEL, Flora Gallup (Mrs.), removed to Roanoke, Virginia on 13 Nov 1893; also see "Virginia G. Michael," q.v. {Ref: Church Records, 1834-1903, p. 202}

MICHAEL, Francis Willis, son of William B. and Rachel E. Michael. [*Ed. Note:* No date of birth or baptism was given, but the baptism was listed among several others in the register between 1872 and 1876]. {Ref: Church Records, 1834-1903, pp. 40-41}

MICHAEL, Frank Pusey, son of James W. and Emily A. Michael, born 5 Sep 1881, private baptism on 4 Mar 1884. {Ref: Church Records, 1834-1903, pp. 4-5}

MICHAEL, George Somers, age 25, buried 31 Mar 1884 in Abingdon M. E. Cemetery. {Ref: Church Records, 1834-1903, p. 100}

MICHAEL, Harriet E. (Mrs.), sponsored the baptism of Ellen Louisa Gibson (colored) and Walter Cook Gibson (colored) on 21 Sep 1881 at St. George's Church; received from All Saints' Church in Baltimore on 9 Apr 1902. {Ref: Church Records, 1834-1903, pp. 2-3, 208}

MICHAEL, Harriet Elizabeth (adult), daughter of ---- [blank], born ---- [blank], baptized 12 Mar 1870, confirmed 14 Mar 1871; also see "Sarah E. Michael," q.v. {Ref: Church Records, 1834-1903, pp. 38-39, 297}

MICHAEL, Harriet Jane, buried 12 Jun 1896, age 8 days. {Ref: Church Records, 1834-1903, p. 103}

MICHAEL, Harry, son of James H. and Lizzie Michael, born 16 Dec 1863, baptized 28 May 1871. {Ref: Church Records, 1834-1903, pp. 38-39}

MICHAEL, Herbert Harlan, son of Dr. J. E. and S. R. Michael, born 18 Jul 1881, baptized 11 Sep 1881 (sponsors: the parents, Dr. H. Harlan and Mrs. V. S. Osborn); received from Grace Church in Baltimore on 10 Apr 1897, church member in 1903; U. S. Navy [no dates given]; also see "Michael Family," q.v. {Ref: Church Records, 1834-1903, pp. 2-3, 206; Parish Register, 1903-1958, p. 107}

MICHAEL, Honora B., wife of Louis T. Michael, sponsored the baptism of William LeRoy Towner on 26 Aug 1900; received 12 Apr 1903; transferred to Trinity Church in Wilmington, Delaware in August, 1913; also see "Edwin B. Michael" and "Louis T. Michael" and "Mary E. Michael" and "---- Michael," q.v. {Ref: Church Records, 1834-1903, pp. 15, 202; Parish Register, 1903-1958, p. 107}

MICHAEL, Honora (Honoria) Blake, daughter of Louis T. and Honora (Honoria) Blake Michael, born 22 Jan 1889, baptized 27 Mar 1889, confirmed 7 Dec 1902, age 14 [sic], church member in 1903, transferred to Trinity Church in Wilmington, Delaware in August, 1913; also see "Michael Family," q.v. {Ref: Church Records, 1834-1903, pp. 8, 303; Parish Register, 1903-1958, p. 107}

MICHAEL, J. E., sponsored the baptism of James Llewellyn Owens on 1 Aug 1915. {Ref: Parish Register, 1903-1958, p. 33}

MICHAEL, J. Edwin, M.D., son of J. J. and Susan Michael, born 13 May 1848, married Susie R. Mitchell on 23 Dec 1875, died 7 Dec 1895, buried 9 Dec 1895; also see "Fannie C. Michael" and "Jacob E. Michael" and "William H. Michael," q.v. {Ref: Church Records, 1834-1903, pp. 103, 148; Tombstone inscription}

MICHAEL, J. H. (Mr.), sponsored the baptism of Martha Laurinda Gallup (adult) on 20 Jul 1884. {Ref: Church Records, 1834-1903, p. 5}

MICHAEL, Jacob (colonel), buried 20 Jan 1853, age 82 years and 5 months; also see "Semelia Ann Michael," q.v. {Ref: Church Records, 1834-1903, p. 92}

MICHAEL, Jacob Edmund, son of Dr. J. Edwin and Susie R. Michael. [*Ed. Note:* No date of birth or baptism was given, but the baptism was listed among several others in the register between 1872 and 1876]; received from Grace Church in Baltimore on 10 Apr 1897; church member in 1903; also see "Michael Family," q.v. {Ref: Church Records, 1834-1903, pp. 40-41, 206; Parish Register, 1903-1958, p. 107}

MICHAEL, Jacob Jackson, son of Col. Jacob Michael, born 11 May 1816, baptized 6 Jun 1857, confirmed 10 May 1860, died 25 Mar 1892, buried 27 Mar 1892, age

76; also see "Charles W. Michael" and "J. Edwin Michael" and "Susan Michael" and "Michael Family," q.v. {Ref: Church Records, 1834-1903, pp. 28-29, 102, 200, 294}

MICHAEL, James, married Lizzie Keen on 12 Feb 1863. {Ref: Church Records, 1834-1903, p. 144}

MICHAEL, James H., sponsored the baptisms of William McDonald Sutton on 3 Aug 1884 and Elizabeth Keen Nelson on 12 Jul 1885 and Virginia Missouri Michael on 8 Oct 1893; also see "Benedict K. Michael" and "Effie C. Michael" and "Harry Michael" and "Mary M. Michael" and "Sarah E. Michael" and "Virginia M. Michael" and "Walter C. Michael," q.v. {Ref: Church Records, 1834-1903, p. 5, 13}

MICHAEL, James Henry, born 1839, baptized 12 Mar 1870, confirmed 14 Mar 1871, removed to Roanoke, Virginia in May, 1890, died 14 Jul 1893, buried 16 Jul 1893. {Ref: Church Records, 1834-1903, pp. 38-39, 102, 200, 297}

MICHAEL, James Henry, Jr., confirmed 6 Aug 1879. {Ref: Church Records, 1834-1903, p. 298}

MICHAEL, James W., sponsored the baptism of Louis Taylor Michael on 12 Apr 1896; buried 12 Nov 1897, age 54. {Ref: Church Records, 1834-1903, pp. 13, 103}

MICHAEL, Jim (Miss), buried 12 Nov 1884, age 32. {Ref: Church Records, 1834-1903, p. 100}

MICHAEL, John H., age 40, buried 29 Sep 1897 in Grove Church Cemetery. {Ref: Church Records, 1834-1903, p. 103}

MICHAEL, John O. (Mr.), buried 12 Oct 1880. {Ref: Church Records, 1834-1903, p. 98}

MICHAEL, Kate Cooley, church member in 1903, later removed [date not given]. {Ref: Parish Register, 1903-1958, p. 107}

MICHAEL, Kate E., see "Michael Family," q.v.

MICHAEL, Lewis David, son of Ethan and Catharine Michael, born 1 Feb 1834, baptized 22 Jul 1838 (sponsors: the parents), married Ella Hollis on 12 Jan 1864. {Ref: Church Records, 1834-1903, pp. 18-19, 145}

MICHAEL, Lizzie, see "Harry Michael" and "Mary M. Michael" and "Sarah E. Michael" and "Walter C. Michael," q.v.

MICHAEL, Louis, see "Michael Family," q.v.

MICHAEL, Louis Taylor, born 1864, married Honoria (Honora) Blake Bonn 20 Jan 1887, confirmed 9 Oct 1887, died 12 Jan 1898, age 33, buried 14 Jan 1898; also see "Honora B. Michael" and "Mary E. Michael" and "Michael Family," q.v. {Ref: Church Records, 1834-1903, pp. 103, 152-153, 202, 300; Tombstone inscription}

MICHAEL, Louis Taylor, Jr., son of Louis Taylor and Honora B. Michael, born 2 Jan 1896, baptized 12 Apr 1896 (sponsors: the father, James W. Malcolm and Mary E. Malcolm), confirmed 11 Dec 1910, transferred to Trinity Church in Wilmington, Delaware in August, 1913, died -- Jan 1915, age 19, buried 9 Jan 1915. {Ref: Church Records, 1834-1903, pp. 12-13; Parish Register, 1903-1958, pp. 88, 110, 159; Tombstone inscription}

MICHAEL, Marcell, see "Nancy Michael," q.v.

MICHAEL, Martha, consort of Ethan Michael, died 1 Feb 1846 in her 34th year; also see "Ethan Michael" and "Martha E. Michael" and "Michael Family," q.v. {Ref: Tombstone inscription}

MICHAEL, Martha B., sponsored the baptism of Edwin Bonn Michael on 8 Feb 1891. {Ref: Church Records, 1834-1903, p. 11}

MICHAEL, Martha E., daughter of Ethan and Martha Michael, born 11 Jan 1848(?), died 27 Mar 1848. {Ref: Tombstone inscription}

MICHAEL, Martha Louisa (Louise), daughter of Walter Cook and Cordelia Michael, born 28 Sep 1902, died 12 Feb 1903, age 4 months and 15 days, buried 14 Feb 1903. {Ref: Church Records, 1834-1903, p. 104; Tombstone inscription}

MICHAEL, Mary, wife of D. Michael, age 51, died 26 Jun 1842. {Ref: Tombstone inscription}

MICHAEL, Mary Ann, confirmed 3 Oct 1858. {Ref: Church Records, 1834-1903, p. 294}

MICHAEL, Mary Catharine, daughter of Benedict Keen and Catharine E. Michael, born 7 Oct 1899, baptized 10 Dec 1899 at Bush River Neck (sponsors: the father,

Mrs. Anna C. Hollis and Mrs. Mary M. Lear); also see "Michael Family," q.v. {Ref: Church Records, 1834-1903, pp. 14-15}

MICHAEL, Mary E. (Ella), confirmed 19 Feb 1878; sponsored the baptism of Louis Taylor Michael on 12 Apr 1896. {Ref: Church Records, 1834-1903, pp. 13, 298}

MICHAEL, Mary Ellen, daughter of Louis T. and Honora B. Michael, born 28 Oct 1892, baptized 11 Dec 1892 (sponsors: Mrs. Gertrude B. Towner, Mrs. Mary E. Mitchell and Mr. J. Street Mitchell); also see "Michael Family," q.v. {Ref: Church Records, 1834-1903, pp. 10-11}

MICHAEL, Mary F., daughter of William C. and Mary L. Michael, born 27 Oct 1885, died 23 Jul 1886. {Ref: Tombstone inscription}

MICHAEL, Mary Martha, daughter of James H. and Lizzie Michael, born 8 Jun 1865, baptized 28 May 1871, confirmed 6 Aug 1879, married Aquila H. Nelson on 10 Jan 1883. {Ref: Church Records, 1834-1903, pp. 38-39, 150, 298}

MICHAEL, Mattie B. (Miss), confirmed 7 Mar 1884, church member in 1903. {Ref: Church Records, 1834-1903, p. 299; Parish Register, 1903-1958, p. 107}

MICHAEL, Mrs., see "Charles W. Michael, Jr.," q.v.

MICHAEL, Mrs. Dr., witnessed the baptism of Edmund Mitchell on 20 Nov 1891. {Ref: Church Records, 1834-1903, p. 11}

MICHAEL, Nancy, daughter of Lt.Cmdr. William Howard and Marcell Michael, born 29 Jul 1920. {Ref: Parish Register, 1903-1958, pp. 34-35}

MICHAEL, Nannie (Miss), confirmed 27 Nov 1886, removed to Roanoke, Virginia on 7 Oct 1892. {Ref: Church Records, 1834-1903, pp. 202, 300}

MICHAEL, Rachel E. (Mrs.), confirmed 9 Feb 1873, buried -- Sep 1878; also see "Archer L. Michael" and "Charles E. Michael" and "Francis W. Michael" and "Sarah A. Michael," q.v. {Ref: Church Records, 1834-1903, pp. 97, 297}

MICHAEL, Robert Lee, son of James W. and Emily A. Michael, born 10 Jul 1879, private baptism on 4 Mar 1884. {Ref: Church Records, 1834-1903, pp. 4-5}

MICHAEL, Sarah Annie, daughter of William B. and Rachel E. Michael. [*Ed. Note:* No date of birth or baptism was given, but the baptism was listed among several others in the register between 1872 and 1876]. {Ref: Church Records, 1834-1903, pp. 40-41}

MICHAEL, Sarah Elizabeth, daughter of James H. and Harriett E. Michael, born 1 Dec 1885, private baptism on 24 Jan 1886 (new born to be received). {Ref: Church Records, 1834-1903, pp. 4-5}

MICHAEL, Semelia Ann, married Thomas Jefferson Murphy on 24 Jun 1840 at Michaelsville. {Ref: Church Records, 1834-1903, p. 138}

MICHAEL, Susan, wife of Jacob Jackson Michael, born 25 Aug 1810, died 17 Apr 1895, buried 19 Apr 1895, age 84; also see "Charles W. Michael" and "J. Edwin Michael" and "William H. Michael" and "Michael Family," q.v. {Ref: Church Records, 1834-1903, p. 102}

MICHAEL, Susan R. (Mrs.), sponsored the baptism of Martha Susanna Osborn on 10 Sep 1882 at St. George's Church; received from Grace Church in Baltimore on 10 Apr 1897. {Ref: Church Records, 1834-1903, pp. 3, 206}

MICHAEL, Susanna Rebecca, daughter of Dr. J. E. and S. R. Michael, born 4 Dec 1877, baptized 11 Sep 1881 (sponsors: the parents); received from Grace Church in Baltimore on 16 Apr 1897, married Dr. Armfield Franklin VanBibber on 16 Oct 1901; church member in 1903; also see "Michael Family," q.v. {Ref: Church Records, 1834-1903, pp. 2-3, 162-163, 206; Parish Register, 1903-1958, p. 107}

MICHAEL, Virginia Gallup, daughter of Charles E. and Flora M. Michael, born 25 Jul 1894, baptized 11 Nov 1894 (sponsors: the parents and Mrs. Annie E. Gallup). {Ref: Church Records, 1834-1903, pp. 12-13}

MICHAEL, Virginia Missouri, daughter of Mrs. James H. Michael, born 14 Jul 1866, baptized 8 Oct 1893 (sponsors: Mrs. Mary M. Nelson and James H. Michael). {Ref: Church Records, 1834-1903, pp. 12-13}

MICHAEL, Walter Cook, son of James H. and Lizzie Michael, born ---- [blank], baptized 21 Apr 1878; sponsored the baptism of John Walter Lear (by proxy) on 5 May 1907; also see "Martha L. Michael," q.v. {Ref: Church Records, 1834-1903, pp. 40-41; Parish Register, 1903-1958, p. 31}

MICHAEL, Walter Keen, born 6 Nov 1897, buried 30 Jun 1898. {Ref: Church Records, 1834-1903, p. 104}

MICHAEL, William B., buried 10 Aug 1879; also see "Archer L. Michael" and "Charles E. Michael" and "Francis W. Michael" and "Sarah A. Michael," q.v. {Ref: Church Records, 1834-1903, p. 98}

MICHAEL, William Bush, son of Ethan and Catharine Michael, born 22 Mar 1832, baptized 22 Jul 1838 (sponsors: the parents). {Ref: Church Records, 1834-1903, pp. 18-19}

MICHAEL, William C., born 26 Apr 1843, died 27 Feb 1912; also see "Mary F. Michael," q.v. {Ref: Tombstone inscription}

MICHAEL, William Emory, buried 29 Feb 1880. {Ref: Church Records, 1834-1903, p. 98}

MICHAEL, William Howard, son of Dr. J. Edwin and Susan R. Michael, born 26 Feb 1888, baptized 5 Aug 1888, confirmed 29 Dec 1901, age 14 *[sic]*, church member in 1903; also see "Nancy Michael" and "Michael Family," q.v. {Ref: Church Records, 1834-1903, pp. 7, 303; Parish Register, 1903-1958, p. 107}

MICHAEL, ---- (unnamed), infant son of Louis T. and Honora B. Michael, buried 22 Feb 1894, age 48 hours. {Ref: Church Records, 1834-1903, p. 102}

MILLER, Annie M. (colored), married Andrew H. Pitt (colored) on 9 Mar 1882. {Ref: Church Records, 1834-1903, p. 150}

MILLER, Elizabeth (Miss), confirmed 9 Oct 1887. {Ref: Church Records, 1834-1903, p. 300}

MILLER, George Henry (colored), married Mary Welsh (colored) on 4 Jun 1891. {Ref: Church Records, 1834-1903, pp. 156-157}

MILLER, Louisa Kate, confirmed 3 Oct 1858. {Ref: Church Records, 1834-1903, p. 294}

MILLER, Mary Elizabeth (colored), daughter of Caroline Monk and H. Miller, born 18 May 1882, private baptism on 31 Oct 1882. {Ref: Church Records, 1834-1903, pp. 2-3}

MILLS, Nicholas (colored), married Octavia Norton (colored) on 23 May 1872. {Ref: Church Records, 1834-1903, p. 147}

MITCHELL FAMILY.

The following family information was entered in the church records under the heading of "Families" circa 1893-1903, but no relationships or ages were indicated, just names. Additional information shown in parenthesis was entered subsequently in the register:

    Edmund Mitchell (dead), J. Street Mitchell (removed to near Baltimore, March, 1897), Mrs. Mary Eliza Mitchell (removed to near Baltimore, March, 1897), and Lamar Mitchell (removed to near Baltimore, March, 1897). {Ref: Church Records, 1834-1903, p. 251}

    Harry E. Mitchell (dead), Mrs. Rosina B. Mitchell (removed to Havre de Grace, died 1911), Edna Mitchell (removed to Havre de Grace), Samuel Mitchell (removed to Havre de Grace), and Edith Mitchell (removed to Havre de Grace). {Ref: Church Records, 1834-1903, p. 251}

    Mallie M. Mitchell (removed to Havre de Grace) and Ethel Mitchell (removed to Havre de Grace). {Ref: Church Records, 1834-1903, p. 251}

MITCHELL, Adele Holmes, daughter of Howard Holmes and Ethel Kennedy Mitchell, born 23 Jan 1904, private baptism on 22 Mar 1904 in Aberdeen, died [5?] May 1905, age 9 months, buried 7 May 1904 in Grove Churchyard. {Ref: Parish Register, 1903-1958, pp. 30-31, 158}

MITCHELL, Amanda (Mrs.), age 64 (mother), died 26 Jan 1885, buried 28 Jan 1885; also see "Bernard Mitchell," q.v. {Ref: Church Records, 1834-1903, p. 100; Tombstone inscription}

MITCHELL, Bernard, oldest son of Paca and Amanda Mitchell, born 15 Oct 1846, died 14 Jan 1876. {Ref: Tombstone inscription}

MITCHELL, Bernard Morean, son of C. P. and Mallie Mitchell, born 5 Jul 1884, private baptism on 10 Aug 1884, buried 12 Aug 1884, age 5 weeks. {Ref: Church Records, 1834-1903, pp. 4-5, 100; Tombstone inscription}

MITCHELL, Cornelius P., born 9 Mar 1849, married Malvine Morean on 13 Jan 1880, died 11 Oct 1888, buried 14 Oct 1888; also see "Bernard M. Mitchell" and "Ethel Mitchell," q.v. {Ref: Church Records, 1834-1903, pp. 101, 149; Tombstone inscription}

MITCHELL, Edith, daughter of H. E. and Rosina B. Mitchell, born 27 Oct 1880, baptized 10 Nov 1889 (sponsors: the parents, Miss Fannie Cole and Mrs. V. S. Osborn); sponsored the baptism of Douglas Elliott Kennedy, Jr. on 2 Sep 1917; also see "Mitchell Family," q.v. {Ref: Church Records, 1834-1903, p. 9; Parish Register, 1903-1958, p. 33}

MITCHELL, Edmund, son of ---- [blank], born 2 Sep 1817, private baptism on 11 Nov 1891 at home ("Witnesses: Mrs. Dr. Michael and Street Mitchel"), died 20 Nov 1891, age 74, buried 23 Nov 1891; also see "James S. Mitchell" and "John P. Mitchell" and "Margaret P. Mitchell" and "Susan R. Mitchell" and "Virginia S. Mitchell" and "Mitchell Family," q.v. {Ref: Church Records, 1834-1903, pp. 10-11, 102; Tombstone inscription}

MITCHELL, Edna, see "Mitchell Family," q.v.

MITCHELL, Elmo, son of Harry E. and Rose E. Mitchell, born 17 Dec 1878, died 11 Sep 1884. {Ref: Tombstone inscription}

MITCHELL, Ethel, daughter of C. P. and M. Mitchell, born 27 Oct 1880, baptized 11 Sep 1881. {Ref: Church Records, 1834-1903, pp. 2-3}

MITCHELL, Ethel (Kennedy), church member in 1903, married Joseph Streett on 8 Nov 1914; also see "Mitchell Family," q.v. {Ref: Parish Register, 1903-1958, p. 107}

MITCHELL, Harry E., born 29 Dec 1851, died 6 Dec 1891, buried 9 Dec 1891; also see "Edith Mitchell" and "Elmo Mitchell" and "Mitchell Family," q.v. {Ref: Church Records, 1834-1903, p. 102; Tombstone inscription}

MITCHELL, Henry Edmund (Mr.), confirmed 27 Jan 1889. {Ref: Church Records, 1834-1903, p. 300}

MITCHELL, Horace Beal, son of J. P. and M. R. Mitchell, born 21 Jun 1889, died 2 Feb 1890. {Ref: Tombstone inscription}

MITCHELL, Howard Holmes, married Ethel Kennedy on 18 Jun 1902 at "Litchfield" in Aberdeen. {Ref: Church Records, 1834-1903, pp. 162-163}

MITCHELL, J. Bernard, son of J. P. and M. P. Mitchell, died 3 Mar 1882, age 13 years and 8 days. {Ref: Tombstone inscription}

MITCHELL, J. P., see "Horace B. Mitchell" and "J. Bernard Mitchell," q.v.

MITCHELL, James Street (Streett), son of Edmund and Martha Mitchell, born 30 Jun 1862, baptized 10 Jul 1864, married Mary Elizabeth Bonn on 16 Feb 1887, sponsored the baptisms of William Osborn Mitchell on 10 Sep 1882 and Mary Ellen Michael on 11 Dec 1892 at St. George's; confirmed 18 Oct 1887 at St. Mary's Church in Emmorton, removed to Orangeville in Baltimore County on 31 May

1897; also see "Mitchell Family," q.v. {Ref: Church Records, 1834-1903, pp. 11, 34-35, 152-153, 202, 300}

MITCHELL, John A., born 2 Jan 1847, died 24 Mar 1914. {Ref: Tombstone inscription}

MITCHELL, John Bernard, son of John P. and Lillie R. Mitchell, born ---- [blank], baptized 13 Jul 1879, buried 2 Apr 1882, age 4 years and 6 months. {Ref: Church Records, 1834-1903, pp. 42-43, 100}

MITCHELL, John Kentucky Sappington, of Havre de Grace, buried 7 Oct 1856. {Ref: Church Records, 1834-1903, p. 92}

MITCHELL, John Paca, son of Edmund and Martha Jane Mitchell, born 24 Oct 1845, baptized 25 May 1851, died 14 Nov 1918, age 73, buried 16 Nov 1918; also see "John B. Mitchell" and "Thomas C. Mitchell" and "William O. Mitchell," q.v. {Ref: Church Records, 1834-1903, pp. 24-25; Parish Register, 1903-1958, p. 159; Tombstone inscription}

MITCHELL, John Sappington, son of Howard H. and Ethel Mitchell, born 3 Apr 1905, baptized 24 Aug 1919 at Mr. H. Mitchell's home (sponsors: the parents and Mr. & Mrs. Douglas Kennedy). {Ref: Parish Register, 1903-1958, pp. 34-35}

MITCHELL, Lamar, daughter of James Street and Mary Elizabeth Mitchell, born 21 Jul 1889, baptized 18 Aug 1889; also see "Mitchell Family," q.v. {Ref: Church Records, 1834-1903, p. 9}

MITCHELL, Lillie, see "John B. Mitchell" and "Thomas C. Mitchell" and "William O. Mitchell," q.v.

MITCHELL, Mallie M. (Mrs.), confirmed 10 Oct 1882, church member in 1903; also see "Bernard M. Mitchell" and "Ethel Mitchell" and "Mitchell Family," q.v. {Ref: Church Records, 1834-1903, p. 299; Parish Register, 1903-1958, p. 107}

MITCHELL, Margaret Priscilla, daughter of Edmund and Martha J. Mitchell, born 8 Mar 1850, baptized 25 May 1851, died 25 Jun 1851, age 1 year, 3 months and 17 days, buried 26 Jun 1851. {Ref: Church Records, 1834-1903, pp. 24-25, 91; Tombstone inscription}

MITCHELL, Martha J., born 30 Mar 1823, died 5 Jul 1890. {Ref: Tombstone inscription}

MITCHELL, Martha Jane (Mrs.), confirmed 27 Apr 1856. {Ref: Church Records, 1834-1903, p. 297}

MITCHELL, Martha P. (Mrs.), age 65, died 5 Jul 1890, buried 7 Jul 1890; also see "James S. Mitchell" and "John P. Mitchell" and "Margaret P. Mitchell" and "Susan R. Mitchell" and "Virginia S. Mitchell" and "Mitchell Family," q.v. {Ref: Church Records, 1834-1903, pp. 101, 200}

MITCHELL, Mary, of Havre de Grace, buried 27 Aug 1857. {Ref: Church Records, 1834-1903, p. 93}

MITCHELL, Mary E. (Mrs. J. Street Mitchell), sponsored the baptism of Mary Ellen Michael on 11 Dec 1892; removed to Orangeville in Baltimore County on 31 May 1897; also see "Mitchell Family," q.v. {Ref: Church Records, 1834-1903, pp. 11, 202}

MITCHELL, Mary Elizabeth, Methodist, confirmed 17 May 1914. {Ref: Parish Register, 1903-1958, pp. 88, 110}

MITCHELL, Matilda Reybold, born 11 Jun 1850, died 15 Jul 1904. {Ref: Tombstone inscription}

MITCHELL, Nancy Carrol, daughter of Howard H. and Ethel Mitchell, born 21 Apr 1917, baptized 24 Aug 1919 at Mr. H. Mitchell's home (sponsors: the parents and Mr. & Mrs. Douglas Kennedy). {Ref: Parish Register, 1903-1958, pp. 34-35}

MITCHELL, Nellie, infant of Cornelius P. and Mollie Mitchell, born 8 Oct 1886, baptized 7 Sep 1887, died 10 Sep 1887, buried 12 Sep 1887. {Ref: Church Records, 1834-1903, pp. 6, 101; Tombstone inscription}

MITCHELL, Paca, born 26 Oct 1808, private baptism 11 Jun 1882, died 14 Jun 1882, buried 16 Jun 1882; also see "Bernard Mitchell, q.v. {Ref: Church Records, 1834-1903, pp. 2-3, 100; Tombstone inscription}

MITCHELL, Priscilla, wife of Richard Mitchell and daughter of Parker and Elizabeth Gilbert, died 18 Mar 1856, age 80 years, 10 months and 7 days, buried 19 Mar 1856. {Ref: Church Records, 1834-1903, p. 92; Tombstone inscription}

MITCHELL, Priscilla (Miss), of Havre de Grace, buried 18 Sep 1856. {Ref: Church Records, 1834-1903, p. 92}

MITCHELL, Rachel, buried 27 Sep 1862. {Ref: Church Records, 1834-1903, p. 93}

MITCHELL, Richard, died 7 Oct 1856, age 84 years, 11 months and 28 days, "buried 8 Oct 1856, age nearly 85"; also see "Priscilla Mitchell," q.v. {Ref: Church Records, 1834-1903, p. 92; Tombstone inscription}

MITCHELL, Rosina Badger, wife of Harry Mitchell, born ---- [blank], baptized 27 Oct 1886, born 26 Dec 1850, confirmed 27 Nov 1886, removed to Havre de Grace on 2 Jul 1890(?) [year unclear], died 19 Mar 1911, age 70+ years, buried 22 Mar 1910; also see "Edith Mitchell" and "Elmo Mitchell" and "Mitchell Family," q.v. {Ref: Church Records, 1834-1903, pp. 6, 202, 251, 300; Parish Register, 1903-1958, p. 158; Tombstone inscription}

MITCHELL, Samuel, see "Mitchell Family," q.v.

MITCHELL, Sarah A., sponsored the baptism of Rachel Louisa Kirby, Thomas Edward Kirby, and Mary Lucretia Kirby on 24 Oct 1839. {Ref: Church Records, 1834-1903, p. 21}

MITCHELL, Street, witnessed the baptism of Edmund Mitchell on 20 Nov 1891; also see "James Street Mitchell," q.v. {Ref: Church Records, 1834-1903, p. 11}

MITCHELL, Susan (Susie) Rebecca, daughter of Edmund and Martha Mitchell, born 28 Aug 1853, baptized 27 Feb 1855, confirmed 14 Mar 1871, married Dr. J. Edwin Michael on 23 Dec 1875; also see "Fannie C. Michael" and "J. Edwin Michael" and "Jacob E. Michael", q.v. {Ref: Church Records, 1834-1903, pp. 26-27, 148, 297}

MITCHELL, Sylvester, married Sarah Ann Dawson (of Talbott) on 24 Oct 1839; sponsored the baptism of Rachel Louisa Kirby, Thomas Edward Kirby, and Mary Lucretia Kirby on 24 Oct 1839). {Ref: Church Records, 1834-1903, pp. 21, 138}

MITCHELL, Thomas Clark, son of John P. and Lillie R. Mitchell, born ---- [blank], baptized 13 Jul 1879. {Ref: Church Records, 1834-1903, pp. 42-43}

MITCHELL, Virginia Sophia, daughter of Edmund and Martha Mitchell, born 15 Apr 1852, baptized 27 Feb 1855, confirmed 14 Mar 1871, married William Osborn on 3 Feb 1880. {Ref: Church Records, 1834-1903, pp. 26-27, 149, 297}

MITCHELL, William Osborn, son of John P. and Lillie R. Mitchell, born 2 Aug 1881, baptized 10 Sep 1882 (sponsors: the parents and J. Street Mitchell). {Ref: Church Records, 1834-1903, pp. 2-3}

MOHR, Mary B., confirmed 9 Feb 1873, married Frederick Guhl on 30 Mar 1880. {Ref: Church Records, 1834-1903, pp. 149, 297}

MOLESTON, James W., church member in 1903, removed in November, 1907. {Ref: Parish Register, 1903-1958, p. 106}

MONK, Caroline (colored), married Daniel Winchester (colored) on 7 Oct 1886. {Ref: Church Records, 1834-1903, pp. 152-153}

MONK, Hampton (colored), married Charlotte Ringgold (colored) on 7 Aug 1864. {Ref: Church Records, 1834-1903, p. 145}

MONK, Isaac J. (colored), married Louisa Christie (colored) on 21 Jul 1895. {Ref: Church Records, 1834-1903, pp. 160-161}

MONK, Jacob H. (colored), married Ella C. D. Frisby (colored) on 28 Jun 1891. {Ref: Church Records, 1834-1903, pp. 156-157}

MONK, James (colored), married Prene Frisby (colored) ---- 1877. [*Ed. Note:* The date was blank, but the marriage was listed between June and December in the register]. {Ref: Church Records, 1834-1903, p. 148}

MONK, Jane (colored), married Alfred Taylor (colored) ---- 1879. [*Ed. Note:* The date was blank, but the marriage was listed between January and April in the register]. {Ref: Church Records, 1834-1903, p. 149}

MONK, John, see "John Monks," q.v.

MONK, John Clark, died 9 Dec 1827, age 67 years, 9 months and 14 days, with "John Clark Monk, a native of Bristol, Gloucestershire, England, who departed this life December 9th Anno Domini 1827, aged 67 years, 9 months, and 14 days" inscribed on the monument; also see "Sarah R. L. Monk," q.v. {Ref: Tombstone inscription}

MONK, Lavinia (colored), married Fernandis Rush Simms (colored) ---- 1879. [*Ed. Note:* The date was blank, but the marriage was listed between January and April in the register]. {Ref: Church Records, 1834-1903, p. 149}

MONK, Lewis H. (colored), married Catherine Price (colored) ---- 1877. [*Ed. Note:* The date was blank, but the marriage was listed between June and December in the register]. {Ref: Church Records, 1834-1903, p. 148}

MONK, Margaret (colored), married Edwin Brandt (colored) on 8 Feb 1872. {Ref: Church Records, 1834-1903, p. 147}

MONK, Margaret (free colored), born ---- [blank], baptized 15 Apr 1837. {Ref: Church Records, 1834-1903, pp. 16-17}

MONK, Mary, see "Mary Monks," q.v.

MONK, Philip, married Susan Holland on 27 Dec 1860. {Ref: Church Records, 1834-1903, p. 143}

MONK, Philip (colored), married Semelia Brown (colored) on 12 Nov 1876. {Ref: Church Records, 1834-1903, p. 148}

MONK, Rachel (free colored), born ---- [blank], baptized 15 Apr 1837. {Ref: Church Records, 1834-1903, pp. 16-17}

MONK, Robert, married Hester Jane Glover on 29 Aug 1858. {Ref: Church Records, 1834-1903, p. 142}

MONK, Sarah Rebecca Lewis, wife of John Clark Monk, died 20 Mar 1854, age 58 years and 12 days; inscribed on monument: "In memory of Sarah Rebecca Lewis, consort of John Clark Monk, who departed this life March the 20th Anno Domini 1854, age 58 years and twelve days." {Ref: Tombstone inscription}

MONK, Thomas T. (colored), married Jane Finch (colored) on 12 Oct 1866. {Ref: Church Records, 1834-1903, p. 146}

MONK, William H., Jr. (colored), married Harriet Rosster (colored) on 4 Sep 1892. {Ref: Church Records, 1834-1903, pp. 158-159}

MONKS, Mary, wife of John Monks, died 14 Oct 1800, age 35. {Ref: Tombstone inscription}

MOON, Catharine, married James Self on 23 Sep 1855 at Havre de Grace. {Ref: Church Records, 1834-1903, p. 140}

MOORE, Edna E., born 1886, died 1906. {Ref: Tombstone inscription}

137

MOORE, Ethel W., born and died in 1888. {Ref: Tombstone inscription}

MOORE, Harriet (colored), married James H. Hall (colored) on 12 Apr 1894. {Ref: Church Records, 1834-1903, pp. 158-159}

MOORE, John, born 13 Dec 1834, died 15 Sep 1907. {Ref: Tombstone inscription}

MOORE, Mary Eliza, daughter of Lloyd and Mary Jane Moore, born 3 Jul 1860, baptized 6 Aug 1860. {Ref: Church Records, 1834-1903, pp. 30-31}

MOORE, Richard (colored), married Milche Griffith (colored) on 28 Nov 1868. {Ref: Church Records, 1834-1903, p. 147}

MOORE, George Victor, born 23 Apr 1885, died 24 Oct 1908. {Ref: Tombstone inscription}

MOREAN, Alexander Columbus, born 19 Sep 1835, died 31 Dec 1891, buried 3 Jan 1892. {Ref: Church Records, 1834-1903, p. 102; Tombstone inscription}

MOREAN, Ellen, born 4 Oct 1836, died 21 May 1908, age 72, buried 24 May 1908 [The register listed her name as "Ellender Morean Marine"]. {Ref: Parish Register, 1903-1958, p. 158; Tombstone inscription}

MOREAN, Ida, married Dr. J. H. Cochran on 28 Nov 1888 at the residence of A. C. Morean. {Ref: Church Records, 1834-1903, pp. 154-155}

MOREAN, Malvine, married Cornelius P. Mitchell on 13 Jan 1880. {Ref: Church Records, 1834-1903, p. 149}

MORGAN FAMILY.
The following family information was entered in the church records under the heading of "Families" circa 1893-1903, but no relationships or ages were indicated, just names. Additional information shown in parenthesis was entered subsequently in the register:
Thomas E. Morgan (removed to Baltimore), Mrs. Annie C. Morgan (removed to Baltimore), Emma Morgan (removed to Baltimore), Thomas Edgar Morgan (dead), and ---- [blank] Morgan. {Ref: Church Records, 1834-1903, p. 255}

MORGAN, Annie C., church member in 1903; also see "Emma B. Morgan" and "Marcus K. Morgan" and "Mildred L. Morgan" and "Miriam P. Morgan" and

"Oscar L. Morgan" and "Thomas E. Morgan" and "Morgan Family," q.v. {Ref: Parish Register, 1903-1958, p. 107}

MORGAN, E. (Mrs.), sponsored the baptism of Nan Lee Porter on 26 Sep 1920. {Ref: Parish Register, 1903-1958, p. 35}

MORGAN, Emily Bay (Gallup), church member in 1905, transferred to Christ Church at Roanoke [Virginia] on 23 Jun 1911. {Ref: Parish Register, 1903-1958, p. 109}

MORGAN, Emily McCay, daughter of Rowland and Mary Gertrude Morgan, born 2 Jun 1910, baptized 19 Sep 1910 at home in Perryman (sponsors: the parents, John Henry Lindsay and Florence Lindsay). {Ref: Parish Register, 1903-1958, pp. 30-31}

MORGAN, Emma B., see "Marcus K. Morgan" and "Miriam P. Morgan," q.v.

MORGAN, Emma Barton, daughter of Thomas and Annie Morgan, born 25 Mar 1888, baptized 1 Apr 1888; also see "Morgan Family," q.v. {Ref: Church Records, 1834-1903, p. 7}

MORGAN, Eva Virginia, Presbyterian, confirmed 11 Dec 1910, married Alexander Shaw Porter on 19 Jan 1918 at Mr. Morgan's residence in Aberdeen. {Ref: Parish Register, 1903-1958, pp. 88, 110, 138-139}

MORGAN, Marcus Kriete (twin of Miriam), son of Thomas E. and Annie C. Morgan, born 7 Dec 1898, baptized 13 Dec 1898 at home in Aberdeen (sponsors: the parents, Emma B. Morgan and Dr. Charles H. Kriete). {Ref: Church Records, 1834-1903, pp. 14-15}

MORGAN, Mary G., see "Emily M. Morgan," q.v.

MORGAN, Mary V., married Joseph M. Simmons on 7 Jun 1884. {Ref: Church Records, 1834-1903, p. 151}

MORGAN, Mildred Louise, daughter of Thomas E. and Annie C. Morgan, born 22 Sep 1896, baptized 31 Jul 1897 at home in Aberdeen (sponsors: the father, Mrs. Rosa C. Brock and Mrs. Sarah L. Scott. {Ref: Church Records, 1834-1903, pp. 12-13}

MORGAN, Miriam Philippa (twin of Marcus), daughter of Thomas E. and Annie C. Morgan, born 7 Dec 1898, baptized 13 Dec 1898 at home in Aberdeen (sponsors: the parents, Emma B. Morgan and Dr. Charles H. Kriete). {Ref: Church Records, 1834-1903, pp. 14-15}

MORGAN, Oscar Leroy, son of Thomas E. and Annie C. Morgan, born 30 Nov 1885, private baptism on 7 Dec 1885 (8 days old, new born to be received). {Ref: Church Records, 1834-1903, pp. 4-5}

MORGAN, Robert Lytle, married Emily Bay Gallup on 15 Nov 1905. {Ref: Parish Register, 1903-1958, pp. 138-139}

MORGAN, Rowland, confirmed 21 Nov 1909; also see "Emily M. Morgan," q.v. {Ref: Parish Register, 1903-1958, p. 87}

MORGAN, S. C. (Mrs.), sponsored the baptism of Shirley Virginia Porter on 26 Sep 1920. {Ref: Parish Register, 1903-1958, p. 35}

MORGAN, Shirley C., sponsored the baptism of Shirley Virginia Porter on 26 Sep 1920. {Ref: Parish Register, 1903-1958, p. 35}

MORGAN, Thomas (Mr.), confirmed 9 Oct 1887; also see "Emma B. Morgan" and "Marcus K. Morgan" and "Mildred L. Morgan" and "Miriam P. Morgan" and "Oscar L. Morgan" and "Thomas E. Morgan" and "Morgan Family," q.v. {Ref: Church Records, 1834-1903, p. 300}

MORGAN, Thomas Edgar, son of Thomas E. and Annie C. Morgan, born 16 Mar 1893, baptized 23 Jul 1893 (sponsors: the parents), church member in 1903, died in 1913; also see "Morgan Family," q.v. {Ref: Church Records, 1834-1903, pp. 12-13; Parish Register, 1903-1958, p. 107}

MORGAN, William E., sponsored the baptism of Nan Lee Porter on 26 Sep 1920. {Ref: Parish Register, 1903-1958, p. 35}

MORRIS FAMILY.
The following family information was entered in the church records under the heading of "Families" circa 1893-1903, but no relationships or ages were indicated, just names. Additional information shown in parenthesis was entered subsequently in the register:
James Morris, Mrs. Lily May Morris, David Ray Morris, and Clarissa Viola Morris (dead). {Ref: Church Records, 1834-1903, p. 262}

MORRIS, Clarissa Viola, daughter of James and Lillie May Morris, born 4 Apr 1902, private baptism on 11 Oct 1902 in a house at Clay Hill; also see "Morris Family," q.v. {Ref: Church Records, 1834-1903, pp. 14-15}

MORRIS, David Ray, son of James and Lillie May Morris, born 22 Mar 1900, baptized 25 May 1902 (sponsors: Mrs. Florence O. Baldwin and Miss Emma J. Moulsdale); also see "Morris Family," q.v. {Ref: Church Records, 1834-1903, pp. 14-15}

MORRIS, James, see "Clarissa V. Morris" and "Morris Family," q.v.

MORRIS, Lily May, see "Clarissa V. Morris" and "Morris Family," q.v.

MORSON, Mary Jane (colored), married Frederick Dorsey (colored) on 15 Oct 1893. {Ref: Church Records, 1834-1903, pp. 158-159}

MORTON, James (colored), married Harriet Ramsey (colored) on 27 Dec 1870. {Ref: Church Records, 1834-1903, p. 147}

MOULSDALE FAMILY.
The following family information was entered in the church records under the heading of "Families" circa 1893-1903, but no relationships or ages were indicated, just names. Additional information shown in parenthesis was entered subsequently in the register:
Mr. ---- [blank] Moulsdale, ---- [blank] Moulsdale, Emma J. Moulsdale, and Florence Moulsdale [which was followed by two empty spaces] and then Miss Eleanor Louise Moulsdale (Abingdon). {Ref: Church Records, 1834-1903, p. 260}

MOULSDALE, Eleanor Louise, age 22, Methodist affiliation, confirmed 18 Nov 1900 at St. George's P. E. Church, church member in 1903, later removed [date not given]; also see "Moulsdale Family," q.v. {Ref: Church Records, 1834-1903, p. 303; Parish Register, 1903-1958, p. 107}

MOULSDALE, Emma Jeff, age 21, Methodist affiliation, confirmed 29 Dec 1901 at St. George's P. E. Church; sponsored the baptisms of David Ray Morris on 25 May 1902 and Dolly May Cullum on 21 Sep 1902; church member in 1903, later removed [date not given]; also see "Moulsdale Family," q.v. {Ref: Church Records, 1834-1903, pp. 15, 303; Parish Register, 1903-1958, p. 107}

MOULSDALE, Florence Olivia, age 17, Methodist affiliation, confirmed 29 Dec 1901 at St. George's P. E. Church, church member in 1903, later removed [date not given]; also see "Moulsdale Family," q.v. {Ref: Church Records, 1834-1903, p. 303; Parish Register, 1903-1958, p. 107}

MOUNT, Annie E., born 1831, died 1908. {Ref: Tombstone inscription}

MOUNT, Charles G., born 1849, died 1902. {Ref: Tombstone inscription}

MOUNT, Russell M., born 1889, died 1912. {Ref: Tombstone inscription}

MOUNT, Willie C., born 1892, died 1894. {Ref: Tombstone inscription}

MURPHY, Anna Maria, daughter of William and Catherine Murphy, died 13 Nov 1856, age 7 years, 3 months and 9 days. {Ref: Tombstone inscription}

MURPHY, Catherine Rosabell, daughter of William and Catherine S. Murphy, died 29 Nov 1856. {Ref: Tombstone inscription}

MURPHY, Catherine S., born 29 Dec 1809, died 25 Sep 1893; also see "Anna M. Murphy" and "Catherine R. Murphy" and "John A. Murphy," q.v. {Ref: Tombstone inscription}

MURPHY, John, son of John and Mary Murphy, died 15 Jan 1826, age 24. {Ref: Tombstone inscription}

MURPHY, John, died 21 Dec 1854, age 74; also see "John Murphy" and "Mary Murphy" and "Philip R. Murphy" and "Mary Sutton," q.v. {Ref: Tombstone inscription}

MURPHY, John A., son of William and Catherine Murphy, died 24 Apr 1855, age 24 years and 4 months. {Ref: Tombstone inscription}

MURPHY, Martha (colored), married James Cooper (colored) on 2 Jun 1870. {Ref: Church Records, 1834-1903, p. 147}

MURPHY, Martha Garretson, confirmed 9 Aug 1867. {Ref: Church Records, 1834-1903, p. 297}

MURPHY, Mary, wife of John Murphy, died 31 Oct 1847, age 67; also see "Mary Murphy" and "Philip R. Murphy" and "Mary Sutton," q.v. {Ref: Tombstone inscription}

MURPHY, Philip R., son of John and Mary Murphy, died 23 Jun 1843, age 23 years, 7 months and 9 days. {Ref: Tombstone inscription}

MURPHY, Semelia Ann, wife of Thomas J. Murphy and daughter of Col. Jacob Michael, born 12 Oct 1809, died 1 Nov 1847, age 38. {Ref: Church Records, 1834-1903, p. 91; Tombstone inscription}

MURPHY, Susan, confirmed 14 May 1865. {Ref: Church Records, 1834-1903, p. 294}

MURPHY, Thomas Jefferson, born 1 Dec 1810, married Semelia Ann Michael on 24 Jun 1840 at Michaelsville, died 16 Jul 1873; also see "Semelia A. Murphy," q.v. {Ref: Church Records, 1834-1903, pp. 97, 138; Tombstone inscription}

MURPHY, William, born 24 Dec 1803, died 11 Jun 1871; also see "Anna M. Murphy" and "Catherine R. Murphy" and "John A. Murphy," q.v. {Ref: Tombstone inscription}

MYERS, Alice E., born 13 Oct 1891, died 25 Oct 1895. {Ref: Tombstone inscription}

MYERS, Bertha May, daughter of Stephen R. and Susan R. Myers, born 1 Apr 1891, private baptism on 10 Dec 1891 at home (child and mother sick). {Ref: Church Records, 1834-1903, pp. 10-11}

MYERS, Charles, see "Charles Meyers," q.v.

MYERS, Elizabeth Ann, daughter of C. H. and M. A. D. Myers, died 6 Mar 1848, buried 8 Mar 1848. [*Ed. Note:* In another Parish Register, 1696-1851, it indicates she was 2 years, 3 months and 13 days old]. {Ref: Church Records, 1834-1903, p. 91}

MYERS, George Washington, son of C. H. and M. A. D. Myers, born ---- [blank], baptized 22 Sep 1850, buried 28 Jan 1851. [*Ed. Note:* In another Parish Register, 1696-1851, it indicates George was the infant son of Christian and Mary Ann Myers]. {Ref: Church Records, 1834-1903, pp. 24-25, 91}

MYERS, Harry E., born 22 Mar 1868, died 8 May 1893. {Ref: Tombstone inscription}

MYERS, John A., married Mary Ann Ergood on 25 Jan 1855 at Havre de Grace. {Ref: Church Records, 1834-1903, p. 140}

MYERS, Mary, see "Mary Meyers," q.v.

MYERS, Mary Ann D. (adult), daughter of ---- [blank], born ---- [blank], baptized 19 May 1850. {Ref: Church Records, 1834-1903, pp. 22-23}

MYERS, Mary Martha, daughter of C. H. and M. A. D. Myers, buried 6 Mar 1848. [*Ed. Note:* In another Parish Register, 1696-1851, it indicates she was 4 years, 11 months and 10 days old]. {Ref: Church Records, 1834-1903, p. 91}

MYERS, Nelson, son of C. H. and M. A. D. Myers, born ---- [blank], baptized 22 Sep 1850. {Ref: Church Records, 1834-1903, pp. 24-25}

MYERS, Oliver Perry, son of C. H. and M. A. D. Myers, born ---- [blank], baptized 22 Sep 1850. {Ref: Church Records, 1834-1903, pp. 24-25}

MYERS, Robert Emory, of Havre de Grace, buried 5 Sep 1854. {Ref: Church Records, 1834-1903, p. 92}

NcCLASKY, Mrs., of Cranberry, died 23 Sep 1839. {Ref: Church Records, 1834-1903, p. 90}

NEILSON, James Crawford, married Rosa Williams on 2 Jun 1840 at Priestsford. {Ref: Church Records, 1834-1903, p. 138}

NELSON FAMILY.
The following family information was entered in the church records under the heading of "Families" circa 1893-1903, but no relationships or ages were indicated, just names. Additional information shown in parenthesis was entered subsequently in the register:
Aquila H. Nelson (dead, name lined out), Mrs. Mary M. Nelson (Mrs. John Lear), Isabell Nelson, Elizabeth K. Nelson, Mary E. Nelson, Emily C. Nelson, Bertha Nelson, Sylvia Lear, Charles Nelson (dead, name lined out), and Mrs. Sarah N. Nelson (name lined out). {Ref: Church Records, 1834-1903, p. 252}
Frederick Nelson, Mrs. Effie Lizzie Nelson, Miss Edith Ruff Nelson (name lined out), Miss Helen Nelson (name lined out), Mary Susannah Nelson, Arthur Nelson (dead, 1910), Dorsey Hayes Nelson, and Effie Louise Nelson. {Ref: Church Records, 1834-1903, p. 253}

NELSON, Aquilla (Aquila), died 10 Oct 1826, age 60 years, 9 months and 15 days; also see "Bertha N. Nelson" and "Elizabeth K. Nelson" and "Emily C. Nelson" and "Frances Nelson" and "Isabel Nelson" and Mary E. Nelson," q.v. {Ref: Tombstone inscription}

NELSON, Aquilla (Aquila) H., born 4 Nov 1841, confirmed 10 Oct 1882, married Mary M. Michael on 10 Jan 1883, died 1 May 1894, buried 3 May 1894; also see "Nelson Family," q.v. {Ref: Church Records, 1834-1903, pp. 102, 150, 201, 299; Tombstone inscription}

NELSON, Arthur, see "Nelson Family," q.v.

NELSON, Bennett, see "Bennett V. Nelson" and "Edwin W. Nelson" and "Laura V. Nelson" and "Martha E. Nelson" and "Mary E. Nelson" and "Mary F. Nelson" and "N. Elizabeth Nelson," q.v.

NELSON, Bennett Vansickle, born 6 Nov 1807, lived at Hopewell, died 17 Dec 1865 of heart disease, buried 20 Dec 1865; also see "N. Elizabeth Nelson," q.v. {Ref: Church Records, 1834-1903, p. 95; Tombstone inscription}

NELSON, Bennett Vansickle (Vansickel), son of Bennett and Elizabeth Nelson, born 27 Sep 1853, baptized 4 Sep 1859, died 22 May 1905. {Ref: Church Records, 1834-1903, pp. 28-29; Tombstone inscription}

NELSON, Bertha N., daughter of Aquila H. and Mary Nelson, born 20 Feb 1891, baptized 31 May 1891 (sponsors: the parents); church member in 1905, confirmed 22 Oct 1905, later removed [date not given]; also see "Nelson Family," q.v. {Ref: Church Records, 1834-1903, pp. 10-11; Parish Register, 1903-1958, pp. 87, 109}

NELSON, Catharine Izannah, daughter of Garrett and Elizabeth Nelson, born 12 Jun 1838, baptized 13 Aug 1838. {Ref: Church Records, 1834-1903, pp. 18-19}

NELSON, Charles, married Sarah Kimble ---- 1879. [*Ed. Note:* The date was blank, but the marriage was listed between January and April in the register]. {Ref: Church Records, 1834-1903, p. 148}

NELSON, Charles B., born 17 Nov 1840, died 13 Jun 1891, age 51, buried 15 Jun 1891; also see "Nelson Family," q.v. {Ref: Church Records, 1834-1903, p. 102; Tombstone inscription}

NELSON, Christie, born 1887, died 1888. {Ref: Tombstone inscription}

NELSON, Dorsey, sponsored the baptism of Sophia Louise Smithson on 20 Apr 1919. {Ref: Parish Register, 1903-1958, p. 35}

NELSON, Dorsey Hayes, son of Frederick and Effie Lizzie Nelson, born 28 Jan 1896, baptized 26 Apr 1899 at home (sponsors: the parents and Miss Edith Ruff

Nelson), confirmed 11 Dec 1910, removed to Perryville, Maryland [date not given]; also see "Nelson Family," q.v. {Ref: Church Records, 1834-1903, pp. 14-15; Parish Register, 1903-1958, pp. 87, 110}

NELSON, Edith (Miss), confirmed 20 Nov 1889, transferred to Epiphany Church, Baltimore, in 1917; also see "Nelson Family" and "Bradford Family," q.v. {Ref: Church Records, 1834-1903, p. 301; Parish Register, 1903-1958, p. 107}

NELSON, Edith Ruff (Miss), sponsored the baptism of Dorsey Hayes Nelson and Effie Louise Nelson on 26 Apr 1899. {Ref: Church Records, 1834-1903, p. 15}

NELSON, Edwin W., son of Bennett and Elizabeth Nelson, born 6 Sep 1847, died 10 Feb 1853. {Ref: Tombstone inscription}

NELSON, Effie, see "Dorsey H. Nelson" and "Effie L. Nelson" and "Mary S. Nelson" and "Nelson Family," q.v.

NELSON, Effie Louise, daughter of Frederick and Effie Lizzie Nelson, born 23 May 1898, baptized 26 Apr 1899 at home (sponsors: the parents and Miss Edith Ruff Nelson), confirmed 11 Dec 1910, married Oliver Porter Boyer on 13 Nov 1920; also see "Nelson Family," q.v. {Ref: Church Records, 1834-1903, pp. 14-15; Parish Register, 1903-1958, pp. 87, 110, 138-139}

NELSON, Elizabeth, see "Harriet Cole" and "Bennett V. Nelson" and "Edwin W. Nelson" and "Laura V. Nelson" and "Martha E. Nelson" and "Mary E. Nelson" and "Mary F. Nelson" and "N. Elizabeth Nelson" and "Catharine I. Nelson" and "Garrett H. Nelson" and "George A. Nelson" and "Hannah Nelson" and "Priscilla F. Nelson" and "Sarah E. Nelson" and "Willie Nelson," q.v.

NELSON, Elizabeth Keen, daughter of Aquilla H. and Mary M. Nelson, born 22 Feb 1885, baptized 12 Jul 1885 (sponsors: the mother, James H. Michael and E. K. Michael), confirmed 30 Apr 1899, church member in 1903, married Joseph M. Streett in 1908 or 1914 [exact date not given, but a later entry indicated 8 Nov 1914], transferred to Holy Cross at The Rocks [date not given]; also see "Nelson Family," q.v. {Ref: Church Records, 1834-1903, pp. 4-5, 302; Parish Register, 1903-1958, pp. 107, 138-139}

NELSON, Emily, infant daughter of H. Nelson, born 28 Apr 1858, died 9 Jul 1859, buried 10 Jul 1859. {Ref: Church Records, 1834-1903, p. 93; Tombstone inscription}

NELSON, Emily Cowan, daughter of A. H. and Mary Nelson, born 18 Apr 1889, baptized 16 Jun 1889, confirmed 7 Dec 1902, age 13, married John Munro Henderson on 24 Jun 1914, transferred to Epiphany Church, Baltimore, in 1917; also see "Nelson Family," q.v. {Ref: Church Records, 1834-1903, pp. 8, 303; Parish Register, 1903-1958, pp. 138-139; Parish Register, 1903-1958, p. 107}

NELSON, Fannie P., born 28 Dec 1832, died 11 May 1868. {Ref: Church Records, 1834-1903, p. 95; Tombstone inscription}

NELSON, Florence M., daughter of Bennett and Elizabeth Nelson, born 11 Mar 1855, baptized 4 Sep 1859, died 11 Nov 1911. {Ref: Church Records, 1834-1903, pp. 28-29; Tombstone inscription}

NELSON, Frances, wife of Aquilla Nelson, died 11 (or 12?) Sep 1847 in her 73rd year. {Ref: Church Records, 1834-1903, p. 91; Tombstone inscription}

NELSON, Frederick, son of Henry and Mary Nelson, baptized 4 Sep 1859, confirmed (adult) 20 Nov 1889; also see "Dorsey H. Nelson" and "Effie L. Nelson" and "Mary S. Nelson" and "Nelson Family," q.v. {Ref: Church Records, 1834-1903, pp. 30-31, 301}

NELSON, Frederick, Jr., born 1886, buried 20 Mar 1889, age 4 *[sic]*. {Ref: Church Records, 1834-1903, p. 101; Tombstone inscription}

NELSON, Frederick (Mrs.), sponsored the baptism of Sophia Louise Smithson on 20 Apr 1919. {Ref: Parish Register, 1903-1958, p. 35}

NELSON, Garrett (Mr.), died in 1875 or 1876 [exact date not given]; also see "Harriet Cole" and "Catharine I. Nelson" and "Garrett H. Nelson" and "George A. Nelson" and "Hannah Nelson" and "Priscilla F. Nelson" and "Sarah E. Nelson," q.v. {Ref: Church Records, 1834-1903, p. 97}

NELSON, Garrett (Mrs.), and an infant (unnamed), died in 1875 or 1876 [exact date not given]. {Ref: Church Records, 1834-1903, p. 97}

NELSON, Garrett Henry, son of Garrett and Elizabeth Nelson, born 10 Apr 1835, baptized 13 Aug 1838, married Georgianna Nelson on 26 Feb 1869. {Ref: Church Records, 1834-1903, pp. 18-19, 147}

NELSON, Garrett V., died 24 Dec 1850 in his 55th year. [*Ed. Note:* In another Parish Register, 1696-1851, it indicates Garret V. Nelson was buried 26 Dec 1850]; also see "Hannah Nelson," q.v. {Ref: Tombstone inscription}

NELSON, George, sponsored the baptism of Rachel Louisa Kirby, Thomas Edward Kirby, and Mary Lucretia Kirby on 24 Oct 1839; also see "Willie Nelson," q.v. {Ref: Church Records, 1834-1903, p. 21}

NELSON, George Alphonso, son of Garrett and Elizabeth Nelson, born 6 Nov 1829, baptized 13 Aug 1838, married Elizabeth A. Gallup on 3 Jan 1861, died 23 Apr 1904. {Ref: Church Records, 1834-1903, pp. 18-19, 143; Tombstone inscription}

NELSON, Georgianna (George Anna), born 22 Jan 1840, baptized 1 Aug 1841, married Garrett H. Nelson on 26 Feb 1869. {Ref: Church Records, 1834-1903, pp. 20-21, 147}

NELSON, H., see "Emily Nelson," q.v.

NELSON, H. Clay, born 7 Mar 1844, died 12 Mar 1911; also see "Harriet Nelson" and "Martha M. Nelson," q.v. {Ref: Tombstone inscription}

NELSON, Hannah, wife of Garrett V. Nelson, died 6 Jan 1862, in her 62nd year, buried 7 Jan 1862. {Ref: Church Records, 1834-1903, p. 93; Tombstone inscription}

NELSON, Harriet, wife of H. Clay Nelson, born 19 Jun 1849, died 10 Mar 1898; also see "Martha M. Nelson," q.v. {Ref: Tombstone inscription}

NELSON, Helen (Miss), confirmed 9 Nov 1890, transferred to Epiphany Church, Baltimore, in 1917; also see "Nelson Family" and "Bradford Family," q.v. {Ref: Church Records, 1834-1903, p. 301; Parish Register, 1903-1958, p. 107}

NELSON, Helen G., died 7 Mar 1920. {Ref: Tombstone inscription}

NELSON, Henry, of Bush River Neck, married Mrs. M. A. Chauncey on 4 Apr 1839; sponsored the baptism of George Anna Nelson on 1 Aug 1841; died 5 Jan 1867 of typhoid pneumonia; also see "Frederick Nelson" and "Louisa A. Nelson" and "Mary A. Nelson" and "Mary B. Nelson," q.v. {Ref: Church Records, 1834-1903, pp. 21, 95, 138}

NELSON, Henry, born 1884, died 1887. {Ref: Tombstone inscription}

NELSON, Isabel (Isabell), daughter of Aquila H. and Mary M. Nelson, born 20 Dec 1883, private baptism on 24 Feb 1884 (sponsors: the parents and Mrs. B. Bradford), confirmed 30 Apr 1899, age 15; sponsored the baptism of Sylvia Lear on 15 Apr 1900; church member in 1903; also see "Nelson Family," q.v. {Ref: Church Records, 1834-1903, pp. 2-3, 302; Parish Register, 1903-1958, p. 107}

NELSON, Laura Virginia, daughter of Bennett and Elizabeth Nelson, born 9 (or 11?) Jun 1851, baptized 4 Sep 1859, died 20 Dec 1874. {Ref: Church Records, 1834-1903, pp. 28-29; Tombstone inscription}

NELSON, Louis (servant of Miss Adaline Hall), born 5 May 1859, baptized 22 Sep 1863. {Ref: Church Records, 1834-1903, pp. 32-33}

NELSON, Louisa, buried 22 Sep 1869. {Ref: Church Records, 1834-1903, p. 96}

NELSON, Louisa Ann, daughter of Henry and Mary Amanda Nelson, born 23 Feb 1846, baptized 6 Dec 1846. {Ref: Church Records, 1834-1903, pp. 22-23}

NELSON, Lydia (Miss), confirmed 9 Jun 1836. {Ref: Church Records, 1834-1903, p. 296}

NELSON, Martha Ella, daughter of Bennett and Elizabeth Nelson, born 28 (or 29?) Nov 1858, baptized 4 Sep 1859, died 13 Mar 1899. {Ref: Church Records, 1834-1903, pp. 28-29; Tombstone inscription}

NELSON, Martha M., daughter of H. Clay and Harriet A. Nelson, born 1860, died 5 Nov 1904, age 34. {Ref: Tombstone inscription}

NELSON, Mary, see "Bertha N. Nelson" and "Elizabeth K. Nelson" and "Emily C. Nelson" and "Isabel Nelson" and Mary E. Nelson" and "Frederick Nelson" and "Louisa A. Nelson" and "Mary B. Nelson" and "Nelson Family," q.v.

NELSON, Mary Amanda, wife of Henry Nelson, born 11 Dec 1816, died 7 Feb 1900, age 83, buried 9 Feb 1900. {Ref: Church Records, 1834-1903, p. 104; Tombstone inscription}

NELSON, Mary Belle, daughter of Henry and Mary Nelson, born 31 May 1852, baptized 4 Sep 1859, married Samuel D. Bradford on 19 Feb 1878. {Ref: Church Records, 1834-1903, pp. 30-31, 148}

NELSON, Mary Ella, daughter of Aquila H. and Mary Nelson, born 23 Dec 1887, baptized 3 Jun 1888, confirmed 29 Dec 1901, age 14, transferred to Epiphany Church, Baltimore, in 1917; also see "Nelson Family," q.v. {Ref: Church Records, 1834-1903, pp. 7 303; Parish Register, 1903-1958, p. 107}

NELSON, Mary Elizabeth, daughter of Bennett and Elizabeth Nelson, born 29 Oct 1857, baptized 4 Sep 1859. {Ref: Church Records, 1834-1903, pp. 28-29}

NELSON, Mary F., daughter of Bennett and Elizabeth, born 20 Jun 1849, died 15 Jan 1853. {Ref: Tombstone inscription}

NELSON, Mary M. (Mrs.), sponsored the baptism of Virginia Missouri Michael and Effie Elizabeth Michael on 8 Oct 1893; also see "Nelson Family," q.v. {Ref: Church Records, 1834-1903, p. 13}

NELSON, Mary Susanna, daughter of Frederick and Effie L. Nelson, born 1 Dec 1883, private baptism on 24 Feb 1884, confirmed 7 Dec 1902, age 19, church member in 1903, married William Preston Smithson on 19 Jan 1918, transferred to Christ Church, Rock Spring [date not given]; also see "Nelson Family," q.v. {Ref: Church Records, 1834-1903, pp. 2-3, 303; Parish Register, 1903-1958, pp. 107, 138-139}

NELSON, N. Elizabeth, wife of Bennett Vansickle Nelson, born 23 Apr 1825, died 23 Nov 1881. {Ref: Tombstone inscription}

NELSON, Priscilla Frances, daughter of Garrett and Elizabeth Nelson, born 28 Dec 1831, baptized 13 Aug 1838. {Ref: Church Records, 1834-1903, pp. 18-19}

NELSON, Ryland, born and died in 1875. {Ref: Tombstone inscription}

NELSON, Sarah (Mrs.), sponsored the baptism of William McDonald Sutton on 3 Aug 1884; also see "Malcolm Family," q.v. {Ref: Church Records, 1834-1903, p. 5}

NELSON, Sarah E., died 10 Aug 1821, age 7. {Ref: Tombstone inscription}

NELSON, Sarah E., died 17 Aug 1914, age 75 years, 5 months and 14 days. {Ref: Parish Register, 1903-1958, pp. 108, 159}

NELSON, Sarah Elizabeth (adult), daughter of Garrett and Elizabeth Nelson, born 18 Sep 1821, baptized 13 Aug 1838. {Ref: Church Records, 1834-1903, pp. 18-19}

NELSON, Sarah N., born 1 Mar 1839, died 15 Aug 1914; also see "Nelson Family," q.v. {Ref: Tombstone inscription}

NELSON, William (colored), married Sarah Carr (colored) on 10 May 1877. {Ref: Church Records, 1834-1903, p. 148}

NELSON, Willie E., son of George A. and Elizabeth Nelson, born 28 Sep 1861, died 18 Oct 1883. {Ref: Tombstone inscription}

NETTLETON, Mary K. (Mrs.), sponsored the baptism of Paul Nettleton Richards on 10 May 1903. {Ref: Church Records, 1834-1903, p. 17}

NOBLE, Eliza, see "James Noble" and "John T. Noble" and "Mary F. Noble" and "William H. Noble," q.v.

NOBLE, Elizabeth (Mrs.), confirmed 26 Jun 1853, buried 9 Dec 1856. {Ref: Church Records, 1834-1903, pp. 93, 296}

NOBLE, James, see "James Noble" and "John T. Noble" and "Mary F. Noble" and "William H. Noble," q.v.

NOBLE, James, son of James and Eliza Noble, born 25 Feb 1831, baptized 21 Jan 1841 (sponsors: John Cole and Parker Gilbert). [*Ed. Note:* The name was mistakenly listed as "Janes" in the register]. {Ref: Church Records, 1834-1903, pp. 20-21}

NOBLE, John Franklin, son of James and Elizabeth Noble, born ---- [blank], baptized 20 May 1849. [*Ed. Note:* In another Parish Register, 1696-1851, it indicates he was about 5 years old]. {Ref: Church Records, 1834-1903, pp. 22-23}

NOBLE, John Thomas, son of James and Eliza Noble, born 7 Aug 1840, baptized 21 Jan 1841 (sponsors: John Cole and Parker Gilbert). {Ref: Church Records, 1834-1903, pp. 20-21}

NOBLE, Mary Frances, daughter of James and Eliza Noble, born 17 Jan 1829, baptized 21 Jan 1841 (sponsors: John Cole and Parker Gilbert). {Ref: Church Records, 1834-1903, pp. 20-21}

NOBLE, William Henry, son of James and Eliza Noble, born 2 Aug 1838, baptized 21 Jan 1841 (sponsors: John Cole and Parker Gilbert). {Ref: Church Records, 1834-1903, pp. 20-21}

NORRIS, Andrew Jackson, age 67 years, 1 month and 17 days, buried 12 May 1920. {Ref: Parish Register, 1903-1958, p. 160}

NORTH, Edward, married Emma P. Paul on 13 Sep 1863. {Ref: Church Records, 1834-1903, p. 145}

NORTON, Frank Ann, married John Henry Lingan on 28 Apr 1863. {Ref: Church Records, 1834-1903, p. 144}

NORTON, Levantia (colored), daughter of Frank and Mary Norton, born 22 Sep 1848, baptized 27 Jul 1864, married Henry Williams (colored) on 24 Dec 1868. {Ref: Church Records, 1834-1903, pp. 34-35, 147}

NORTON, Octavia (colored), married Nicholas Mills (colored) on 23 May 1872. {Ref: Church Records, 1834-1903, p. 147}

NORTON, Ruth, married Horace Wilmer on 25 Jul 1858. {Ref: Church Records, 1834-1903, p. 142}

NOWLAND, Peregrine, born -- Jul 1763, died -- Oct 1810 in his 48th year. {Ref: Tombstone inscription}

NUMBERS, Harlan C., son of J. H. and M. A. Numbers, born 30 Jun 1895, died 24 Nov 1896. {Ref: Tombstone inscription}

NUMBERS, James, born 6 Jun 1833, died 20 Dec 1868; also see "Sarah J. Numbers" and "Thomas B. Numbers," q.v. {Ref: Tombstone inscription}

NUMBERS, J. R. (Mrs.), sponsored the baptism of James Llewellyn Owens on 1 Aug 1915. {Ref: Parish Register, 1903-1958, p. 33}

NUMBERS, Sarah Jane, wife of James Numbers, born 10 Jan 1838, died 15 Dec 1917; also see "Malcolm Family," q.v. {Ref: Tombstone inscription}

NUMBERS, M. A., see "Harlan C. Numbers," q.v.

NUMBERS, Thomas B., son of James and Sarah Numbers, born 7 Dec 1866, died 10 Oct 1889. {Ref: Tombstone inscription}

O'BRIEN, Isabella (Mrs.), sponsored the baptism of Robert Clinton Cronin, Jr. on 24 Feb 1895. {Ref: Church Records, 1834-1903, p. 13}

OLIVER, Anna Virginia, daughter of James and Ann Oliver, born 3 Jun 1840, baptized 10 Jan 1858. {Ref: Church Records, 1834-1903, pp. 28-29}

OLIVER, Charles Ellsworth, married Caroline Laport Taylor on 14 Aug 1902 at 9:30 a.m. {Ref: Church Records, 1834-1903, pp. 162-163}

OLIVER, James, see "Anna V. Oliver," q.v.

ORRICK, S. H., deacon in charge, 1907-1908; sponsored the baptism of Lawrence Matthew Taylor on 26 Apr 1908. {Ref: Parish Register, 1903-1958, pp. ii, 31}

OSBORN FAMILY.
The following family information was entered in the church records under the heading of "Families" circa 1893-1903, but no relationships or ages were indicated, just names:
William D. Osborn, Mrs. Virginia S. Osborn, Walter C. Osborn, Virginia M. Osborn, and Mabel S. Osborn. {Ref: Church Records, 1834-1903, p. 251}

OSBORN, Annie M., wife of Charles Osborn, born 5 Jan 1840, died 22 Jun 1885. {Ref: Tombstone inscription}

OSBORN, B., see "Drusilla Osborn" and "Lottie Osborn," q.v.

OSBORN, Bennett, born 13 Dec 1832, died 14 Feb 1907; also see "Harriet M. J. Osborn" and "Annie Aaronson," q.v. {Ref: Tombstone inscription}

OSBORN, Charles, born 17 Jun 1836, died 27 Aug 1910; also see "Annie M. Osborn," q.v. {Ref: Tombstone inscription}

OSBORN, Cyrus, age 82, buried 19 Mar 1895 in Grove Church Cemetery. {Ref: Church Records, 1834-1903, p. 102}

OSBORN, Drusilla M., daughter of B. and H. Osborn, born 6 Sep 1870, died 18 Mar 1872. {Ref: Tombstone inscription}

OSBORN, George A., born 15 Nov 1828, died 5 Apr 1876, age 47 years and 4 months. {Ref: Tombstone inscription}

OSBORN, George B., see "Mollie A. Osborn," q.v.

OSBORN, H., see "Drusilla Osborn" and "Lottie Osborn," q.v.

OSBORN, Harriet M. (neé Jackson), wife of Bennett Osborn, born 24 Feb 1839, died 19 Dec 1875. {Ref: Tombstone inscription}

OSBORN, Jane, buried 26 Mar 1866. {Ref: Church Records, 1834-1903, p. 94}

OSBORN, Lottie, daughter of B. Osborn and H. M. Jackson, born 14 Apr 1872, died 8 Jun 1872. {Ref: Tombstone inscription}

OSBORN, Mabel Street (or Streett), daughter of William D. and Virginia Osborn, born ---- [blank], baptized 11 Sep 1887, confirmed 18 Nov 1900, age 13, church member in 1903, married ---- Cooper [date not given]; also see "Osborn Family," q.v. {Ref: Church Records, 1834-1903, pp. 6, 300; Parish Register, 1903-1958, p. 107}

OSBORN, Martha Susanna, daughter of William D. and Virginia S. Osborn, born 2 Jul 1882, baptized 10 Sep 1882 (sponsors: the parents and Mrs. Susan R. Michael), died 15 Mar 1883, age 8 months and 13 days, buried 17 Mar 1883. {Ref: Church Records, 1834-1903, pp. 2-3, 100; Tombstone inscription}

OSBORN, Mary Virginia, daughter of William D. and Virginia S. Osborn, born 27 Nov 1892, baptized 28 May 1893 (sponsors: the parents), confirmed 25 Apr 1908. {Ref: Church Records, 1834-1903, pp. 10-11; Parish Register, 1903-1958, pp. 87, 109}

OSBORN, Mister, see "Hester Griffin," q.v.

OSBORN, Mollie A., wife of George B. Osborn, born 8 Aug 1854, died 13 Oct 1884. {Ref: Tombstone inscription}

OSBORN, Virginia Mitchell, daughter of William D. and Virginia Osborn, born 1 Jun 1886, baptized 14 Aug 1886; also see "Osborn Family," q.v. {Ref: Church Records, 1834-1903, p. 6}

OSBORN, Virginia S., sponsored the baptism of Herbert Harlan Michael and Ethel Mitchell on 11 Sep 1881; church member in 1903; also see "Mabel S. Osborn" and "Martha S. Osborn" and "Mary V. Osborn" and "Virginia M. Osborn" and "Walter C. Osborn" and "Osborn Family," q.v. {Ref: Church Records, 1834-1903, p. 3; Parish Register, 1903-1958, p. 107}

OSBORN, Walter Cochran, son of William D. and Virginia S. Osborn, born 11 Jan 1884, baptized 29 Jun 1884 (sponsors: the parents and Mr. Charles W. Michael), confirmed 30 Apr 1899, age 15; church member in 1903, later removed or dropped [date not given]; also see "Osborn Family," q.v. {Ref: Church Records, 1834-1903, pp. 4-5, 302; Parish Register, 1903-1958, p. 107}

OSBORN, William, married Virginia S. Mitchell on 3 Feb 1880; also see "Mabel S. Osborn" and "Martha S. Osborn" and "Mary V. Osborn" and "Virginia M.

Osborn" and "Walter C. Osborn" and "Osborn Family," q.v. {Ref: Church Records, 1834-1903, p. 149}

OSBORN, William Davis, Presbyterian, confirmed 18 Jun 1916. {Ref: Parish Register, 1903-1958, pp. 88, 111}

OSBORN, ---- [blank], infant of W. G. Osborn, buried 26 Sep 1886. {Ref: Church Records, 1834-1903, p. 101}

OWENS, Herbert Malcolm, son of James Herbert and A. Mabel Owens, born 18 Apr 1917, baptized 14 Oct 1917 (sponsors: Cornelius Cole, George W. Thomas and Gertrude Thomas). {Ref: Parish Register, 1903-1958, pp. 32-33}

OWENS, James Herbert, married Annie Mabel Hyde on 1 Aug 1914; also see "Herbert M. Owens" and "J. Herbert Owens," q.v. {Ref: Parish Register, 1903-1958, pp. 138-139}

OWENS, James Llewellyn, son of J. Herbert and A. Mabel (Hyde) Owens, born 13 Jun 1915, baptized 1 Aug 1915 (sponsors: J. E. Michael, R. C. Cronin and Mrs. J. R. Numbers). {Ref: Parish Register, 1903-1958, pp. 32-33}

OZBURN, Mary (colored), married Albert Clark (colored) on 30 Dec 1865. {Ref: Church Records, 1834-1903, p. 146}

OZBURN, Sallie, married Freeborn Rice on 7 Apr 1859. {Ref: Church Records, 1834-1903, p. 142}

PACA, James Wesley, married Martha C. Sims on 16 Oct 1862. {Ref: Church Records, 1834-1903, p. 144}

PAINE, Zacharia, married Fannie Harris on 4 Jun 1864. {Ref: Church Records, 1834-1903, p. 145}

PALMER FAMILY.
The following family information was entered in the church records under the heading of "Families" circa 1893-1903, but no relationships or ages were indicated, just names. Additional information shown in parenthesis was entered subsequently in the register:
Walter M. H. Palmer (dead, name lined out), Mrs. Belle C. Palmer, Marion Herbert Palmer, Mary Lena Palmer, John Loehning, and Mary Guerney. {Ref: Church Records, 1834-1903, p. 253}

PALMER, Belle C., witnessed the baptism of Walter Palmer on 7 Jan 1893; church member in 1903, buried 1 Jul 1906; also see "Mary L. Palmer" and "Walter M. H. Palmer" and "Palmer Family," q.v. {Ref: Church Records, 1834-1903, p. 11; Parish Register, 1903-1958, pp. 108, 158}

PALMER, Daniel, died 1 Oct 1845 in his 73rd year. {Ref: Tombstone inscription}

PALMER, Edgar Marion, son of Marion Herbert and Helen Groton (Taylor) Palmer, born 12 Sep 1905, baptized 24 Jun 1906 (sponsors: the parents), confirmed 14 Mar 1920. {Ref: Parish Register, 1903-1958, pp. 30-31, 89, 111}

PALMER, Elizabeth G., born 1814, died 1894. {Ref: Tombstone inscription}

PALMER, H. L., see "William Palmer," q.v.

PALMER, Helen Groton (Mrs.), Presbyterian, confirmed 13 Jun 1915; also see "Edgar M. Palmer" and "Ruth T. Palmer," q.v. {Ref: Parish Register, 1903-1958, pp. 88, 110}

PALMER, Isabella Coe, born 11 Sep 1831, died 29 Jun 1906. {Ref: Tombstone inscription}

PALMER, Joshua H., age 71, died 23 Mar 1879, buried 25 Mar 1879. {Ref: Church Records, 1834-1903, p. 97; Tombstone inscription}

PALMER, M. Herbert, witnessed the baptism of Walter Palmer on 7 Jan 1893. {Ref: Church Records, 1834-1903, p. 11}

PALMER, Mahlon, born 1812, died 1895. {Ref: Tombstone inscription}

PALMER, Marion Herbert (Mr.), confirmed 9 Nov 1890, member in 1906; also see "Edgar M. Palmer" and "Ruth T. Palmer" and "Palmer Family," q.v. {Ref: Church Records, 1834-1903, p. 301; Parish Register, 1903-1958, p. 109}

PALMER, Mary L., died 16 Sep 1884, age 81. {Ref: Tombstone inscription}

PALMER, Mary Lena, daughter of Walter M. H. and Belle Palmer, born 28 May 1871, baptized 18 Jan 1872, confirmed 15 Nov 1885; witnessed the baptism of Walter Palmer on 7 Jan 1893 and sponsored the baptism of Louise Loehning on 18 Nov 1900; also see "Palmer Family" and "Mary Lena Anderson," q.v. {Ref: Church Records, 1834-1903, pp. 11, 15, 38-39, 201, 299}

PALMER, Ruth Taylor, daughter of M. Herbert and Helen D. Palmer, born 3 Feb 1911, private baptism on 27 Jan 1913 at Perryman. {Ref: Parish Register, 1903-1958, pp. 30-31}

PALMER, S. Webster, see "William Palmer," q.v.

PALMER, Samuel W., born 1851, died 1902. {Ref: Tombstone inscription}

PALMER, Susannah A., died 9 Jun 1854, age 48. {Ref: Tombstone inscription}

PALMER, Walter M. H., born 12 Oct 1814, married Isabella (Belle) E. Coe on 9 Sep 1869, private baptism on 7 Jan 1893, age 78, at home (witnesses: Mrs. Belle C. Palmer, M. Herbert Palmer and M. Lena Palmer), died 14 Jan 1893, buried 15 Jan 1893; also see "Mary L. Palmer" and "Palmer Family," q.v. {Ref: Church Records, 1834-1903, pp. 10-11, 102, 147; Tombstone inscription}

PALMER, William, son of S. Webster and H. L. Palmer, died 10 Mar 1882, age 2 years, 5 months and 3 days. {Ref: Tombstone inscription}

GILBERT, Gilbert, sponsored the baptism of Mary Frances Noble, James Noble, William Henry Noble and John Thomas Noble on 21 Jan 1841. {Ref: Church Records, 1834-1903, pp. 20-21}

PARKER, Margaret (adult), daughter of Robert and Rachel Parker, born ---- [blank], baptized 1 May 1853, confirmed 26 Jun 1853. {Ref: Church Records, 1834-1903, pp. 26-27, 296}

PARKER, William, son of Robert and Rachel Parker, born 16 Feb 1841, baptized 22 Aug 1854. {Ref: Church Records, 1834-1903, pp. 26-27}

PATTERSON FAMILY.
The following family information was entered in the church records under the heading of "Families" circa 1893-1903, but no relationships or ages were indicated, just names. Additional information shown in parenthesis was entered subsequently in the register:
Frederick E. Patterson, Mrs. Lillie P. Patterson (die 1909, name lined out), Ethel Patterson (married Cary Ruffin Randolph on 11 Oct 1899, removed to Charlottesville, Virginia), and Lillie Patterson (married Dr. Jay H. Stier). {Ref: Church Records, 1834-1903, p. 254}

PATTERSON, Anna, see "Jane B. Patterson," q.v.

PATTERSON, Cordelia Phillips, daughter of William A. and Sarah (Sally) S. Patterson, born 13 Jul 1848, baptized 27 Oct 1848, confirmed 9 Aug 1867, buried 29 Aug 1868. {Ref: Church Records, 1834-1903, pp. 22-23, 96, 297}

PATTERSON, Edward, son of William P. and Frances Patterson, died 5 Apr 1835 in his 18th year. {Ref: Tombstone inscription}

PATTERSON, Ella C., married John A. Barker on 18 Jun 1874. {Ref: Church Records, 1834-1903, p. 148}

PATTERSON, Ethel, see "Patterson Family," q.v.

PATTERSON, F. Ethel, married Cary Ruffin Randolph on 11 Oct 1899 at "Brinfield" in Perryman. {Ref: Church Records, 1834-1903, pp. 160-161}

PATTERSON, F. G. (Frances), see "Frederick E. Patterson" and "George G. Patterson," q.v.

PATTERSON, Fannie B., married George Airey on 21 Jun 1870. {Ref: Church Records, 1834-1903, p. 147}

PATTERSON, Frances, wife of William P. Patterson, died 21 Jan 1860, age 68. {Ref: Tombstone inscription}

PATTERSON, Frances Barthia, daughter of William A. and Sally S. Patterson, born 4 Aug 1850, baptized 16 Oct 1850, confirmed 14 May 1865. {Ref: Church Records, 1834-1903, pp. 24-25, 294}

PATTERSON, Francis Whiting Powell, son of Frederick E. and Olivia C. Patterson, born 25 Apr 1878, baptized 1 Sep 1878, buried 23 Sep 1879. {Ref: Church Records, 1834-1903, pp. 42-43, 98; Tombstone inscription}

PATTERSON, Frederica Etheldred, daughter of Frederick E. and Olivia C. Patterson, born 29 Feb 1872, baptized 8 Sep 1872; "Frederica Etheldred Patterson (Mrs. Randolph)" transferred to Charlottesville, Virginia in April, 1901. {Ref: Church Records, 1834-1903, pp. 40-41, 203}

PATTERSON, Frederick, see "Francis W. P. Patterson" and "Frederick E. Patterson" and "Lillie P. Patterson" and "Olivia C. Patterson," q.v.

PATTERSON, Frederick Ethelred, son of William P. and F. G. Patterson, born 2 Jul 1822; sponsored the baptism of Ridgely Patterson Stier on 9 Aug 1895;

Presbyterian affiliation, confirmed 29 Dec 1901, age 79, at St. George's P. E. Church; church member in 1903; died 20 Mar 1914, buried 22 Mar 1914; also see "Olivia C. Patterson" and "Patterson Family," q.v. {Ref: Church Records, 1834-1903, pp. 13, 303; Parish Register, 1903-1958, pp. 108, 159; Tombstone inscription}

PATTERSON, George G., son of William P. and Frances Patterson, died 9 Jan 1835 in his 24th year. {Ref: Tombstone inscription}

PATTERSON, Isabella Sophia, daughter of William A. and Sally S. Patterson, born 28 Oct 1852, baptized 1 May 1853, confirmed 14 Mar 1871. {Ref: Church Records, 1834-1903, pp. 26-27, 297}

PATTERSON, J. O., see "James O. Patterson" and "Jane B. Patterson" and "John F. Patterson" and "Mary B. Patterson" and "Sophia Patterson" and "William A. Patterson," q.v.

PATTERSON, James Orville, son of J. O. and Jane Patterson, born 12 Mar 1865, baptized 21 Jun 1865. {Ref: Church Records, 1834-1903, pp. 34-35}

PATTERSON, Jane, see "James O. Patterson" and "Jane B. Patterson" and "John F. Patterson" and "Mary B. Pattersob" and "Sophia Patterson" and "William A. Patterson," q.v.

PATTERSON, Jane Belt, daughter of J. O. and Anna Jane Patterson, born 10 Jul 1854, baptized 5 May 1855. {Ref: Church Records, 1834-1903, pp. 26-27}

PATTERSON, Jane Hepburn, daughter of William A. and Sally S. Patterson, born 25 Apr 1859, baptized 15 Oct 1859. {Ref: Church Records, 1834-1903, pp. 30-31}

PATTERSON, John Fulford, son of J. O. and Jane Patterson, born 6 Aug 1861, baptized 2 Dec 1861. {Ref: Church Records, 1834-1903, pp. 30-31}

PATTERSON, Lillie Powell, daughter of Frederick E. and Olivia C. Patterson, church member in 1903, died 6 Jun 1907. [*Ed. Note:* No date of birth or baptism was given, but the baptism was listed among several others in the register between 1872 and 1876]; also see "Patterson Family," q.v. {Ref: Church Records, 1834-1903, pp. 40-41; Parish Register, 1903-1958, p. 108}

PATTERSON, Mary Bates, infant daughter of J. O. and Jane Patterson, buried 6 May 1871, age 9 months. {Ref: Church Records, 1834-1903, p. 96}

PATTERSON, Mary Hawkins, daughter of William A. and Sarah (Sally) S. Patterson, born 3 Oct 1856, baptized 6 Jun 1857, died 25 Dec 1862; tombstone indicates 25 Dec 1866(?). {Ref: Church Records, 1834-1903, pp. 28-29, 93; Tombstone inscription}

PATTERSON, Olivia Claggett, wife of Frederick E. Patterson and daughter of F. W. and H. H. Powell, born 16 Jul 1843, died 6 Jun 1907; also see "Francis W. P. Patterson" and "Frederick E. Patterson" and "Lillie P. Patterson" and "Olivia C. Patterson," q.v. {Ref: Tombstone inscription}

PATTERSON, Priscilla Christie, daughter of William A. and Sarah (Sally) S. Patterson, born 22 Nov 1855(?) *[sic]*, baptized 5 May 1855, confirmed 14 Mar 1871. {Ref: Church Records, 1834-1903, pp. 26-27, 297}

PATTERSON, Rebecca, see "William F. Patterson," q.v.

PATTERSON, Rebecca Newkirk, daughter of William A. and Sarah (Sally) S. Patterson, born 14 Aug 1846, baptized 25 Oct 1846, died 29 Feb 1848, age 18 months, buried 1 Mar 1848. {Ref: Church Records, 1834-1903, pp. 22-23, 91; Tombstone inscription}

PATTERSON, Robert Pinkney, son of William A. and Sarah (Sallie) S. Patterson, born 2 Aug 1863, baptized 15 Jul 1864, buried 11 Aug 1872. {Ref: Church Records, 1834-1903, pp. 34-35, 96}

PATTERSON, Sally (Sarah), see "Cordelia P. Patterson" and "Frances B. Patterson" and "Isabella S. Patterson" and "Jane H. Patterson" and "Mary H. Patterson" and "Priscilla C. Patterson" and "Rebecca N. Patterson" and "Robert Patterson," q.v.

PATTERSON, Sarah, daughter of William A. and Sarah (Sallie) S. Patterson, born 3 May 1861, baptized 20 Jul 1862, died 7 Nov 1866; register states died 6 Nov 1866 of dysentery, age 5. {Ref: Church Records, 1834-1903, pp. 32-33, 95; Tombstone inscription}

PATTERSON, Sophia de la Roche, daughter of J. Orvill and Jane Patterson, born 10 Jan 1859, baptized 2 Aug 1859. {Ref: Church Records, 1834-1903, pp. 30-31}

PATTERSON, William, see "Frederick E. Patterson" and "George G. Patterson" and "William F. Patterson," q.v.

PATTERSON, William A., see "Cordelia P. Patterson" and "Frances B. Patterson" and "Isabella S. Patterson" and "Jane H. Patterson" and "Mary H. Patterson" and "Priscilla C. Patterson" and "Rebecca N. Patterson" and "Robert Patterson" and "Sarah Patterson," q.v.

PATTERSON, William Alfred, son of J. O. and Anna Jane Patterson, born 19 Apr 1857, baptized 6 Jun 1857. {Ref: Church Records, 1834-1903, pp. 28-29}

PATTERSON, William Alfred, died 14 Jan 1864, age 52. {Ref: Church Records, 1834-1903, p. 94; Tombstone inscription}

PATTERSON, William Francis, son of William and Rebecca Patterson, died 9 Jun 1838, age 1 month. {Ref: Tombstone inscription}

PATTERSON, William P., died 14 Nov 1865, age 77; also see "Frances Patterson," q.v. {Ref: Tombstone inscription}

PAUL, Emma P., married Edward North on 13 Sep 1863. {Ref: Church Records, 1834-1903, p. 145}

PEARCE, John Franklin, son of ---- [blank], born 25 Jul 1901(?). [*Ed. Note:* The actual date was recorded as "July 25, 1801," but it is an obvious mistake since he was baptized at his home on December 7, 1937]. {Ref: Parish Register, 1903-1958, pp. 38-39}

PEARSON, Franklin D., born 1828, married Susanna E. Cook on 14 Dec 1858, died 1897. {Ref: Church Records, 1834-1903, p. 142; Tombstone inscription}

PEARSON, S. Augusta, born 1862, died 1880. {Ref: Tombstone inscription}

PEARSON, Susannah S., born 1834, died 1874. {Ref: Tombstone inscription}

PENNINGTON, Harry O., died 28 Jul 1895, age 39. {Ref: Tombstone inscription}

PENNINGTON, Henry O. H., died 19 Jan 1892, age 79. {Ref: Tombstone inscription}

PENNINGTON, Mary E., born 9 Jan 1824, died 19 Feb 1900. {Ref: Tombstone inscription}

PENNYPACKER, Nathaniel Ramsay, second son of Isaac R. and Charlotte W. Pennypacker, born 28 Sep 1881 at Mt. Pleasant, Harford County, Maryland, died

20 Aug 1911, buried 23 Aug 1911. {Ref: Parish Register, 1903-1958, p. 158; Tombstone inscription}

PENTZ, Alleine R., born 1878, died 1913; see "Mary Alleine Pentz," q.v. {Ref: Tombstone inscription}

PENTZ, Louise Raymond, daughter of William H. and Mary A. Pentz, born 27 May 1903, baptized 4 Oct 1903 (sponsors: the parents and Miss F. May Cole). {Ref: Church Records, 1834-1903, pp. 16-17}

PENTZ, Mary Alleine (neé Raymond), sponsored the baptism of Ellen Lee Kloman on 13 Apr 1902; church member in 1903, later removed [date not given]; also see "Alleine R. Pentz," q.v. {Ref: Church Records, 1834-1903, p. 15; Parish Register, 1903-1958, p. 108}

PENTZ, William Henry, married Mary Alleine Raymond on 2 Aug 1901 at Mr. Henry Raymond's in Aberdeen; also see "Louise R. Pentz," q.v. {Ref: Church Records, 1834-1903, pp. 160-161}

PERRYMAN, Ann, died 7 Oct 1837, age 75. {Ref: Tombstone inscription}

PERRYMAN, Belle, confirmed 27 Apr 1856, married Rev. S. W. Crampton on 2 Feb 1858. {Ref: Church Records, 1834-1903, pp. 141, 297}

PERRYMAN, Charles W., died -- Jul 1835, age 30. {Ref: Tombstone inscription}

PERRYMAN, Edward Griffith (reverend), born 20 Jul 1836, confirmed 26 Jun 1853, married Isabella H. Fitzhugh on 8 May 1862, died 30 Apr 1888; also see "Julia J. Perryman," q.v. {Ref: Church Records, 1834-1903, p. 144, 296; Tombstone inscription}

PERRYMAN, Elizabeth A., married Col. Thomas Hendrickson (U.S.A.) at Fort Smith, Arkansas, by Rev. Washburn, on 25 Apr 1853. [*Ed. Note:* This information was entered in the register at St. George's in 1885]. {Ref: Church Records, 1834-1903, pp. 152-153}

PERRYMAN, George, see "Henry Perryman" and "Isaac Perryman" and "Isabella Perryman," q.v.

PERRYMAN, Henry, son of George and Isabella Perryman, died -- Aug 1834, age 10 months. {Ref: Tombstone inscription}

PERRYMAN, Isaac, died 30 Jun 1831, age 72. {Ref: Tombstone inscription}

PERRYMAN, Isaac, son of George and Isabella Perryman, died -- Aug 1835, age 4 months. {Ref: Tombstone inscription}

PERRYMAN, Isabella A., relict of George H. Perryman, born 26 Jul 1806, died 12 May 1876, age 70; also see "Henry Perryman" and "Isaac Perryman," q.v. {Ref: Church Records, 1834-1903, p. 97; Tombstone inscription}

PERRYMAN, Julia Johns, wife of Rev. E. G. Perryman, died 7 Jun 1873, age 39. {Ref: Church Records, 1834-1903, p. 97; Tombstone inscription}

PERRYMAN, Mrs., see "Fanny ----" and "William Henry Hall," q.v.

PERRYMAN, Sallie Gover, confirmed 22 Aug 1854. {Ref: Church Records, 1834-1903, p. 296}

PETERS, Jesse T. (Mr.), confirmed 7 Mar 1884. {Ref: Church Records, 1834-1903, p. 299}

PETERS, Louisa, buried 7 Nov 1883. {Ref: Church Records, 1834-1903, p. 100}

PETERS, Nathan (colored), married Susan Winchester (colored) on 2 May 1883. {Ref: Church Records, 1834-1903, p. 150}

PETERS, ---- [blank], infant of Mr. Peters, died in 1875 or 1876 [exact date not given]. {Ref: Church Records, 1834-1903, p. 97}

PEYTON, ----, "infant son of Mr. Peyton at Mr. A. Hall's," born ---- [blank], baptized 12 Dec 1880. {Ref: Church Records, 1834-1903, pp. 42-43}

PEYTON, Rosa Elizabeth, daughter of George and ---- [blank] Peyton, born ---- [blank], private baptism on 11 Feb 1883, died 13 Feb 1883. {Ref: Church Records, 1834-1903, pp. 2-3, 100}

PHILLIPS, Cordelia, died 24 Jan 1876, age 82. {Ref: Tombstone inscription}

PHILLIPS, James, see "Cordelia Giles," q.v.

PHILLIPS, LeBamey T. (reverend), sponsored the baptism of Paul Nettleton Richards on 10 May 1903. {Ref: Church Records, 1834-1903, p. 17}

PIGMAN, B. Smallwood, buried 10 Jan 1855. {Ref: Church Records, 1834-1903, p. 92}

PINION, Ann, buried 29 Aug 1863. {Ref: Church Records, 1834-1903, p. 94}

PINION, Elizabeth (servant of Miss Adaline Hall), born -- Jul 1847, baptized 22 Sep 1863, buried 1 Oct 1863. {Ref: Church Records, 1834-1903, pp. 32-33, 94}

PINION, John Lewis (colored), married Carrie Collins (colored) on 24 Jan 1884 at the residence of Mr. John H. Michael in Perryman. {Ref: Church Records, 1834-1903, p. 151}

PINION, Lewis (colored), married Henrietta Hopkins (colored) on 26 Jan 1867. {Ref: Church Records, 1834-1903, p. 146}

PINION, Mary Eliza (colored), married Thomas Henry Haycock (colored) on 12 Mar 1891. {Ref: Church Records, 1834-1903, pp. 156-157}

PINION, Philip (colored), married Mary M. Webster (colored) on 2 Oct 1890. {Ref: Church Records, 1834-1903, pp. 156-157}

PITT, Alfred (colored), married Mary Stansbury (colored) ---- 1877. [*Ed. Note:* The date was blank, but the marriage was listed between June and December in the register]. {Ref: Church Records, 1834-1903, p. 148}

PITT, Andrew H. (colored), married Annie M. Miller (colored) on 9 Mar 1882. {Ref: Church Records, 1834-1903, p. 150}

PITT, Charles W., married Carrie (Corrie) *[sic]* A. Brown on 30 Dec 1880. {Ref: Church Records, 1834-1903, p. 149}

PITT, John T. (colored), married Fannie E. Churchill (colored) on 9 Feb 1882. {Ref: Church Records, 1834-1903, p. 150}

PITT, John W. (colored), married Frances Harris (colored) on 16 Apr 1865. {Ref: Church Records, 1834-1903, p. 146}

PITT, Peter (colored), married Elizabeth Dallam (colored) on 11 Dec 1885. {Ref: Church Records, 1834-1903, pp. 152-153}

PITTS, James Amos, married Elizabeth Lisby on 14 Feb 1861. {Ref: Church Records, 1834-1903, p. 143}

PLASKITT, Joshua, born 14 Feb 1831, died 15 Oct 1903, age 72, buried 19 Oct 1903. {Ref: Parish Register, 1903-1958, p. 158; Tombstone inscription}

PLASKITT, Sophia Catherine, wife of Joshua Plaskitt, died 15 Mar 1890. {Ref: Tombstone inscription}

POALK, Caroline Preston, daughter of William L. and Charlotte O. Poalk, born 8 Apr 1858, baptized 16 Oct 1858. {Ref: Church Records, 1834-1903, pp. 28-29}

POALK, Lewis Griffith, son of William L. and Charlotte O. Poalk, born 25 Jan 1861, baptized 2 Sep 1863. {Ref: Church Records, 1834-1903, pp. 32-33}

POLK, Lizzie, daughter of Dr. John L. and Elizabeth O. Polk, born 28 Nov 1845, baptized 4 May 1850. {Ref: Church Records, 1834-1903, pp. 22-23}

POLK, Mary, daughter of Dr. John L. and Elizabeth O. Polk, born 24 Aug 1849, baptized 4 May 1850. {Ref: Church Records, 1834-1903, pp. 22-23}

PORTER FAMILY.
The following family information was entered in the church records under the heading of "Families" circa 1893-1903, but no relationships or ages were indicated, just names:
G. Ellis Porter, Katherine K. Porter, Alexander S. Porter, Mina Porter, Sidney Porter, and Willie Johnson. {Ref: Church Records, 1834-1903, p. 252}

PORTER, Alexander S., M.D., married Ella Keen on 10 Jun 1890; also see "Gabriel E. Porter" and "Katharine K. Porter" and "Nan Lee Porter" and "Shirley V. Porter," q.v. {Ref: Church Records, 1834-1903, pp. 156-157}

PORTER, Alexander Shaw, confirmed 21 Nov 1909, married Eva Virginia Morgan on 19 Jan 1918 at Mr. Morgan's residence in Aberdeen; also noted "removed to Baltimore - Philadelphia" [date not given]; also see "Porter Family," q.v. {Ref: Parish Register, 1903-1958, pp. 87, 109, 138-139}

PORTER, Elizabeth P. (Miss), sponsored the baptism of Ella Keen Johnson on 11 Apr 1910. {Ref: Parish Register, 1903-1958, p. 31}

PORTER, Ella Keen, church member in 1903; also see "Ella Keen Johnson" and "Keen Family" and "Alexander S. Porter" and "Gabriel E. Porter" and "Katharine K. Porter," q.v. {Ref: Parish Register, 1903-1958, p. 108}

PORTER, Eva V., see "Alexander S. Porter" and "Nan Lee Porter" and "Shirley V. Porter," q.v.

PORTER, Gabriel Ellis, son of Alexander S. and Ella Keen Porter, born 29 Mar 1891, baptized 12 Jul 1891 (sponsors: Dr. M. Gibson Porter, Lawrence Griffith and Mrs. A. C. Rishel); confirmed 10 Apr 1904, removed to Philadelphia [date not given]; also see "Porter Family," q.v. {Ref: Church Records, 1834-1903, pp. 10-11; Parish Register, 1903-1958, p. 87}

PORTER, Katharine Keen, daughter of Alexander S. and Ella Keen Porter, born 7 Dec 1892, baptized 2 Jul 1893 (sponsors: the parents and Mrs. Mary C. Keen), confirmed 25 Apr 1908, married Charles Lowndes Steel on 28 Dec 1916; later note indicated "U. S. Army, moved to Chicago" [date not given]; also see "Porter Family," q.v. {Ref: Church Records, 1834-1903, pp. 12-13; Parish Register, 1903-1958, pp. 87, 109, 138-139}

PORTER, Margarite (Mrs.), sponsored the baptism of Ella Keen Steel on 1 Aug 1920. {Ref: Parish Register, 1903-1958, p. 35}

PORTER, M. Gibson, M.D., sponsored the baptism of Garbiel Ellis Porter on 12 Jul 1891. {Ref: Church Records, 1834-1903, p. 11}

PORTER, Mary Beatrice (adult from Newark, Delaware), daughter of Mr. Porter, born ---- [blank], baptized 2 Mar 1856, confirmed 27 Apr 1856. {Ref: Church Records, 1834-1903, pp. 26-27, 297}

PORTER, Minor (Mina) Gibson, confirmed 17 May 1914, married Maurice Gaylord Steele on 7 Aug 1919; also see "Porter Family" and "Minor Steele," q.v. {Ref: Parish Register, 1903-1958, pp. 88, 110, 138-139}

PORTER, Nan Lee, daughter of Alexander S. and Eva Virginia Porter, born 29 Aug 1919, baptized 26 Sep 1920 at William Morgan's in Aberdeen (sponsors: William E. Morgan, Mrs. Paul Tabb and Miss E. Morgan). {Ref: Parish Register, 1903-1958, pp. 34-35}

PORTER, Shirley Virginia, daughter of Alexander S. and Eva Virginia Porter, born 3 Sep 1920, baptized 26 Sep 1920 at William Morgan's in Aberdeen (sponsors: the mother, Shirley C. Morgan and Mrs. S. C. Morgan). {Ref: Parish Register, 1903-1958, pp. 34-35}

PORTER, Sidney, see "Porter Family," q.v.

PORTER, Sydney Wynne, confirmed 18 Jun 1916; sponsored the baptism of Minor Porter Steele on 5 Sep 1920. {Ref: Parish Register, 1903-1958, pp. 35, 89}

POWELL, F. W., see "Olivia Patterson," q.v.

POWELL, H. H., see "Olivia Patterson," q.v.

PRESTON, Achsah, see "Alexander Preston" and "Caroline Preston" and "Robert L. Preston," q.v.

PRESTON, Achsah Ridgely, born 1838, died 1917. {Ref: Tombstone inscription}

PRESTON, Alexander, son of J. Alex and Achsah Preston, born 7 Jan 1867 in Baltimore, baptized 31 May 1867. {Ref: Church Records, 1834-1903, pp. 36-37}

PRESTON, C. E., see "Lucy Ringold," q.v.

PRESTON, Caroline E. (neé Perryman), died 23 Sep 1861, age 60. {Ref: Church Records, 1834-1903, p. 93; Tombstone inscription}

PRESTON, Caroline, daughter of J. Alexander and Achsah Preston, born 22 Apr 1864, baptized 10 Aug 1864. {Ref: Church Records, 1834-1903, pp. 34-35}

PRESTON, Charles Carrol, buried 26 Aug 1863. {Ref: Church Records, 1834-1903, p. 94}

PRESTON, Doctor, see "Harriet Ringold" and "Sally Ringold," q.v.

PRESTON, Emily P., confirmed 10 May 1860. {Ref: Church Records, 1834-1903, p. 294}

PRESTON, Fanny, daughter of Dr. Jacob A. and Caroline Elizabeth Preston, born 2 Sep 1837, baptized 12 Aug 1838 (sponsors: the parents). {Ref: Church Records, 1834-1903, pp. 18-19}

PRESTON, Fanny, daughter of J. A. and Caroline Preston, born 15 Apr 1839, baptized 29 Sep 1839 (sponsors: the parents). {Ref: Church Records, 1834-1903, pp. 20-21}

PRESTON, J. A., see "Lucy ----" and "Harriet Johnson" and "Lucy Ringold," q.v.

PRESTON, Jacob A. (doctor), confirmed 1 Nov 1846, died 2 Aug 1868, age 72, buried 3 Aug 1868. {Ref: Church Records, 1834-1903, pp. 95, 296; Tombstone inscription}

PRESTON, Jacob Alexander, son of Dr. Jacob A. and Caroline Elizabeth Preston, born 3 Mar 1836, baptized 12 Aug 1838 (sponsors: the parents); died -- Jan 1904, age 69 *[sic]*, buried 19 Jan 1904. {Ref: Church Records, 1834-1903, pp. 18-19; Parish Register, 1903-1958, p. 158; tombstone inscription}

PRESTON, James, sponsored the baptism of Nathaniel Howard Thayer on 15 Mar 1840. {Ref: Church Records, 1834-1903, p. 21}

PRESTON, James Carroll, born 1 Nov 1861, died 24 Aug 1863. {Ref: Tombstone inscription}

PRESTON, John Fisher, son of J. A. and C. E. Preston, born 27 Nov 1840, baptized 4 Jul 1841 (sponsor: Mary Fisher). {Ref: Church Records, 1834-1903, pp. 20-21}

PRESTON, Lloyd (colored), married Mary Lizzie Brown (colored) ---- 1877. [*Ed. Note:* The date was blank, but the marriage was listed between June and December in the register]. {Ref: Church Records, 1834-1903, p. 148}

PRESTON, Mary, confirmed 27 Apr 1856. {Ref: Church Records, 1834-1903, p. 297}

PRESTON, Robert Ludlow, son of J. A. Jr. and Achsah Preston, born 26 Apr 1869, baptized 10 Jul 1871. {Ref: Church Records, 1834-1903, pp. 38-39}

PRICE, Catherine (colored), married Lewis H. Monk (colored) ---- 1877. [*Ed. Note:* The date was blank, but the marriage was listed between June and December in the register]. {Ref: Church Records, 1834-1903, p. 148}

PRICE, David, son of John H. and Mary R. Price, born 27 Jan 1837, baptized 22 Aug 1854. {Ref: Church Records, 1834-1903, pp. 26-27}

PRICE, Elizabeth, from the Forest, died 23 Jan 1872. {Ref: Church Records, 1834-1903, p. 96}

PRICE, John, see "David Price" and "Mary Price," q.v.

PRICE, Mary, daughter of John H. and Mary R. Price, born 2 Jul 1853, baptized 22 Aug 1854. {Ref: Church Records, 1834-1903, pp. 26-27}

PRINCE, Isaac, buried 21 Nov 1900, age 77 years, 7 months and 26 days. {Ref: Church Records, 1834-1903, p. 104}

PROTZMAN, Charles W., born 15 Dec 1854, died 4 Oct 1900. {Ref: Tombstone inscription}

PURNELL, Isabella (colored), daughter of Stephen and Mary F. Purnell (colored), born 22 Oct 1869, baptized 28 Jul 1870, buried 29 Jul 1870. {Ref: Church Records, 1834-1903, pp. 38-39, 96}

PURNELL, Stephen (colored), married Mary F. Ringgold (colored) on 20 Jun 1869. {Ref: Church Records, 1834-1903, p. 147}

QUILLAN, Thomas B., married Margaret Burns on 28 May 1912. {Ref: Parish Register, 1903-1958, pp. 138-139}

QUINN, James, see "Martha Quinn," q.v.

QUINN, Martha, wife of James Quinn, born ---- [blank], baptized 22 May 1853. {Ref: Church Records, 1834-1903, pp. 26-27}

QUINN, Mary, married Thomas Wilson on 14 Jun 1860. {Ref: Church Records, 1834-1903, p. 142}

QUINN, Thomas M., died 2 Jan 1877, age 27. {Ref: Tombstone inscription}

RAISIN FAMILY.
 The following family information was entered in the church records under the heading of "Families" circa 1893-1903, but no relationships or ages were indicated, just names. Additional information shown in parenthesis was entered subsequently in the register:
 William H. Raisin, Mrs. Fannie M. Raisin (dead, name lined out, followed by a question mark), Claude N. Raisin, and Florence Aleine Raisin. {Ref: Church Records, 1834-1903, p. 253}

RAISIN, Claude N., see "Claude Reasin" and "Raisin Family," q.v.

RAISIN, Fannie N. (Mrs.), age 42, died 16 Jan 1897, buried 19 Jan 1897; also see "Raisin Family," q.v. {Ref: Church Records, 1834-1903, pp. 103, 200}

RAISIN, Florence Aleine, daughter of William H. and Fannie N. Raisin, born 27 Aug 1892, private baptism on 12 Sep 1892 (sick) at home of Henry Raymond; also see "Raisin Family," q.v. {Ref: Church Records, 1834-1903, pp. 10-11}

RAISIN, William H., see "William H. Reasin" and "Raisin Family," q.v.

RAMSAY, Ellen, see "Charlotte Sheaff," q.v.

RAMSAY (RAMSY), Emily, married John Lewis on 7 Jun 1862. {Ref: Church Records, 1834-1903, p. 144}

RAMSAY, Harriet (colored), married Samuel Ramsay (colored) on 23 Sep 1869. {Ref: Church Records, 1834-1903, p. 147}

RAMSAY (RAMSEY), Harriet (colored), married James Morton (colored) on 27 Dec 1870. {Ref: Church Records, 1834-1903, p. 147}

RAMSAY, James Henry (servant of Mrs. Chauncey of "Primrose"), son of ---- [blank], born 1825, baptized 30 Jun 1837. {Ref: Church Records, 1834-1903, pp. 18-19}

RAMSAY (RAMSY), Janetta (colored), died 23 Dec 1866 at Woodlawn and was interred in the cemetery at colored people's meeting house. {Ref: Church Records, 1834-1903, p. 95}

RAMSAY, Philip (slave of Edward and Mary Griffith), son of ---- [blank], born -- Mar 1837, baptized 14 Oct 1838. {Ref: Church Records, 1834-1903, pp. 18-19}

RAMSAY, Samuel (colored), slave of Edward and Mary Griffith, born 1833, baptized 14 Oct 1838, married Harriet Ramsay (colored) on 23 Sep 1869. {Ref: Church Records, 1834-1903, pp. 18-19, 147}

RAMSAY (RAMSY), Samuel, married Janetta Brown on 29 Dec 1863. {Ref: Church Records, 1834-1903, p. 145}

RAMSAY (RAMSEY), William, born 29 Nov 1792, died 26 Dec 1831. {Ref: Tombstone inscription}

RAMSAY, William W., see "Charlotte Sheaff," q.v.

RANDOLPH, Cary Ruffin, married F. Ethel Patterson on 11 Oct 1899 at "Brinfield" in Perryman; also see "Patterson Family," q.v. {Ref: Church Records, 1834-1903, pp. 160-161}

RANSON, Kane (colored), married Sarah C. Dallam (colored) on 17 Oct 1867. {Ref: Church Records, 1834-1903, p. 146}

RATHER, Laura V., wife of Austin S. Rather, born 1872, died 1904. {Ref: Tombstone inscription}

RAYMOND FAMILY.
The following family information was entered in the church records under the heading of "Families" circa 1893-1903, but no relationships or ages were indicated, just names. Additional information shown in parenthesis was entered subsequently in the register:
Fletcher Raymond (removed to Baltimore, words then lined out) Mrs. ---- [blank] Raymond (removed to Baltimore, words then lined out) Maud Raymond (removed to Baltimore, words then lined out) Mannie Raymond (removed to Baltimore, words then lined out). {Ref: Church Records, 1834-1903, p. 257}
Henry Raymond, Mrs. Mary V. Raymond, Mary A. Raymond (married W. H. Pentz? *[sic]*), and Henry Raymond, Jr. {Ref: Church Records, 1834-1903, p. 254}

RAYMOND, Fletcher, born 3 Jan 1846, died 15 Jan 1905; also see "Raymond Family," q.v. {Ref: Tombstone inscription}

RAYMOND, Henry, see "Mary Allen Raymond" and "Florence A. Raisin" and "William H. Pentz" and "Raymond Family," q.v.

RAYMOND, Mannie, see "Raymond Family," q.v.

RAYMOND, Mary Allene (Aleine), daughter of Henry and Mollie Raymond, born ---- [blank], baptized 27 Apr 1879, confirmed 9 Jun 1893, married William Henry Pentz on 20 Aug 1901 at Mr. Henry Raymond's in Aberdeen; also see "Mary A. Pentz," q.v. {Ref: Church Records, 1834-1903, pp. 42-43, 160-161, 204-205 301}

RAYMOND, Mary (Mollie) V. (Mrs.), born 1850, confirmed 7 Mar 1884, church member in 1903, died in 1904. {Ref: Church Records, 1834-1903, p. 299; Parish Register, 1903-1958, p. 108; Tombstone inscription}

RAYMOND, Maude, received from the Church of the Holy Innocents in Baltimore on 21 May 1901, church member in 1903; also see "Raymond Family," q.v. {Ref: Church Records, 1834-1903, p. 206; Parish Register, 1903-1958, p. 108}

RAYMOND, Mollie, see "Mary A. Raymond" and "Mary V. Raymond," q.v.

READ, George H. (colored), married Mary Eliza Bass (colored) on 14 Dec 1882. {Ref: Church Records, 1834-1903, p. 150}

READ, Joshua (colored), married Harriet Wilmer (colored) ---- 1877. [*Ed. Note:* The date was blank, but the marriage was listed between June and December in the register]. {Ref: Church Records, 1834-1903, p. 148}

READ(?), Andrew Harrison, son of John Thomas and Mary E. Read(?) *[sic]*, born ---- [blank], baptized 23 Oct 1874 (1877?). {Ref: Church Records, 1834-1903, pp. 40-41}

READ(?), Caroline Frances, daughter of John Thomas and Mary E. Read(?) *[sic]*, born ---- [blank], baptized 23 Oct 1874 (1877?). {Ref: Church Records, 1834-1903, pp. 40-41}

REASIN, Claude, son of William H. and Fannie W. Reasin, born 29 Mar 1889, private baptism on 16 Sep 1889; also see "Claude Raisin," q.v. {Ref: Church Records, 1834-1903, p. 9}

REASIN, Fannie B., wife of William H. Reasin, Jr., born 1 Sep 1854, died 17 Jan 1897. {Ref: Tombstone inscription}

REASIN, Martha E., daughter of William and Sarah Reasin, born 6 Sep 1825, died 8 Aug 1858, buried 9 Aug 1858. {Ref: Church Records, 1834-1903, p. 93; Tombstone inscription}

REASIN, Sarah A., wife of William D. Reasin, born 29 Sep 1794, died 5 Mar 1835. {Ref: Tombstone inscription}

REASIN, William H., born 1855, died 1917; also see "Fannie B. Reasin," q.v. {Ref: Tombstone inscription}

REDDON, Maggie, married Joseph Stephenson on 22 Apr 1879. {Ref: Church Records, 1834-1903, p. 149}

REED, Andrew, married Martha Frisby on 4 Jul 1857. {Ref: Church Records, 1834-1903, p. 141}

REED, Caleb (colored), married Harriet Harris (colored) on 3 Mar 1871. {Ref: Church Records, 1834-1903, p. 147}

REED, Frances (colored), married Wesley Harris (colored) ---- 1877. [*Ed. Note:* The date was blank, but the marriage was listed between June and December in the register]. {Ref: Church Records, 1834-1903, p. 148}

REED, Henny, see "Mary Reed," q.v.

REED, Isaac (colored), married Milley Ann Gibson (colored) on 18 Mar 1869. {Ref: Church Records, 1834-1903, p. 147}

REED, Jacob, see "Thomas A. Reed," q.v.

REED, Mary, daughter of Isaac and Henny Reed, born 29 Dec 1864, baptized 28 Apr 1865. {Ref: Church Records, 1834-1903, pp. 34-35}

REED, Sarah J., married George H. Matthews on 29 Aug 1872. {Ref: Church Records, 1834-1903, p. 147}

REED, Sophia, see "Thomas A. Reed," q.v.

REED, Thomas Arthur (colored), son of Jacob and Sophia Reed, born 11 Oct 1871, baptized 14 Jan 1872. {Ref: Church Records, 1834-1903, pp. 38-39}

REESE, St. Louis, sponsored the baptism of Winthrop Parkhurst Buttrick on 19 Oct 1919. {Ref: Parish Register, 1903-1958, pp. 34-35}

REHREN, Theresa M., married John W. Hayn on 1 Oct 1881. {Ref: Church Records, 1834-1903, p. 150}

REID, Hattie (colored), married George Griffith (colored) on 11 Oct 1883. {Ref: Church Records, 1834-1903, p. 151}

REISHEL, Abia Clark, married Mary Keen on 17 Jan 1878. {Ref: Church Records, 1834-1903, p. 148}

173

REISHEL, Warren Keen, son of A. C. and M. K. Reishel, born 8 Jul 1881, baptized 25 Sep 1881 (sponsors: the parents and Mr. & Mrs. B. H. Keen). {Ref: Church Records, 1834-1903, pp. 2-3}

RELLENSMAN, Julius, buried Trinity Sunday, 27 May 1893, "age about 60." {Ref: Church Records, 1834-1903, p. 102}

REYNOLDS, Anna Susie, daughter of M. V. and Anna D. Reynolds, born 26 May 1912, private baptism 28 Jan 1913 at "Romney Royal." {Ref: Parish Register, 1903-1958, pp. 30-31}

REYNOLDS, Annie, born 1901, died 1903. {Ref: Tombstone inscription}

REYNOLDS, Annie (Mrs.), sponsored the baptism of Asa Alexander Taylor, Ida May Taylor, Lawrence Matthew Taylor and Willie Thomas Taylor on 13 Aug 1882. {Ref: Church Records, 1834-1903, p. 3}

RHODES, Clara Scisco, daughter of William and Matilda Rhodes, born 28 Jun 1860, baptized 24 Apr 1864. {Ref: Church Records, 1834-1903, pp. 34-35}

RHODES, Harriet, see "John L. Rhodes," q.v.

RHODES, James, married Sarah W. Washington Bond on 27 Dec 1856. {Ref: Church Records, 1834-1903, p. 141}

RHODES, John Lloyd, son of Harriet Rhodes (servant of Dr. Dallam), born ---- [blank], baptized 21 Jun 1837. {Ref: Church Records, 1834-1903, pp. 18-19}

RHODES, Matilda, see "Clara S. Rhodes," q.v.

RHODES, William, buried 10 Jul 1863; also see "Clara S. Rhodes," q.v. {Ref: Church Records, 1834-1903, p. 94}

RICE, Abraham Lincoln (colored), married Georgeanna Tinson (colored) on 30 Sep 1886. [*Ed. Note:* His name was actually written "Ab: Lincoln Rice" in the register]. {Ref: Church Records, 1834-1903, pp. 152-153}

RICE, Araminta (slave of J. Sidney Hall), daughter of ---- [blank], born 16 Sep 1837, baptized 23 Aug 1838. {Ref: Church Records, 1834-1903, pp. 18-19}

RICE, Charlotte (colored), married William Clark (colored) on 5 Dec 1867. {Ref: Church Records, 1834-1903, p. 146}

RICE, Freeborn, married Sallie Ozburn on 7 Apr 1859; also see "George W. Rice" and "Jacob A. Rice" and "John W. Rice" and "Mary E. Rice" and "Mary M. Rice" and "Robert A. Rice" and "Semelia A. Rice" and "William H. Rice," q.v. {Ref: Church Records, 1834-1903, p. 142}

RICE, George Washington (colored), son of Freeborn and Sarah A. Rice, born 24 May 1872, baptized 12 Jun 1872. {Ref: Church Records, 1834-1903, pp. 38-39}

RICE, Jacob (colored), married Dinah Clark (colored) on 27 Dec 1883. {Ref: Church Records, 1834-1903, p. 151}

RICE, Jacob Albert, son of Freeborn and Sarah Ann Rice, born 14 Feb 1857, baptized 13 Oct 1863. {Ref: Church Records, 1834-1903, pp. 32-33}

RICE, Jacob Lewis (colored), son of Nancy Rice, born 13 Aug 1841, baptized 11 Jul 1848. {Ref: Church Records, 1834-1903, pp. 22-23}

RICE, James (colored), buried 7 Jun 1848. [*Ed. Note:* In another Parish Register, 1696-1851, it indicates he was about 10 years old]. {Ref: Church Records, 1834-1903, p. 91}

RICE, John Wesley, son of Freeborn and Sarah Ann Rice, born 26 Sep 1859, baptized 13 Oct 1863. {Ref: Church Records, 1834-1903, pp. 32-33}

RICE, Lloyd (colored), married Ella Dallam (colored) on 22 Dec 1887. {Ref: Church Records, 1834-1903, p. 154}

RICE, Mary Elizabeth, daughter of Freeborn and Sarah Ann Rice, born -- Apr 1856, baptized 13 Oct 1863. {Ref: Church Records, 1834-1903, pp. 32-33}

RICE, Mary Maria, daughter of Freeborn and Sarah Ann Rice, born 28 Jan 1861, baptized 13 Oct 1863. {Ref: Church Records, 1834-1903, pp. 32-33}

RICE, Nancy, see "Jacob L. Rice," q.v.

RICE, Nancy, married Robert Dallam on 2 Jan 1858. {Ref: Church Records, 1834-1903, p. 141}

RICE, Robert Alexander (colored), son of Freeborn and Sarah A. Rice, born 1 Mar 1871, baptized 12 Jun 1872. {Ref: Church Records, 1834-1903, pp. 38-39}

RICE, Ruth Roberta (neé McCrory), born 30 Jun 1915. {Ref: Parish Register, 1903-1958, p. 44}

RICE, Sarah, see "George W. Rice" and "Jacob A. Rice" and "John W. Rice" and "Mary E. Rice" and "Mary M. Rice" and "Robert A. Rice" and "Semelia A. Rice" and "William H. Rice," q.v.

RICE, Semelia Elizabeth, daughter of Freeborn and Sarah Rice, born ---- [blank], baptized -- Jul 1878. {Ref: Church Records, 1834-1903, pp. 40-41}

RICE, William Henry, son of Freeborn and Sarah Ann Rice, born 27 Nov 1863, baptized 13 Oct 1863. {Ref: Church Records, 1834-1903, pp. 32-33}

RICHARDS, A. G. (reverend), sponsored the baptisms of William LeRoy Towner on 26 Aug 1900 and Louise Loehning on 18 Nov 1900. {Ref: Church Records, 1834-1903, p. 15}

RICHARDS, Grace N. (Mrs.), received from St. John's Church in Baltimore on 12 Dec 1900, transferred to Trinity Church in Chicago, Illinois on 15 Dec 1903. {Ref: Church Records, 1834-1903, p. 206; Parish Register, 1903-1958, p. 108}

RICHARDS, Paul Nettleton, son of Albert Glenn and Grace Nettleton Richards, born 4 Feb 1903, baptized 10 May 1903 (sponsors: Rev. LeBamey T. Phillips, Mr. Charles W. Michael, Mrs. Harriet E. Yarnall and Mrs. Mary K. Nettleton). {Ref: Church Records, 1834-1903, pp. 16-17}

RICHARDSON, Agnes (colored), daughter of Lovinia Richardson, born 1st Sunday in April, 1862, baptized 28 Apr 1864 at Belvidere. {Ref: Church Records, 1834-1903, pp. 34-35}

RICHARDSON, Avarilla, see "Mary Richardson," q.v.

RICHARDSON, Cassey, married Andrew Banks on 8 Aug 1863. {Ref: Church Records, 1834-1903, p. 145}

RICHARDSON, David, see "Elizabeth C. Richardson" and "James L. Richardson" and "Jamima Richardson" and "John W. Richardson," q.v.

RICHARDSON, Elizabeth, see "Elizabeth C. Richardson" and "James L. Richardson" and "Jamima Richardson" and "John W. Richardson," q.v.

RICHARDSON, Elizabeth Christiana, daughter of David and Elizabeth Richardson, born 26 Feb 1834, baptized 2 Jun 1837. {Ref: Church Records, 1834-1903, pp. 16-17}

RICHARDSON, Ellen, daughter of Rilla Richardson (servant to Albert Davis), born 12 Feb 1854, baptized 27 Sep 1856. {Ref: Church Records, 1834-1903, pp. 28-29}

RICHARDSON, Hannah (colored), daughter of Rilla Richardson, born 1st Sunday in April, 1862, baptized 28 Apr 1864 at Belvidere. {Ref: Church Records, 1834-1903, pp. 34-35}

RICHARDSON, James Leach, son of David and Elizabeth Richardson, born 2 Jan 1827, baptized 2 Jun 1837, died 10 Aug 1907. {Ref: Church Records, 1834-1903, pp. 16-17; Tombstone inscription}

RICHARDSON, Jamima, daughter of David and Elizabeth Richardson, born 16 Aug 1838 [error made in register; actually born in 1836], baptized 2 Jun 1837. {Ref: Church Records, 1834-1903, pp. 16-17}

RICHARDSON, John Wesley, son of David and Elizabeth Richardson, born 10 Sep 1832, baptized 2 Jun 1837. {Ref: Church Records, 1834-1903, pp. 16-17}

RICHARDSON, Lewis (slave), born ---- [blank], private baptism on 9 Mar 1836 at "The Dairy" (sponsor: Mrs. Dr. Davidge, mistress). {Ref: Church Records, 1834-1903, pp. 16-17}

RICHARDSON, Lovinia, see "Agnes Richardson," q.v.

RICHARDSON, Mary (colored), daughter of Avarilla Richardson, born 30 Mar 1865, baptized 5 Feb 1866. {Ref: Church Records, 1834-1903, pp. 36-37}

RICHARDSON, Mary E., born 3 Sep 1835, died 1 Nov 1907. {Ref: Tombstone inscription}

RICHARDSON, Rilla, see "Ellen Richardson" and "Hannah Richardson" and "Mary Richardson," q.v.

RICHARDSON, William, married Rachel McClure Cobourn on 1 May 1861. {Ref: Church Records, 1834-1903, p. 143}

177

RICKEY, Annie W., died 1 Mar 1866, age 21 years, 3 months and 23 days. {Ref: Tombstone inscription}

RICKEY, Joseph R., born 3 Jul 1811, died 1 Nov 1876. {Ref: Tombstone inscription}

RICKEY, Rachel, wife of Joseph R. Rickey, born 17 Jul 1812, died 11 Jun 1870, buried 14 Jun 1870. {Ref: Church Records, 1834-1903, p. 96; Tombstone inscription}

RILEY, Daniel W., born 29 May 1850, died 16 Sep 1863. {Ref: Tombstone inscription}

RILEY, John, see "Nancy Riley," q.v.

RILEY, Nancy, wife of John Riley, born 25 Nov 1815, died 7 Jun 1867, buried 8 Jun 1867. {Ref: Church Records, 1834-1903, p. 95; Tombstone inscription}

RILEY, Nancy C., born 26 May 1845, died 20 Oct 1855. {Ref: Tombstone inscription}

RILEY, Sarah B., born 9 May 1842, died 9 Aug 1847. {Ref: Tombstone inscription}

RINGGOLD, Alice Hawthorn, daughter of Lucy Ringgold, born 28 Jul 1860, baptized 10 Dec 1861. {Ref: Church Records, 1834-1903, pp. 30-31}

RINGGOLD, Blanche, daughter of John and Sarah Ringgold, born age 4 months, baptized ---- [blank] 1860. {Ref: Church Records, 1834-1903, pp. 30-31}

RINGGOLD, Caroline, married Charles Heath on 20 Sep 1856. {Ref: Church Records, 1834-1903, p. 140}

RINGGOLD, Charles, married Mary Johnson on 26 Dec 1857; also see "Emily Ringold," q.v. {Ref: Church Records, 1834-1903, p. 141}

RINGGOLD, Charlotte (colored), married Hampton Monk (colored) on 7 Aug 1864. {Ref: Church Records, 1834-1903, p. 145}

RINGGOLD, Eliza, married Henry Frizby on 26 May 1848. {Ref: Church Records, 1834-1903, p. 139}

RINGGOLD, Emily, daughter of Charles and Mary Ringgold, buried 18 Nov 1861. {Ref: Church Records, 1834-1903, p. 93}

RINGGOLD, Emory (colored), married Eliza A. Lewis (colored) on 7 Jul 1867. {Ref: Church Records, 1834-1903, p. 146}

RINGGOLD, Jane (colored), married Henry Tilden (colored) on 21 Jul 1867. {Ref: Church Records, 1834-1903, p. 146}

RINGGOLD, John, see "John Ringold," q.v.

RINGGOLD, John (colored child), buried 27 Jan 1857. {Ref: Church Records, 1834-1903, p. 93}

RINGGOLD, Lucy (colored), married William Lee (colored) on 5 Dec 1867; also see "Alice Ringgold," q.v. {Ref: Church Records, 1834-1903, p. 146}

RINGGOLD, Marian V. (colored), married James Henry Stansbury (colored) on 10 Feb 1887. {Ref: Church Records, 1834-1903, pp. 152-153}

RINGGOLD, Martha, married Philip Brown on 16 Jan 1848. {Ref: Church Records, 1834-1903, p. 139}

RINGGOLD, Mary F. (colored), married Stephen Purnell (colored) on 20 Jun 1869. {Ref: Church Records, 1834-1903, p. 147}

RINGGOLD, Rachel, buried 14 Mar 1850. {Ref: Church Records, 1834-1903, p. 91}

RINGGOLD, Sarah (colored), buried 29 Mar 1869. {Ref: Church Records, 1834-1903, p. 95}

RINGGOLD, Sophie Cummings, daughter of John and Sarah Ringgold, age 4 years, baptized ---- [blank] 1860. {Ref: Church Records, 1834-1903, pp. 30-31}

RINGGOLD, Washington, married Aminta Wilmer on 26 Dec 1857. {Ref: Church Records, 1834-1903, p. 141}

RINGOLD, Charles (colored), son of William and Mary Ringold, born -- Apr 1841, baptized 10 Jul 1848. {Ref: Church Records, 1834-1903, pp. 22-23}

RINGOLD, Francis (colored), son of John and Sarah Ringold, born ---- [blank], baptized 8 Sep 1849. {Ref: Church Records, 1834-1903, pp. 22-23}

RINGOLD, Harriet, daughter of John and Sarah Ringold (servants of Dr. Preston), born ---- [blank], baptized 6 Jan 1857. {Ref: Church Records, 1834-1903, pp. 28-29}

RINGOLD, Howard Brice (colored), son of Nathan and Susan A. Ringold, born 25 Feb 1893, baptized 1 Feb 1896 (sponsor: the mother). {Ref: Church Records, 1834-1903, pp. 12-13}

RINGOLD, Jane Hepburn (colored), daughter of John and Sarah Ringold, born ---- [blank], baptized 8 Sep 1849. {Ref: Church Records, 1834-1903, pp. 22-23}

RINGOLD, John, see "John Ringgold" and "Blanche Ringgold" and "Sophie Ringgold" and "Francis Ringold" and "Harriet Ringold" and "Jane Ringold" and "Rachel Ringold" and "Sally Ringold," q.v.

RINGOLD, John (colored), son of John and Sarah Ringold, born 8 Jul 1852, baptized 16 Jan 1853. {Ref: Church Records, 1834-1903, pp. 24-25}

RINGOLD, Lucy (slave of Jacob A. and C. E. Preston), born 29 Dec 1840, baptized 4 Jul 1841. {Ref: Church Records, 1834-1903, pp. 20-21}

RINGOLD, Nathan, see "Howard B. Ringold," q.v.

RINGOLD, Rachel (colored), daughter of John and Sarah Ringold, born ---- [blank], baptized 8 Sep 1849. {Ref: Church Records, 1834-1903, pp. 22-23}

RINGOLD, Rachel (colored), daughter of John and Sarah Ringold, born 14 Nov 1850, baptized 16 Jan 1853. {Ref: Church Records, 1834-1903, pp. 24-25}

RINGOLD, Sally, daughter of John and Sarah Ringold (servants of Dr. Preston), born ---- [blank], baptized 6 Jan 1857. {Ref: Church Records, 1834-1903, pp. 28-29}

RINGOLD, Sarah, see "Blanche Ringgold" and "Sophie Ringgold" and "Francis Ringold" and "Harriet Ringold" and "Jane Ringold" and "Rachel Ringold" and "Sally Ringold," q.v.

RINGOLD, Susan, see "Howard B. Ringold," q.v.

RINGOLD, William, see "Charles Ringold," q.v.

RISCHEL, Mamie K., sponsored the baptism of Willie Warburton Nelson on 25 Aug 1907 (by proxy). {Ref: Parish Register, 1903-1958, p. 31}

RISHEL, A. C. (Mrs.), sponsored the baptism of Garbiel Ellis Porter on 12 Jul 1891. {Ref: Church Records, 1834-1903, p. 11}

ROBERSON, Tissue, daughter of Israel and Eliza Roberson, buried 23 Oct 1861. {Ref: Church Records, 1834-1903, p. 93}

ROBERTS, Jane, consort of Owen Roberts, died 3 Apr 1824, age 44. {Ref: Tombstone inscription}

ROBERTSON, Israel, married Eliza Izer on 13 Mar 1848. [*Ed. Note:* In another Parish Register, 1696-1851, it indicates Israel Roberson, a servant man of Mr. Mitchel, married Elizer Iser, a free woman, on 13 Mar 1847, both "persons of color"]. {Ref: Church Records, 1834-1903, p. 139}

ROBINSON, Joseph (reverend), born 26 May 1825 in Moalefield, England, died 18 Feb 1893 in Perryman, Harford County, Maryland. {Ref: Church Records, 1834-1903, p. 102; Tombstone inscription}

ROCKWELL, Hermione, married J. Murray Maynadier on 24 Jul 1872. {Ref: Church Records, 1834-1903, p. 147}

RODES, Eliza Hepburn (colored), daughter of John Thomas and Maria Rodes, born 7 Aug 1862, baptized 23 Jun 1865. {Ref: Church Records, 1834-1903, pp. 34-35}

RODGERS, Delia, wife of Alexander Rodgers, died 7 Sep 1827 in her 45th year. {Ref: Tombstone inscription}

ROGERS, James (Mr. & Mrs.), sponsored the baptism of Evelyn Caldwell Hume on 14 Nov 1916. {Ref: Parish Register, 1903-1958, pp. 32-33}

ROGERS, Jane Perry, daughter of Robert and Sarah Rogers, born 26 May 1852, baptized 18 Sep 1852. {Ref: Church Records, 1834-1903, pp. 24-25}

ROLLASON, James H., married Frances S. Kimble on 9 Apr 1868. {Ref: Church Records, 1834-1903, p. 146}

ROSS, Benjamin A., married Ida May Lee on 4 Nov 1897. {Ref: Church Records, 1834-1903, pp. 160-161}

ROSSTER, Harriet (colored), married William H. Monk, Jr. on 4 Sep 1892. {Ref: Church Records, 1834-1903, pp. 158-159}

ROUSE, Maude, married William T. Taylor on 25 Jun 1896; also see "Isabel F. Taylor" and "Ida Virginia Taylor," q.v. {Ref: Church Records, 1834-1903, pp. 160-161}

ROWLEY, John Henry, married Florence Lindsay White on 15 Dec 1909 at Perryman. {Ref: Parish Register, 1903-1958, pp. 138-139}

RUE, George Howard Kennedy (colored), married Ellenora Webster (colored) on 9 Jun 1887. {Ref: Church Records, 1834-1903, p. 154}

RUFF, Cyrus N., died 25 Apr 1851, age 29. {Ref: Tombstone inscription}

RUFF, Elizabeth F., died 15 Feb 1911, age 82. {Ref: Tombstone inscription}

RUFF, Mrs., see "Matthews Family," q.v.

RUMSBY, Martha (colored), married John R. Taylor (colored) on 25 Oct 1883. {Ref: Church Records, 1834-1903, p. 151}

RUMSEY, Amy, married Welton Curtis on 18 May 1862. {Ref: Church Records, 1834-1903, p. 144}

RUMSEY, Mary, married Jacob Dallam on 15 Oct 1863. {Ref: Church Records, 1834-1903, p. 145}

RUMSEY, Sabina (colored), married Jacob H. Christie (colored) on 21 Dec 1865. {Ref: Church Records, 1834-1903, p. 146}

RUSSELL FAMILY.
The following family information was entered in the church records under the heading of "Families" circa 1893-1903, but no relationships or ages were indicated, just names:
William T. Russell, Catharine C. Russell, Harry Russell, Eddie Russell, and Helen Elizabeth Russell. {Ref: Church Records, 1834-1903, p. 262}

RUSSELL, Catharine, see "Russell Family," q.v.

RUSSELL, Eddie, see "Russell Family," q.v.

RUSSELL, Harry, see "Russell Family," q.v.

RUSSELL, Helen Elizabeth, daughter of William Thompson and Catharine Christina Russell, born 11 Feb 1903, baptized 12 Apr 1903 (sponsors: Mrs. Mary Elizabeth Dashield, Mr. James W. Malcolm and Miss Helen E. Malcolm); also see "Russell Family," q.v. {Ref: Church Records, 1834-1903, pp. 16-17}

RUSSELL, Mabel, see "---- Russell," q.v.

RUSSELL, William, see "Russell Family," q.v.

RUSSELL, ----, infant daughter of Harry and Mabel Russell, age 8 hours, buried 20 Apr 1913. {Ref: Parish Register, 1903-1958, p. 158}

RUSSELL, ----, infant son of Harry and Mabel Russell, died at birth, buried 8 May 1914. {Ref: Parish Register, 1903-1958, p. 159}

RYAN, Mary Virginia, daughter of John and Laura Ryan, born 23 Jul 1886, baptized 19 Nov 1886. {Ref: Church Records, 1834-1903, p. 6}

SANDERS, Joseph E., of Havre de Grace, son of Joseph and Harriet F. Sanders, died 16 May 1872, age 22 years, 6 months and 5 days, buried 18 May 1872. {Ref: Church Records, 1834-1903, p. 96; Tombstone inscription}

SANDERS, Nannie, married Alphonso N. McGaw on 15 Dec 1885. {Ref: Church Records, 1834-1903, pp. 152-153}

SANK, Jane L., died 30 Apr 1869, age 56. {Ref: Tombstone inscription}

SANNER, Martha A., in her 61st year, buried 29 Apr 1884 in Greenmount Cemetery in Baltimore. {Ref: Church Records, 1834-1903, p. 100}

SAPPINGTON, Florence, daughter of John and Mary A. Sappington, born 16 Oct 1841, baptized 22 Aug 1854. {Ref: Church Records, 1834-1903, pp. 26-27}

SAPPINGTON, John, son of John and Mary A. Sappington, born 19 Oct 1846, baptized 22 Aug 1854. {Ref: Church Records, 1834-1903, pp. 26-27}

SAPPINGTON, Walter, son of John and Mary A. Sappington, born 5 Jul 1849, baptized 22 Aug 1854. {Ref: Church Records, 1834-1903, pp. 26-27}

SAUMENIG, Henry (Harry) Fields (reverend), rector in 1903 and 1904, transferred to Church of the Ascension in Baltimore on 7 Jul 1904. {Ref: Parish Register, 1903-1958, pp. ii, 108}

SAUMENIG, Rosalie Q.(?), church member in 1903, transferred to Church of the Ascension in Baltimore, 7 Jul 1904. {Ref: Parish Register, 1903-1958, p. 108}

SAVOY, Mary Ann (colored), daughter of Richard and Ellen Savoy, born 15 Sep 1869, baptized 10 May 1870. {Ref: Church Records, 1834-1903, pp. 38-39}

SAVOY, Richard (colored), married Ellen Stevenson (colored) on 15 Apr 1869. {Ref: Church Records, 1834-1903, p. 147}

SCHERLING, Amanda Jenetta, daughter of Ernest and Caroline Scherling, born 7 Jun 1868, baptized 25 Dec 1868. {Ref: Church Records, 1834-1903, pp. 36-37}

SCHERLING, Catharine Christiana, daughter of Ernest and Caroline Scherling, born 30 Jun 1865, baptized 15 Sep 1866. {Ref: Church Records, 1834-1903, pp. 36-37}

SCHERLING, Ernst, buried 30 Mar 1896, age 67. [*Ed. Note:* His name was also spelled "Earnest Schirling" and "Ernest Scherling" in the register]. {Ref: Church Records, 1834-1903, p. 103}

SCHERLING, Mary Amanda, daughter of Ernst and Caroline Scherling, born 24 Apr 1859, baptized 15 Jul 1860, buried 20 Sep 1860. {Ref: Church Records, 1834-1903, pp. 30-31, 93}

SCHERLING, William Groderlrick Simpson, son of Ernst and Caroline Scherling, born 6 Nov 1861, baptized 1 Jan 1862. {Ref: Church Records, 1834-1903, pp. 32-33}

SCHOFIELD, Bessie Virginia, daughter of Robert H. and Virginia Schofield, born 28 Mar 1913, baptized 11 Jul 1913 "near St. George's Church" (sponsors: the parents). {Ref: Parish Register, 1903-1958, pp. 32-33}

SCHOFIELD, Harold (Howard?) Edward, son of William R. and Lacey C. Schofield, born 11 Feb 1913, baptized 27 Jun 1913 in the church rectory, died -- Sep 1913, age 7 months, buried 27 Sep 1913. {Ref: Parish Register, 1903-1958, pp. 32-33, 159}

SCHOFIELD, Helen Elizabeth, daughter of William R. and Lacey C. Schofield, born 2 Apr 1917, baptized 9 Jun 1917 in the church rectory (sponsor: Mrs. Lacy C. Schofield). {Ref: Parish Register, 1903-1958, pp. 32-33}

SCHOFIELD, Katherine Virginia, daughter of William R. and Lacey C. Schofield, born 2 Dec 1915, baptized 22 Jul 1916 in the church rectory (sponsor: Mrs. Lacey C. Schofield). {Ref: Parish Register, 1903-1958, pp. 32-33}

SCHOFIELD, Lacey C. (Mrs.), sponsored the baptisms of Katherine Virginia Schofield on 2 Jul 1916, Helen Elizabeth Schofield on 9 Jun 1917 and Katherine Elizabeth Baldwin on 28 Jul 1917; also see "Harold (Howard?) Schofield" and "Helen E. Schofield" and "Katherine V. Schofield," q.v. {Ref: Parish Register, 1903-1958, pp. 32-33}

SCHOFIELD, Robert, see "Bessie V. Schofield" and "Russell S. Schofield," q.v.

SCHOFIELD, Russell Sylvester, son of Robert H. and Virginia Schofield, born 16 Feb 1911, baptized 11 Jul 1913 "near St. George's Church" (sponsors: the parents). {Ref: Parish Register, 1903-1958, pp. 32-33}

SCHOFIELD, Samuel L., born 2 Jun 1895, died 6 Oct 1918 in France, M. G. Company, 115th Infantry [29th Division]. {Ref: Tombstone inscription}

SCHOFIELD, William, married Lacey Baldwin on 25 Sep 1912; also see "Harold (Howard?) Schofield" and "Helen E. Schofield" and "Katherine V. Schofield," q.v. {Ref: Parish Register, 1903-1958, pp. 138-139}

SCHOLTZ, Albert, son of Albert and Lizzie Scholtz, born 8 Aug 1889, private baptism on 8 Aug 1889. {Ref: Church Records, 1834-1903, p. 9}

SCOTT, Sarah L. (Mrs.), sponsored the baptism of Mildred Louise Morgan on 31 Jul 1897. {Ref: Church Records, 1834-1903, p. 13}

SELF, James, married Catharine Moon on 23 Sep 1855 at Havre de Grace; also see "William B. Self," q.v. {Ref: Church Records, 1834-1903, p. 140}

SELF, William, confirmed 9 Feb 1873. {Ref: Church Records, 1834-1903, p. 297}

SELF, William Barnabas, son of James and Catharine Self, born 25 Feb 1857, baptized 12 Apr 1857. {Ref: Church Records, 1834-1903, pp. 28-29}

SELFE, Lee Webster, married Helen Opall Wright on 5 May 1917 at Mr. Wright's residence in Stepney. {Ref: Parish Register, 1903-1958, pp. 138-139}

SEWELL, Ann Olevia, daughter of James Munro and Ann O. Sewell, born 12 Jun 1868, baptized 4 Nov 1869. {Ref: Church Records, 1834-1903, pp. 38-39}

SEWELL, Charles S. (colonel), of Abingdon, buried 5 Nov 1848. [*Ed. Note:* In another Parish Register, 1696-1851, it indicates he was 70 years old when he died]. {Ref: Church Records, 1834-1903, p. 91}

SEWELL, Charles Smith, son of Septimus D. and Maria L. Sewell, born 10 Feb 1853, baptized 26 Mar 1853. {Ref: Church Records, 1834-1903, pp. 26-27}

SEWELL, Clement Kegry, son of Septimus and Maria Sewell, born 22 May 1861, baptized 22 May 1862. {Ref: Church Records, 1834-1903, pp. 32-33}

SEWELL, Jacob (doctor), of Abingdon, buried on Good Friday 17 Apr 1840. {Ref: Church Records, 1834-1903, p. 90}

SEWELL, James M., see "Ann O. Sewell," q.v.

SEWELL, Maria, see "Benjamin King" and "Martha Susan ----" and "Charles S. Sewell" and "Clement K. Sewell" and Maria C. Sewell" and "Mary S. Sewell" and Septimas E. Sewell" and "William H. Sewell," q.v.

SEWELL, Maria Catherine, daughter of Septimus D. and Maria L. Sewell, born 22 Aug 1856, baptized 6 Jun 1857. {Ref: Church Records, 1834-1903, pp. 28-29}

SEWELL, Mary Smith, daughter of Septimus D. and Maria L. Sewell, born 17 Apr 1859, baptized 30 Dec 1859. {Ref: Church Records, 1834-1903, pp. 30-31}

SEWELL, Septimas Eloize, daughter of Septimus D. and Maria Sewell, born 7 Oct 1869, baptized 4 Nov 1869. {Ref: Church Records, 1834-1903, pp. 38-39}

SEWELL, Septimus, see "Benjamin King" and "Martha Susan ----" and "Charles S. Sewell" and "Clement K. Sewell" and Maria C. Sewell" and "Mary S. Sewell" and Septimas E. Sewell" and "William H. Sewell," q.v.

SEWELL, William Hyde, son of Septimus and Maria Sewell, born 30 Sep 1862, baptized 19 Jun 1864. {Ref: Church Records, 1834-1903, pp. 34-35}

SHALBURG, John Howard, married Christina W. Anderson ---- 1877. [*Ed. Note:* The date was blank, but the marriage was listed between June and December in the register]. {Ref: Church Records, 1834-1903, p. 148}

SHANE, Sarah B., born 1838, died 1903. {Ref: Tombstone inscription}

SHAY, Alice, wife of Bennett Shay, born 11 May 1812, died 30 May 1895, buried 1 Jun 1895, age 84 [*sic*]. {Ref: Church Records, 1834-1903, p. 103; Tombstone inscription}

SHAY, Bennett, died 9 Mar 1881, age 74; also see "Alice Shay," q.v. {Ref: Tombstone inscription}

SHAY, Emma V., buried -- Aug 1885, age 37; also see "Howard C. Shay" and "Ida I. Shay" and "William W. Shay," q.v. {Ref: Church Records, 1834-1903, p. 101}

SHAY, Fannie (Miss), sponsored the baptism of Howard Chapman Shay, Ida Isabel Shay, and William Wallace Shay on 25 Sep 1881. {Ref: Church Records, 1834-1903, p. 3}

SHAY, Howard Chapman, son of William T. and Emma V. Shay, born 2 Nov 1880, baptized 25 Sep 1881 (sponsors: the parents and Miss Fannie Shay). {Ref: Church Records, 1834-1903, pp. 2-3}

SHAY, Ida Isabel, daughter of William T. and Emma V. Shay, born 8 May 1876, baptized 25 Sep 1881 (sponsors: the parents and Miss Fannie Shay). {Ref: Church Records, 1834-1903, pp. 2-3}

SHAY, Mr., buried 11 Mar 1880, age about 75 years. {Ref: Church Records, 1834-1903, p. 98}

SHAY, Mrs., died in 1873 [exact date not given]. {Ref: Church Records, 1834-1903, p. 97}

SHAY, William T., see "Howard C. Shay" and "Ida I. Shay" and "William W. Shay," q.v.

SHAY, William Wallace, son of William T. and Emma V. Shay, born 4 Jul 1878, baptized 25 Sep 1881 (sponsors: the parents and Miss Fannie Shay). {Ref: Church Records, 1834-1903, pp. 2-3}

SHEAFF, Charlotte, wife of John A. Sheaff and daughter of Col. William W. and Ellen Ramsay (or Ramsey), born 30 Mar 1822. died 8 May 1852, buried 9 May 1852. {Ref: Church Records, 1834-1903, p. 92; Tombstone inscription}

SHEEP, Maggie, married Christian Lay ---- 1877. [*Ed. Note:* The date was blank, but the marriage was listed between June and December in the register]. {Ref: Church Records, 1834-1903, p. 148}

SHEPPERD, Ganowfeen (colored), married Jacob Giles (colored) on 1 Jan 1893. {Ref: Church Records, 1834-1903, pp. 158-159}

SHOLLER, Dorothy, see "Dorothy Littlefield," q.v.

SHRIVER, Henrietta, sponsored the baptism of Harry Herbert Buck on 16 Nov 1882. {Ref: Church Records, 1834-1903, p. 3}

SILVER, Esther, see "Esther Jaeger," q.v.

SIMMONS FAMILY.
The following family information was entered in the church records under the heading of "Families" circa 1893-1903, but no relationships or ages were indicated, just names. Additional information shown in parenthesis was entered subsequently in the register:
Mr. ---- [blank] Simmons, Mrs. Mary V. Simmons (removed), and ---- [blank] Simmons (removed). {Ref: Church Records, 1834-1903, p. 258}

SIMMONS, Carrie Naudine, daughter of Joseph M. and Mary V. Simmons, age 6 years, baptized 6 Nov 1892 (sponsors: the mother, Robert H. Smith, Jr. and Mrs. India Martin). {Ref: Church Records, 1834-1903, pp. 10-11}

SIMMONS, Joseph M., married Mary V. Morgan on 7 Jun 1884; also see "Carrie N. Simmons," q.v. {Ref: Church Records, 1834-1903, p. 151}

SIMMONS, Mary V. (Mrs.), received from Havre de Grace on 14 Nov 1892; also see "Simmons Family," q.v. {Ref: Church Records, 1834-1903, p. 204}

SIMMONS, ----, see "Simmons Family," q.v.

SIMMS, Charles W. (colored), married Cassandra Stansbury (colored) on 29 Oct 1868. {Ref: Church Records, 1834-1903, p. 146}

SIMMS, Charlott, married Aquila Frisby on 14 Feb 1852. {Ref: Church Records, 1834-1903, p. 140}

SIMMS, Eliza J. (colored), married John C. Dennison (colored) on 3 Oct 1867. {Ref: Church Records, 1834-1903, p. 146}

SIMMS, Fernandis Rush (colored), married Lavinia Monk (colored) ---- 1879. [*Ed. Note:* The date was blank, but the marriage was listed between January and April in the register]. {Ref: Church Records, 1834-1903, p. 149}

SIMMS (SIMS), Martha C., married James Wesley Paca on 16 Oct 1862. {Ref: Church Records, 1834-1903, p. 144}

SIMONS, Wesley, of Harford Furnace, buried 21 Mar 1870. {Ref: Church Records, 1834-1903, p. 96}

SIMSON, ---- [blank], removed [no date was given, but apparently after 1892]. {Ref: Church Records, 1834-1903, p. 258}

SINGLETON, Charles, son of William and M. E. Singleton, born -- Jul 1846, baptized 22 Aug 1854. {Ref: Church Records, 1834-1903, pp. 26-27}

SLEE FAMILY.
The following family information was entered in the church records under the heading of "Families" circa 1893-1903, but no relationships or ages were indicated, just names:
George Slee, Meth. *[sic]*, and Mrs. Martha L. Slee. {Ref: Church Records, 1834-1903, p. 254}

SLEE, Albert W., born 18 Apr 1848, died 19 Aug 1909. {Ref: Tombstone inscription}

SLEE, Coleman, born 18 Nov 1847, died 8 Aug 1892. {Ref: Tombstone inscription}

SLEE, Cornelia Crocket (adult), daughter of John Slee, born ---- [blank], baptized and died 28 Sep 1849. [*Ed. Note:* In another Parish Register, 1696-1851, it indicates she was about 17 years old]. {Ref: Church Records, 1834-1903, pp. 22-23, 91}

SLEE, Eliza, buried 22 Dec 1865. {Ref: Church Records, 1834-1903, p. 94}

SLEE, George, married Mattie L. Gallup on 15 Aug 1888; also see "Slee Family," q.v. {Ref: Church Records, 1834-1903, p. 154}

SLEE, George Washington, son of William and Mary Slee, died 12 Mar 1860, age 1 year, 3 months and 5 days, buried 13 Mar 1860. {Ref: Church Records, 1834-1903, p. 93; Tombstone inscription}

SLEE, George Willerd, son of N. Lipton and Sadie Slee, born 1892, died 1909. {Ref: Tombstone inscription}

SLEE, John, buried 9 Apr 1860, age 82; also see "Cornelia C. Slee," q.v. {Ref: Church Records, 1834-1903, p. 93}

SLEE, Laura Cassandra, buried 2 May 1901, age 84 years and 27 days. {Ref: Church Records, 1834-1903, p. 104}

SLEE, Martha Lourinda (neé Gallup), church member in 1903; sponsored the baptism of Catherine Gallup Sutton on 11 Sep 1910; also see "Slee Family," q.v. {Ref: Parish Register, 1903-1958, pp. 31, 108}

SLEE, Mary, wife of the late William Slee, born 14 Jun 1822, died 5 Feb 1872 in her 50th year; also see "George W. Slee," q.v. {Ref: Tombstone inscription}

SLEE, N. Lipton, see "George W. Slee," q.v.

SLEE, Sadie, see "George W. Slee," q.v.

SLEE, William, born 20 Jun 1812, died 22 Jul 1868 of billious dysentery; also see "George W. Slee" and "Mary Slee," q.v. {Ref: Church Records, 1834-1903, p. 95; Tombstone inscription}

SMITH FAMILY.
The following family information was entered in the church records under the heading of "Families" circa 1893-1903, but no relationships or ages were indicated, just names. Additional information shown in parenthesis was entered subsequently in the register:
Robert H. Smith, Sr., Robert H. Smith, Jr. (dead, name lined out), Mrs. Margaret B. Smith (dead), Robert Smith, Mary Smith, J. Donald Smith (dead, name lined out), Mrs. J. Donald Smith, and Ellen Smith. {Ref: Church Records, 1834-1903, p. 255}

SMITH, Alexander Lawson (colonel), died 24 Jan 1801 in his 48th year. {Ref: Tombstone inscription}

SMITH, Ann, wife of Basil L. Smith, died 22 May 1851, age 81. {Ref: Tombstone inscription}

SMITH, Anna Moore, daughter of Robert H. and Mary M. Smith (of Spesutia Island), born 22 Jul 1865, baptized 17 Sep 1865. {Ref: Church Records, 1834-1903, pp. 36-37}

SMITH, Anna Moore (Miss), sponsored the baptism of Nannie Moore Smith on 10 Jul 1892. {Ref: Church Records, 1834-1903, p. 11}

SMITH, Barney (colored), married Semelia Ann McComas (colored) on 30 Jan 1868. {Ref: Church Records, 1834-1903, p. 146}

SMITH, Basil L., see "Ann Smith," q.v.

SMITH, Benjamin M. (colored), married Mary Eliza Taylor (colored) on 20 Oct 1887. {Ref: Church Records, 1834-1903, p. 154}

SMITH, Caroline, see "Sarah R. Smith," q.v.

SMITH, Daniel, see "Sarah R. Smith," q.v.

SMITH, Daniel A. (colored), married Lizzie Winchester (colored) on 10 Jun 1883. {Ref: Church Records, 1834-1903, p. 151}

SMITH, Edwin, see "Margaret R. Smith," q.v.

SMITH, Elizabeth (colored), married Philip Stansbury (colored) on 30 Dec 1866. {Ref: Church Records, 1834-1903, p. 146}

SMITH, Ellen, see "Smith Family," q.v.

SMITH, Ellen Moore, daughter of John D. and Maud B. Smith, born 9 Sep 1901, baptized 23 Aug 1903 (sponsors: Phillips M. Hall and Martha P. Hall). {Ref: Church Records, 1834-1903, pp. 16-17}

SMITH, Elmer Thomas, son of Thomas B. and Ida C. (Webb) Smith, born 17 Sep 1900, baptized 26 Apr 1908 at Perryman (sponsors: David N. Webb, Charles W. Michael and John Webb). {Ref: Parish Register, 1903-1958, pp. 30-31}

SMITH, Frederick, see "Robert J. W. Smith," q.v.

SMITH, Frenetta F., age 62, died 10 Feb 1860, buried 12 Feb 1860. {Ref: Church Records, 1834-1903, p. 93; Tombstone inscription}

SMITH, Harriett (colored), married Charles Holmes (colored) on 22 Dec 1887. {Ref: Church Records, 1834-1903, pp. 154-155}

SMITH, Harriett J., see "Margaret R. Smith," q.v.

SMITH, Henry (colored), married Martha Williams (colored) on 15 Sep 1869; also see "Mary Margaret Smith," q.v. {Ref: Church Records, 1834-1903, p. 147}

SMITH, Ida C., see "Elmer T. Smith," q.v.

SMITH, J. Donald, see "Smith Family," q.v.

SMITH, J. Donnell, see "Ellen M. Smith," q.v.

SMITH, John Donnell, son of Robert H. and Mary M. Smith, born 1 Feb 1867, baptized 6 Jun 1869. {Ref: Church Records, 1834-1903, pp. 38-39}

SMITH, John Donnell, son of Robert H. and Mary M. Smith, born 3 Mar 1871, baptized 30 Jun 1872, died 24 Jan 1903, buried 26 Jan 1903, age 31 years, 10 months and 21 days. {Ref: Church Records, 1834-1903, pp. 40-41, 104; Tombstone inscription}

SMITH, John Donnell, sponsored the baptism of Chapman Stuart Clark on 11 Sep 1910. {Ref: Parish Register, 1903-1958, p. 31}

SMITH, Julian Chatard, son of Robert H. and Mary M. Smith, born 1 Mar 1869, baptized 6 Jun 1869. {Ref: Church Records, 1834-1903, pp. 38-39}

SMITH, Louise R., married Perrin Kemp on 8 Nov 1866. {Ref: Church Records, 1834-1903, p. 146}

SMITH, M. A., see "Mary Ann Harlan," q.v.

SMITH, Margaret Baldwin, wife of Robert H. Smith, Jr., born 11 Sep 1866, died 7 Feb 1892, buried 9 Feb 1892; also see "Nannie M. Smith" and "Robert H. Smith" and "Smith Family," q.v. {Ref: Church Records, 1834-1903, pp. 102, 202; Tombstone inscription}

SMITH, Margaret Rebecca (colored), daughter of Edwin and Harriett Jane Smith, born 4 Sep 1886, baptized 23 May 1887. {Ref: Church Records, 1834-1903, p. 7}

SMITH, Maria, daughter of Maria Smith (servant of Mrs. Davidge), born 19 Apr 1839, baptized 19 Jan 1840 at "The Dairy." {Ref: Church Records, 1834-1903, pp. 20-21}

SMITH, Maria M., died 14 Sep 1860, age 61. {Ref: Church Records, 1834-1903, p. 93; Tombstone inscription}

SMITH, Martha, see "Mary Margaret Smith," q.v.

SMITH, Martha, relict of Thomas L. Smith and also of Samuel Jay, died 1 Aug 1817, age 76. {Ref: Tombstone inscription}

SMITH, Mary M., see "Anna M. Smith" and "John D. Smith" and "Julian C. Smith" and "Margaret B. Smith" and "Nannie M. Smith" and "Smith Family," q.v.

SMITH, Mary Margaret (colored), daughter of Henry and Martha Smith, born ---- [blank], baptized 23 Oct 1874 (1877?). {Ref: Church Records, 1834-1903, pp. 40-41}

SMITH, Mary Stuart, member in June, 1911, transferred from St. Luke's, later removed [date not given]. {Ref: Parish Register, 1903-1958, p. 110}

SMITH, Maud, see "Ellen M. Smith," q.v.

SMITH, Nannie Moore, daughter of Robert H. Jr. and Margaret B. Smith, born 7 Oct 1891, baptized 10 Jul 1892 (sponsors: Miss Anna Moore Smith, Mrs. Martha P. Hall, and Mr. Chapman Clark); church member in June, 1911, later removed [date not given]. {Ref: Church Records, 1834-1903, pp. 10-11; Parish Register, 1903-1958, p. 110}

SMITH, Robert, see "Anna M. Smith" and "John D. Smith" and "Julian C. Smith" and "Margaret B. Smith" and "Nannie M. Smith" and "Smith Family," q.v.

SMITH, Robert H., married Mary Moore Hall on 12 Dec 1861 at St. George's, confirmed 27 Feb 1880 in Winchester, Virginia; also see "Smith Family," q.v. {Ref: Church Records, 1834-1903, pp. 143, 298}

SMITH, Robert Hall, son of Robert H. Jr. and Margaret Baldwin Smith, born 10 Mar 1888, baptized 17 Jun 1888, member in June, 1911, transferred to Christ

Church in Roanoke, Virginia on 1 Mar 1921; also see "Smith Family," q.v. {Ref: Church Records, 1834-1903, p. 7; Parish Register, 1903-1958, p. 110}

SMITH, Robert Hall, Jr., son of Robert H. and Mary M. Smith, born 26 May 1863, baptized 12 Jun 1863; sponsored the baptism of Carrie Naudine Simmons on 6 Nov 1892; died 18 Feb 1895, buried 21 Feb 1895; also see "Margaret B. Smith" and "Smith Family," q.v. {Ref: Church Records, 1834-1903, pp. 11, 32-33, 102, 202; Tombstone inscription}

SMITH, Robert James Washington (colored), son of Frederick and Sarah Rebecka Smith, born 26 Dec 1905, private baptism on 20 Jul 1906 (sick). {Ref: Parish Register, 1903-1958, pp. 30-31}

SMITH, Rosa (colored), married Robert Garrison (colored) on 12 Aug 1883. {Ref: Church Records, 1834-1903, p. 151}

SMITH, Samuel Griffith, died 18 Apr 1845, age 30 (50?). {Ref: Tombstone inscription}

SMITH, Sarah E., married Raymond F. Hanson on 29 Jul 1916. {Ref: Parish Register, 1903-1958, pp. 138-139}

SMITH, Sarah Rebecca, daughter of Daniel and Caroline Smith, born ---- [blank], baptized 1 Sep 1878. {Ref: Church Records, 1834-1903, pp. 42-43}

SMITH, Thomas B., see "Elmer T. Smith," q.v.

SMITH, Thomas L., see "Martha Smith," q.v.

SMITH, Winston, died 2 Oct 1822, age 50. {Ref: Tombstone inscription}

SMITHSON, Sophia Louise, daughter of William Preston and M. Susanna Smithson, born 26 Jan 1919, baptized 20 Apr 1919 at Mr. Frederick Nelson's home (sponsors: Frank Holloway, Mrs. Frederick Nelson and Dorsey Nelson). {Ref: Parish Register, 1903-1958, pp. 34-35}

SMITHSON, William Preston, married Mary Susanna Nelson on 19 Jan 1918. {Ref: Parish Register, 1903-1958, pp. 138-139}

SPANGLER, William, married Margaret Bellomy on 20 Nov 1889. {Ref: Church Records, 1834-1903, pp. 156-157}

STANSBURY, Abram (colored), married Elizabeth Lisbury (colored) on 26 Dec 1882. {Ref: Church Records, 1834-1903, p. 150}

STANSBURY, Cassandra (colored), married Charles W. Simms (colored) on 29 Oct 1868. {Ref: Church Records, 1834-1903, p. 146}

STANSBURY, Cora (colored), married Theodore Gibson (colored) on 8 Sep 1892. {Ref: Church Records, 1834-1903, pp. 158-159}

STANSBURY, Eliza, married Robert Griffin on 26 Feb 1880. {Ref: Church Records, 1834-1903, p. 149}

STANSBURY, James Henry (colored), married Marian V. Ringgold (colored) on 10 Feb 1887. {Ref: Church Records, 1834-1903, pp. 152-153}

STANSBURY, Mary (colored), married Alfred Pitt (colored) ---- 1877. [*Ed. Note:* The date was blank, but the marriage was listed between June and December in the register]. {Ref: Church Records, 1834-1903, p. 148}

STANSBURY, Olivia J. (colored), married Benjamin S. Johnson (colored) on 14 Jan 1879. {Ref: Church Records, 1834-1903, p. 148}

STANSBURY, Philip (colored), married Elizabeth Smith (colored) on 30 Dec 1866. {Ref: Church Records, 1834-1903, p. 146}

STANSBURY, Robert (colored), married Cassie Warfield (colored) on 14 Mar 1867. {Ref: Church Records, 1834-1903, p. 146}

STANSBURY, Solomon (colored), married Henrietta Johnes (colored) on 15 Aug 1878. {Ref: Church Records, 1834-1903, p. 148}

STANSBURY, Stephen (colored), married Sophia Brown (colored) on 11 May 1877. {Ref: Church Records, 1834-1903, p. 148}

STANSBURY, William (colored), married Rebecca Warfield (colored) on 28 Oct 1869. {Ref: Church Records, 1834-1903, p. 147}

STANSBURY, William Henry, married Delia Griffith on 16 Aug 1860. {Ref: Church Records, 1834-1903, p. 142}

STEEL, Charles Lowndes, married Katharine Keen Porter on 28 Dec 1916. {Ref: Parish Register, 1903-1958, pp. 138-139}

STEEL, Ella Keen, daughter of Capt. Charles L. and Katharine P. Steel, born 2 Jul 1920, baptized 1 Aug 1920 (sponsors: Thomas G.(?) Steel, Mrs. Margarite Porter, Miss Willie(?) Johnson and Mrs. Katherine P. Steel). {Ref: Parish Register, 1903-1958, pp. 34-35}

STEEL, Katharine P. (Mrs.), sponsored the baptism of Ella Keen Steel on 1 Aug 1920. {Ref: Parish Register, 1903-1958, p. 35}

STEEL, Thomas G.(?), sponsored the baptism of Ella Keen Steel on 1 Aug 1920. {Ref: Parish Register, 1903-1958, p. 35}

STEELE, Eliza H. (neé Kimble), church member in 1903, "moved away" [date not given]. {Ref: Parish Register, 1903-1958, p. 108}

STEELE, Elizabeth Millicent, confirmed 19 Aug 1917. {Ref: Parish Register, 1903-1958, pp. 89, 111}

STEELE, Gertrude Margarite, confirmed 19 Aug 1917, later removed [date not given]. {Ref: Parish Register, 1903-1958, pp. 89, 111}

STEELE, Hattie Kimble, confirmed 19 Aug 1917, later removed [date not given]. {Ref: Parish Register, 1903-1958, pp. 89, 111}

STEELE, Joseph, see "Eliza Hattie Kimble" and "Botts Family," q.v.

STEELE, Maurice Gaylord, married Mina Gibson Porter on 7 Aug 1919. {Ref: Parish Register, 1903-1958, pp. 138-139}

STEELE, Minor Porter, child of Maurice G. and Mina (Porter) Steele, born 31 Jul 1920, baptized 5 Sep 1920 (sponsors: Sydney W. Porter and Mrs. Gertrude S. Thomas). {Ref: Parish Register, 1903-1958, pp. 34-35}

STENGEL, Susan, born 9 Feb 1895. {Ref: Parish Register, 1903-1958, p. 36}

STEPHENS, Harriet Jane (colored), daughter of John and Nancy Stephens, born 26 Nov 1848, baptized 29 Jan 1849. {Ref: Church Records, 1834-1903, pp. 22-23}

STEPHENSON, Joseph, married Maggie Reddon on 22 Apr 1879. {Ref: Church Records, 1834-1903, p. 149}

STEPHENSON, Lizzie, buried 7 Apr 1866. {Ref: Church Records, 1834-1903, p. 94}

STEVENSON, Ellen (colored), married Richard Savoy (colored) on 15 Apr 1869. {Ref: Church Records, 1834-1903, p. 147}

STEVENSON, John L., married Maria Bowzer on 24 Dec 1856. {Ref: Church Records, 1834-1903, p. 140}

STEVENSON, Martha, daughter of John and Maria Stevenson, born 24 Feb 1861, baptized 14 Oct 1861. {Ref: Church Records, 1834-1903, pp. 30-31}

STEWARD, Charlotte (colored), buried 20 Nov 1857. {Ref: Church Records, 1834-1903, p. 93}

STEWARD, Harriet, married Stepney York on 27 May 1855. {Ref: Church Records, 1834-1903, p. 140}

STEWARD, Rachel, married James Edward Taylor on 13 Jun 1857. {Ref: Church Records, 1834-1903, p. 141}

STEWARD, Sidney (colored), married John Crosen (colored) on 19 Aug 1869. {Ref: Church Records, 1834-1903, p. 147}

STEWARD, Thomas, buried 19 Oct 1871. {Ref: Church Records, 1834-1903, p. 96}

STEWART, A. (Mrs.), confirmed 19 Feb 1878, removed circa 1893-1903 [date not given]. {Ref: Church Records, 1834-1903, pp. 253, 298}

STEWART, Albert, died suddenly in Jersey City and was interred at Spesutia [St. George's Churchyard] on 23 Aug 1868. {Ref: Church Records, 1834-1903, p. 95}

STEWART, Albertine, born 7 Nov 1852, died 12 Jun 1913. {Ref: Tombstone inscription}

STEWART, Alfred, born 7 Jun 1822, died 20 Aug 1868. {Ref: Tombstone inscription}

STEWART, Avarilla, see "John W. W. Stewart," q.v.

STEWART, Charles (slave of Edward and Mary Griffith), son of ---- [blank], born -- Jul 1828, baptized 14 Oct 1838. {Ref: Church Records, 1834-1903, pp. 18-19}

STEWART, Charlotte R. (colored), married Henry V. Holland (colored) on 8 May 1884. {Ref: Church Records, 1834-1903, p. 151}

STEWART, Elizabeth, see "Frederick Stewart," q.v.

STEWART, Frederick Henry, son of William and Elizabeth Stewart (servants of Mr. E. Griffith), born ---- [blank], baptized 8 Aug 1858. {Ref: Church Records, 1834-1903, pp. 28-29}

STEWART, Harriet (slave of Edward and Mary Griffith), daughter of ---- [blank], born 1833, baptized 14 Oct 1838. {Ref: Church Records, 1834-1903, pp. 18-19}

STEWART, Henry, buried 30 Jun 1836. {Ref: Church Records, 1834-1903, p. 90}

STEWART, J. R., see "Mary E. Stewart," q.v.

STEWART, John Wesley Wilson, son of Thomas W. and Avarilla Stewart, born 6 Sep 1862, baptized 10 Jun 1868. {Ref: Church Records, 1834-1903, pp. 36-37}

STEWART, Louisa, born 8 Oct 1822, died 3 Nov 1871. {Ref: Tombstone inscription}

STEWART, Luther M., born 13 Sep 1815, died 23 Apr 1884. {Ref: Tombstone inscription}

STEWART, Mary, married William Wilmer on 17 Jan 1862. {Ref: Church Records, 1834-1903, p. 144}

STEWART, Mary E., wife of J. R. Stewart, died 25 Mar 1883, age 31 years and 16 days. {Ref: Tombstone inscription}

STEWART, Rachel (slave of Edward and Mary Griffith), daughter of ---- [blank], born 1835, baptized 14 Oct 1838. {Ref: Church Records, 1834-1903, pp. 18-19}

STEWART, Thomas, see "John W. W. Stewart," q.v.

STEWART, William, married Elizabeth Flint on 11 Apr 1857; also see "Frederick H. Stewart," q.v. {Ref: Church Records, 1834-1903, p. 141}

STICKNEY, Henry C., married Margaret Deaver on 12 May 1901. {Ref: Church Records, 1834-1903, pp. 160-161}

STIER FAMILY.
The following family information was entered in the church records under the heading of "Families" circa 1893-1903, but no relationships or ages were indicated, just names:
Dr. Jay H. Stier, Mrs. Lily P. P. Stier, H. Douglas Stier, and Ridgely P. Stier. {Ref: Church Records, 1834-1903, p. 257}

STIER, Hugh Douglas, son of Dr. Jay Hugh and Lily Patterson Stier, born 14 May 1893, baptized 30 Jul 1893 (sponsors: the parents and Wilton Greenway), confirmed 21 Nov 1909; also noted "moved to Baltimore" [date not given]; also see "Stier Family," q.v. {Ref: Church Records, 1834-1903, pp. 12-13; Parish Register, 1903-1958, pp. 87, 109}

STIER, J. H. (Dr. & Mrs.), sponsored the baptism of Henry Stier Dulaney and Josephine Estelle Dulaney on 31 Dec 1914. {Ref: Parish Register, 1903-1958, p. 33}

STIER, Jay Hugh (doctor), Methodist, confirmed 17 May 1914; also see "Stier Family" and "Patterson Family," q.v. {Ref: Parish Register, 1903-1958, pp. 88, 110}

STIER, Lily Powell Patterson (Mrs.), confirmed 1 May 1892, church member in 1903; also see "Stier Family," q.v. {Ref: Church Records, 1834-1903, p. 301; Parish Register, 1903-1958, p. 108}

STIER, Ridgely Patterson, son of Dr. Jay Hugh and Lily Patterson Stier, born 13 Jun 1895, baptized 9 Aug 1895 at home in Perryman (sponsors: the parents and Frederick E. Patterson), confirmed 21 Nov 1909; also noted "moved to Baltimore" [date not given]; also see "Stier Family," q.v. {Ref: Church Records, 1834-1903, pp. 12-13; Parish Register, 1903-1958, pp. 87, 109}

STOCKHAM, Algernon S., son of John and Elizabeth Stockham, age 18, died 27 May 1853. {Ref: Tombstone inscription}

STOCKHAM, Charles, died 4 Sep 1882, age 4. {Ref: Tombstone inscription}

STOCKHAM, Elizabeth, wife of John Stockham, born 22 Dec 1801, died 26 Oct 1878. {Ref: Tombstone inscription}

STOCKHAM, E. V., sponsored the baptism of Marion Stockham on 11 May 1914. {Ref: Parish Register, 1903-1958, p. 33}

STOCKHAM, Georgie, married Horace G. Githens on 5 Jun 1895. {Ref: Church Records, 1834-1903, pp. 160-161}

STOCKHAM, Harteauft, confirmed 18 Jun 1916, "moved away" [date not given]. {Ref: Parish Register, 1903-1958, pp. 89, 111}

STOCKHAM, John, died 19 Sep 1855, age 72; also see "Elizabeth Stockham," q.v. {Ref: Tombstone inscription}

STOCKHAM, John F., see "Marion Stockham," q.v.

STOCKHAM, Margaret E., born 27 Nov 1842, died 4 Feb 1904. {Ref: Tombstone inscription}

STOCKHAM, Marion, son of John F. and Sallie D. (Harteauft) Stockham, born 19 Sep 1869, baptized 11 May 1914 at "Angel Hill" (sponsors: E. V. Stockham and Gertrude E. Thomas), confirmed 22 May 1914. {Ref: Parish Register, 1903-1958, pp. 32-33, 88}

STOCKHAM, Mrs. Marion (neé Harteauft), member in May, 1914. {Ref: Parish Register, 1903-1958, p. 110}

STOCKHAM, Nettie Horton, daughter of Charles and Annie Stockham, died 30 Sep 1882, age 1 year and 7 days. {Ref: Tombstone inscription}

STOCKHAM, Sallie, see "Marion Stockham," q.v.

STOCKHAM, Thomas, born 12 May 1807, died 30 Sep 1881. {Ref: Tombstone inscription}

STOKES, Bradford, married Rachel Anderson on 18 May 1889. {Ref: Church Records, 1834-1903, p. 154}

STOKES, Eleanor Roger, died 7 Aug 1791 in her 8th year. {Ref: Tombstone inscription}

STREET, H. H. (Dr. & Mrs.), sponsored the baptism of Mary Alice Henderson on 11 Jun 1916. {Ref: Parish Register, 1903-1958, p. 33}

STREETT, Joseph M., married Elizabeth Keen Nelson on 8 Nov 1914 [although an earlier entry indicated 1908]; also see "Elizabeth Keen Nelson," q.v. {Ref: Parish Register, 1903-1958, p. 107}

STRONG, James Thomas, son of William Edward and Mary Ann Strong, born 7 Dec 1905, baptized 6 Jul 1909 at home, mother sick (sponsors: the mother and Myrtle May Way). {Ref: Parish Register, 1903-1958, pp. 30-31}

STRONG, Martha Viola, daughter of William Edward and Mary Ann Strong, born 21 May 1909, baptized 6 Jul 1909 at home, mother sick (sponsors: the mother and Myrtle May Way). {Ref: Parish Register, 1903-1958, pp. 30-31}

STUMP, Ann (Miss), confirmed 9 Jun 1836. {Ref: Church Records, 1834-1903, p. 296}

STUMP, Cassandra (Miss), confirmed 9 Jun 1836. {Ref: Church Records, 1834-1903, p. 296}

STUMP, Sarah, sponsored the baptism of Sarah Bias Griffith on 29 Jan 1841. {Ref: Church Records, 1834-1903, pp. 20-21}

STUMP, Sarah, confirmed 14 May 1865. {Ref: Church Records, 1834-1903, p. 294}

STUMP, Sidney (colored), married Jane Dorsey (colored) on 19 Mar 1865. {Ref: Church Records, 1834-1903, p. 146}

STUMP, W. H., sponsored the baptism of Sidney Hall on 23 Oct 1838. {Ref: Church Records, 1834-1903, p. 19}

STUMP, William Herman, age 83, died 21 Jun 1880. {Ref: Tombstone inscription}

SULLIVAN, James T., married Harriett M. Elliott on 8 Feb 1835. {Ref: Church Records, 1834-1903, p. 138}

SULLIVAN, Josaphine, of Havre de Grace, buried 12 Jun 1858. {Ref: Church Records, 1834-1903, p. 93}

SULLIVAN, Mary E., married Samuel A. House on 10 Oct 1861. {Ref: Church Records, 1834-1903, p. 143}

SUTOR, Catharine (Mrs.), buried 20 Apr 1838. {Ref: Church Records, 1834-1903, p. 90}

SUTOR, Henry P., age 71, died 7 Jan 1880; also see "Margaret S. Sutor" and "Mary C. Sutor," q.v. {Ref: Tombstone inscription}

SUTOR, J. Nicholas, born 4 Dec 1756, died 23 Mar 1831, age 75; also see "Mary Sutor," q.v. {Ref: Tombstone inscription}

SUTOR, Jacob, born 25 Jul 1791, died 12 Jul 1840 in his 49th year. {Ref: Tombstone inscription}

SUTOR, Margaret S., wife of Henry P. Sutor, born 9 Jun 1835, died 5 Nov 1907. {Ref: Tombstone inscription}

SUTOR, Mary (mother), consort of J. Nicholas Sutor, died at Havre de Grace on 17 Jun 1832, age 71, and inscribed on the same tombstone: "Also her grandchild Henrietta A., dau. of Thomas and Elizabeth Cook(?), died in Havre de Grace -- Jun 1832, age -- [illegible]. {Ref: Tombstone inscription}

SUTOR, Mary C., consort of Henry P. Sutor, born 2 Sep 1812, died 17 Feb 1863. {Ref: Tombstone inscription}

SUTOR, Thomas (Mr.), buried 24 Aug 1878. {Ref: Church Records, 1834-1903, p. 97}

SUTTON, Annie Virginia (neé Gallup), member in 1906. {Ref: Parish Register, 1903-1958, p. 109}

SUTTON, Catherine Gallup, daughter of Samuel and Annie Virginia Sutton, born 19 Jul 1910, baptized 11 Sep 1910 (sponsors: the parents and Martha Lourinda Slee). {Ref: Parish Register, 1903-1958, pp. 30-31}

SUTTON, Frank, see "Mary F. Sutton," q.v.

SUTTON, Frankie, son of Frank G. and Mary F. Sutton, died 21 Mar 1862, age 2. {Ref: Tombstone inscription}

SUTTON, Ida Matilda, confirmed 15 Nov 1885. {Ref: Church Records, 1834-1903, p. 299}

SUTTON, J. H., see "William M. Sutton," q.v.

SUTTON, John, see "Mary Sutton," q.v.

SUTTON, Jonathan, died 19 Jan 1825, age 65 years, 2 months and 2 days. {Ref: Tombstone inscription}

SUTTON, Jonathan, born 1 Jan 1797, died 6 Oct 1882; also see "Ruth A. Sutton" and "Martha Sutton" and "Mary Sutton" and "Samuel Sutton," q.v. {Ref: Tombstone inscription}

SUTTON, Jonathan H., buried 14 Dec 1890, age 89. {Ref: Church Records, 1834-1903, p. 102}

SUTTON, Lora, died 25 Jan 1839, age 12 years and 8 months. {Ref: Tombstone inscription}

SUTTON, Martha, consort of Samuel Sutton, died 10 Jun 1824, age 30 years, 1 month and 11 days. {Ref: Tombstone inscription}

SUTTON, Mary, consort of Jonathan Sutton and daughter of John and Mary Murphy, died 30 Mar 1854, age 48 years, 4 months and 25 days; also see "Samuel Sutton," q.v. {Ref: Tombstone inscription}

SUTTON, Mary E., buried 18 May 1884; also see "William M. Sutton,". {Ref: Church Records, 1834-1903, p. 100}

SUTTON, Mary F., wife of Frank G. Sutton, died 12 Feb 1866, age 23; also see "Frankie Sutton," q.v. {Ref: Tombstone inscription}

SUTTON, Oliver Perry, born 30 Sep 1813, died 7 Jul 1851. [*Ed. Note:* The foregoing information is on his tombstone, but the church register indicates that "Perry Sutton died 29 Jun 1851"]. {Ref: Church Records, 1834-1903, p. 92; Tombstone inscription}

SUTTON, Ruth A., wife of Jonathan Sutton, born 9 Feb 1812, died 11 Nov 1897. {Ref: Tombstone inscription}

SUTTON, Samuel, son of Jonathan and Mary Sutton, born 17 Jun 1847, died 20 Aug 1862. {Ref: Tombstone inscription}

SUTTON, Samuel (Mr.), died in 1876. [*Ed. Note:* The exact date was not given in register, but the grave marker indicates he died 8 Mar 1876, age 83]; also see "Susan Sutton," q.v. {Ref: Church Records, 1834-1903, p. 97; Tombstone inscription}

SUTTON, Samuel (Mr.), confirmed 9 Nov 1890, church member in 1903. {Ref: Church Records, 1834-1903, pp. 257, 301; Parish Register, 1903-1958, p. 108}

SUTTON, Samuel S., married Annie Virginia Gallup on 30 Jun 1906; also see "Catherine G. Gallup," q.v. {Ref: Parish Register, 1903-1958, pp. 138-139}

SUTTON, Sarah, died 5 Dec 1824, age 56 years, 8 months and 17 days. {Ref: Tombstone inscription}

SUTTON, Susan, wife of Samuel Sutton, died 2 Jun 1879, age 87. {Ref: Church Records, 1834-1903, p. 98; Tombstone inscription}

SUTTON, William, age 34, buried 16 Aug 1910. {Ref: Parish Register, 1903-1958, p. 158}

SUTTON, William McDonald, son of J. H. and Mary E. Sutton, born 8 Apr 1877, baptized 3 Aug 1884 (sponsors: Mr. James H. Michael and Mrs. Sarah Nelson). {Ref: Church Records, 1834-1903, pp. 4-5}

SWEETING, Benjamin Henry (C.S.A.), buried 7 Jan 1896, age 52. {Ref: Church Records, 1834-1903, p. 103}

SWEETING, Margaret (Mrs.), buried 3 Jan 1899, age 82. {Ref: Church Records, 1834-1903, p. 104}

SWIFT FAMILY.
The following family information was entered in the church records under the heading of "Families" circa 1893-1903, but no relationships or ages were indicated, just names:
Nathan Swift and Mrs. Rose Swift. {Ref: Church Records, 1834-1903, p. 250}

SWIFT, Nathan, age not indicated, buried 30 Apr 1906 in Loudon Park Cemetery in Baltimore; also see "Swift Family," q.v. {Ref: Parish Register, 1903-1958, p. 158}

SWIFT, Rose, church member in 1903, later removed [date not given]; also see "Swift Family," q.v. {Ref: Parish Register, 1903-1958, p. 108}

SWOAP, Frederick William, son of Frederick and Mary Swoap (German) *[sic]*, born 11 Dec 1866? *[sic]*, baptized 21 Apr 1867(?) *[sic]*. {Ref: Church Records, 1834-1903, pp. 36-37}

TABB, Paul (Mrs.), sponsored the baptism of Nan Lee Porter on 26 Sep 1920. {Ref: Parish Register, 1903-1958, p. 35}

TANNER, Lynn DeLancey, married Mary [Stockham] Walker on 29 Sep 1909 at "The Park Home [Home]" *[sic]*. {Ref: Parish Register, 1903-1958, pp. 138-139}

TARRING, H. W., sponsored the baptism of Malcolm Yarnall Tarring on 1 Jun 1913. {Ref: Parish Register, 1903-1958, p. 33}

TARRING, Henry, son of Henry W. and Annie M. Tarring, born 28 May 1908, baptized 19 Jul 1908 (sponsors: Henry Tarring, M. G. Yarnall and Mabel Hyde). {Ref: Parish Register, 1903-1958, pp. 30-31}

TARRING, Malcolm Yarnall, son of Henry W. and Annie M. Tarring, born 22 Jul 1912, baptized 1 Jun 1913 (sponsors: Jacob P. Yarnall, H. W. Tarring and Mabel Hyde). {Ref: Parish Register, 1903-1958, pp. 32-33}

TAYLOR FAMILY.
The following family information was entered in the church records under the heading of "Families" circa 1893-1903, but no relationships or ages were indicated, just names. Additional information shown in parenthesis was entered subsequently in the register:

D. Wesley Taylor (dead), Mrs. Amelia Taylor (removed), Mollie Taylor (removed), Edith Taylor (dead), Bessie Taylor (removed), Howard Taylor (removed), Robert Taylor (removed), and Raymond Taylor (removed). {Ref: Church Records, 1834-1903, p. 256}

Mr. Joseph W. Taylor, Mrs. Anna E. Taylor, Mary Stockham Taylor (Mrs. A. Raymond Walker, married again), Helen W. Taylor, and John Howard Taylor. {Ref: Church Records, 1834-1903, p. 259}

William H. Taylor, Mrs. Isabel Taylor, William Thomas Taylor, Asa A. Taylor, Ida May Taylor (married Charles W. Byrd), Lawrence M. Taylor, Laura B. Taylor (Mrs. Keen), and Norval Chapman Taylor. {Ref: Church Records, 1834-1903, p. 250}

TAYLOR, Alfred (colored), married Jane Monk (colored) ---- 1879. [*Ed. Note:* The date was blank, but the marriage was listed between January and April in the register]. {Ref: Church Records, 1834-1903, p. 149}

TAYLOR, Amelia, church member in 1903, removed to Suffolk, Virginia in 1917; also see "Taylor Family," q.v. {Ref: Parish Register, 1903-1958, p. 108}

TAYLOR, Amelia Thornton (Mrs.), born 2 Jul 1845, confirmed 27 Jan 1889, died 15 Jun 1909; also see "Annie Taylor" and "John R. Taylor" and "Wesley R. Taylor" and "Taylor Family," q.v. {Ref: Church Records, 1834-1903, p. 300; Tombstone inscription}

TAYLOR, Ann W., born 1 Jan 1814, died 2 Feb 1896. {Ref: Tombstone inscription}

TAYLOR, Anna Elizabeth (Mrs.), confirmed 27 Oct 1894; church member in 1903; sponsored the baptism of Anna Hazlett Walker on 3 Jul 1904; removed to Suffolk, Virginia in 1917; also see "Helen W. Taylor" and "John H. Taylor" and "Mary S. Taylor" and "Taylor Family," q.v. {Ref: Church Records, 1834-1903, p. 302; Parish Register, 1903-1958, p. 31, 108}

TAYLOR, Annie, daughter of D. Wesley and Amelia T. Taylor, born 23 Oct 1882, baptized 23 Jun 1883 (sponsors: Mrs. C. E. Buck and Mrs. Martha A. Hopkins), died 27 Feb 1885. {Ref: Church Records, 1834-1903, pp. 2-3; Tombstone inscription}

TAYLOR, Asa A., see "Asa C. Taylor" and "Charles A. Taylor" and "Taylor Family," q.v.

TAYLOR, Asa Alexander, son of William H. and Isabel Taylor, born ---- [blank], baptized 1 May 1879. {Ref: Church Records, 1834-1903, pp. 42-43}

TAYLOR, Asa Alexander, son of William H. and Isabel Taylor, born ---- [blank], baptized 13 Aug 1882 (sponsors: the mother and Mrs. Annie Reynolds). {Ref: Church Records, 1834-1903, pp. 2-3}

TAYLOR, Asa Carr, son of Asa Alexander and Sarah L. Taylor, born 31 Mar 1910, baptized 1 Apr 1916 at the home of Mr. W. H. Taylor (sponsors: Mrs. William H. Taylor, Mrs. Byrd and Lawrence M. Taylor). {Ref: Parish Register, 1903-1958, pp. 32-33}

TAYLOR, Asa W., buried 4 Feb 1896, age 83. {Ref: Church Records, 1834-1903, p. 103}

TAYLOR, Bessie, see "Taylor Family," q.v.

TAYLOR, Caroline Laport, married Charles Ellsworth Oliver on 14 Aug 1902 at 9:30 a.m. {Ref: Church Records, 1834-1903, pp. 162-163}

TAYLOR, Charles Alexander, son of Asa Alexander and Sarah Lavinia C. Taylor, born 30 Apr 1901, private baptism on 1 Apr 1903 in the church yard, noting in register "This child was supposed to have been brought under the influence of the contagion of smallpox." {Ref: Church Records, 1834-1903, pp. 16-17}

TAYLOR, Charles Henry, son of James and Rachel Taylor, born 18 Oct 1861, 14 Jul 1863. {Ref: Church Records, 1834-1903, pp. 32-33}

TAYLOR, Clara Rebecca, daughter of Hammond and Georgianna Taylor, born 28 Sep 1862, baptized 10 Jul 1863. {Ref: Church Records, 1834-1903, pp. 32-33}

TAYLOR, Clifford, sponsored the baptism of Mary Virginia Taylor on 26 Nov 1914. {Ref: Parish Register, 1903-1958, p. 33}

TAYLOR, D. Wesley, see "Annie Taylor" and "John R. Taylor" and "Wesley R. Taylor" and "Taylor Family," q.v.

TAYLOR, Daniel Wesley, born 29 Jul 1845, confirmed 27 Jan 1889, died 16 Aug 1898, buried 18 Aug 1898; also see "Taylor Family," q.v. {Ref: Church Records, 1834-1903, pp. 104, 202, 300; Tombstone inscription}

TAYLOR, Edith, see "Taylor Family," q.v.

TAYLOR, Emory, see "R. Emory Taylor," q.v.

TAYLOR, Fannie, buried 29 Mar 1861. {Ref: Church Records, 1834-1903, p. 93}

TAYLOR, Fannie A., wife of R. Emory Taylor and daughter of E. W. and M. A. Gallup, born 14 Jul 1851, died 20 Oct 1879, buried 21 Oct 1879; also see "Francis E. Taylor," q.v. {Ref: Church Records, 1834-1903, p. 98; Tombstone inscription}

TAYLOR, Francis Emory, infant son of R. Emory and Fannie A. Taylor, born 6 Oct 1879, died 10 Dec 1879, buried 11 Dec 1879. {Ref: Church Records, 1834-1903, p. 98; Tombstone inscription}

TAYLOR, Francis James, son of James Franklin and Sarah Frances Taylor, born 26 Oct 1863, baptized 21 Jun 1865. {Ref: Church Records, 1834-1903, pp. 34-35}

TAYLOR, Frances Rosebelle, daughter of Joseph and Rebecca Taylor, died 27 Mar 1861, age 11. {Ref: Tombstone inscription}

TAYLOR, G. Lillian, born 2 Dec 1871, died 9 Jan 1890. {Ref: Tombstone inscription}

TAYLOR, Georgianna, see "Clara R. Taylor" and "Robert H. Taylor" and "Sarah L. Taylor," q.v.

TAYLOR, Hammond, see "Clara R. Taylor" and "Robert H. Taylor" and "Sarah L. Taylor," q.v.

TAYLOR, Helen G., see "Edgar M. Palmer," q.v.

TAYLOR, Helen Woolman, daughter of Joseph W. and Anna E. Taylor, born 4 Jan 1889, baptized 7 Oct 1894 (sponsors: the parents); confirmed 7 Dec 1902, age 14; church member in 1903; also see "Taylor Family," q.v. {Ref: Church Records, 1834-1903, pp. 12-13, 303; Parish Register, 1903-1958, p. 108}

TAYLOR, Howard, see "Taylor Family," q.v.

TAYLOR, Ida May, daughter of William H. and Isabel Taylor, born 2 Apr 1878, baptized 1 May 1879, died 1 May 1879. {Ref: Church Records, 1834-1903, pp. 42-43; Tombstone inscription}

TAYLOR, Ida May, daughter of William H. and Isabel Taylor, born ---- [blank], baptized 13 Aug 1882 (sponsors: the mother and Mrs. Annie Reynolds), confirmed 20 Nov 1889, married Charles W. Byrd on 15 Dec 1898 at "Union Farm" near Perryman; also see "Taylor Family," q.v. {Ref: Church Records, 1834-1903, pp. 2-3, 160-161, 301}

TAYLOR, Ida Virginia, daughter of William Thomas and Maude (Rouse) Taylor, born 30 Dec 1912, baptized 1 Apr 1916 at the home of Mr. W. H. Taylor (sponsors: Mrs. William H. Taylor, Mrs. Byrd and Lawrence M. Taylor). {Ref: Parish Register, 1903-1958, pp. 32-33}

TAYLOR, Isabel, wife of William H. Taylor, born 4 Mar 1848, confirmed 6 Aug 1879; sponsored the baptisms of William Stephen Taylor on 3 Dec 1897 and Ralph Byrd Taylor on 15 Dec 1898; church member in 1903; died 15 Jul 1916, age 68, buried 17 Jul 1916; also see "Asa A. Taylor" and "Ida M. Taylor" and "Isabel Taylor" and "Lawrence M. Taylor" and "Norval C. Taylor" and "William T. Taylor" and "Willie T. Taylor" and "---- Taylor" and "Taylor Family," q.v. {Ref: Church Records, 1834-1903, pp. 13, 15, 298; Parish Register, 1903-1958, pp. 108, 159; Tombstone inscription}

TAYLOR, Isabel Frances, daughter of William Thomas and Maud Rouse Taylor, born 18 May 1903, baptized 4 Jul 1906 at William Taylor's house (sponsors: Mrs. William Taylor, Mrs. Ida T. Byrd and Mr. Lawrence Taylor). {Ref: Parish Register, 1903-1958, pp. 30-31}

TAYLOR, James, see "Charles H. Taylor" and "James A. Taylor" and "John R. Taylor" and "Lottie Taylor," q.v.

TAYLOR, James Alfred, son of James and Rachel Taylor, born 18 Apr 1859, 14 Jul 1863. {Ref: Church Records, 1834-1903, pp. 32-33}

TAYLOR, James Edward, married Rachel Steward on 13 Jun 1857. {Ref: Church Records, 1834-1903, p. 141}

TAYLOR, James F., buried 28 Aug 1863. {Ref: Church Records, 1834-1903, p. 94}

TAYLOR, James F., see "Francis J. Taylor" and "John T. J. Taylor" and "Sarah F. Taylor," q.v.

TAYLOR, James R., see "Joseph L. Taylor" and "Seth B. Taylor," q.v.

TAYLOR, John Howard, son of Joseph W. and Anna E. Taylor, born 20 Jan 1880, baptized 7 Oct 1894 (witnesses: the parents) at St. George's Church; confirmed 27 Oct 1894; church member in 1903, removed to Suffolk, Virginia in 1917; also see "Taylor Family," q.v. {Ref: Church Records, 1834-1903, pp. 12-13, 302; Parish Register, 1903-1958, p. 108}

TAYLOR, John R. (colored), married Martha Rumsby (colored) on 25 Oct 1883. {Ref: Church Records, 1834-1903, p. 151}

TAYLOR, John Robert, son of D. W. and Amelia Taylor, born ---- [blank], baptized 10 Apr 1887. {Ref: Church Records, 1834-1903, p. 9}

TAYLOR, John Roberts, son of James and Rachel Taylor, born 11 Jan 1863, 14 Jul 1863. {Ref: Church Records, 1834-1903, pp. 32-33}

TAYLOR, John Thomas Jefferson, son of James Franklin and Sarah Frances Taylor, born 26 Oct 1863, baptized 21 Jun 1865. {Ref: Church Records, 1834-1903, pp. 34-35}

TAYLOR, Joseph, see "Frances R. Taylor," q.v.

TAYLOR, Joseph Lee, son of James R. and Martha H. Taylor, of Hopewell, born 1 Jan 1863, baptized 2 Sep 1863, died 17 Jul 1865 of brain fever; also see "Taylor Family," q.v. {Ref: Church Records, 1834-1903, pp. 32-33 96}

TAYLOR, Joseph Woolman, confirmed 27 Oct 1894; church member in 1903; sponsored the baptism of Anna Hazlett Walker on 3 Jul 1904; also see "Helen W. Taylor" and "John H. Taylor" and "Mary S. Taylor" and "Taylor Family," q.v. {Ref: Church Records, 1834-1903, p. 302; Parish Register, 1903-1958, pp. 31, 108}

TAYLOR, Julia Edith, buried 24 Sep 1894, age 18. {Ref: Church Records, 1834-1903, p. 102}

TAYLOR, Laura Blanche, age 15, confirmed 29 Dec 1901, church member in 1903, married Robert Keen, Jr. [date not given]; also see "Taylor Family," q.v. {Ref: Church Records, 1834-1903, p. 303; Parish Register, 1903-1958, p. 108}

TAYLOR, Lawrence (Mr.), sponsored the baptism of Isabel Frances Taylor on 4 Jul 1906. {Ref: Parish Register, 1903-1958, p. 31}

TAYLOR, Lawrence Matthew, son of William H. and Isabel Taylor, born 1 Oct 1880, baptized 13 Aug 1882 (sponsors: the mother and Mrs. Annie Reynolds), confirmed 12 Mar 1896, church member in 1903; sponsored the baptism of Lawrence Matthew Taylor, Raymond Rouse Taylor and William Henry Taylor on 26 Apr 1908 and Asa Carr Taylor, John Robert Keen, III, and Ida Virginia Taylor on 1 Apr 1916; also see "Taylor Family," q.v. {Ref: Church Records, 1834-1903, pp. 2-3, 302; Parish Register, 1903-1958, pp. 31, 33, 108}

TAYLOR, Lawrence Matthew, son of William T. and Maude Taylor, born and died 3 May 1901, age 9 hours, buried 5 May 1901. {Ref: Church Records, 1834-1903, p. 104}

TAYLOR, Lawrence Matthew, son of Lawrence M. and Maude L. Taylor, born 24 Sep 1907, baptized 26 Apr 1908 at Perryman. {Ref: Parish Register, 1903-1958, pp. 30-31}

TAYLOR, Lily (Miss), confirmed 18 Oct 1887 at St. Mary's Church in Emmorton, died 9 Jan 1890. {Ref: Church Records, 1834-1903, pp. 202, 300}

TAYLOR, Lottie, daughter of James Edward and Rachel Taylor (servants of Mr. E. Griffith), born ---- [blank], baptized 8 Aug 1858. {Ref: Church Records, 1834-1903, pp. 28-29}

TAYLOR, Margaret, wife of Richard M. Taylor, born -- May 1836, died -- Jan 1909. {Ref: Tombstone inscription}

TAYLOR, Martha, see "Joseph L. Taylor" and "Seth B. Taylor," q.v.

TAYLOR, Mary Eliza (colored), married Benjamin M. Smith (colored) on 20 Oct 1887. {Ref: Church Records, 1834-1903, pp. 154-155}

TAYLOR, Mary Frances (Mrs.), sponsored the baptism of Louise Trezevant Wigfall Marshall on 12 Sep 1916. {Ref: Parish Register, 1903-1958, p. 33}

TAYLOR, Mary Stockham, daughter of Joseph W. and Anna E. Taylor, born 2 Apr 1878, baptized 7 Oct 1894 (witnesses: the parents) at St. George's Church; confirmed 27 Oct 1894; married Albert Raymond Walker on 15 Oct 1902 at "Pleasant Hill" in Perryman; also see "Taylor Family" and "Anna H. Walker," q.v. {Ref: Church Records, 1834-1903, pp. 12-13, 162-163, 302}

TAYLOR, Mary Virginia, daughter of Lawrence M. and Maude Taylor, born 12 Apr 1914, baptized 26 Nov 1914 at parents' home at Boothby Hill (sponsors: Clifford Taylor, Mrs. E. M. Cooley and Miss --?-- Martin). {Ref: Parish Register, 1903-1958, pp. 32-33}

TAYLOR, Maud L., Presbyterian, confirmed 11 Dec 1910. {Ref: Parish Register, 1903-1958, pp. 87, 110}

TAYLOR, Maude (Maud), see "Ida V. Taylor" and "Isabel F. Taylor" and "Lawrence M. Taylor" and "Ralph B. Taylor" and "Raymond R. Taylor" and "William S. Taylor," q.v.

TAYLOR, Minerva J., married Allan Hoffman on 21 Jun 1865. {Ref: Church Records, 1834-1903, p. 146}

TAYLOR, Minnie (Miss), confirmed 18 Oct 1887 at St. Mary's Church in Emmorton, removed in 1889. {Ref: Church Records, 1834-1903, pp. 202, 300}

TAYLOR, Mollie, see "Taylor Family," q.v.

TAYLOR, Norval (Norvell) Chapman, son of William H. and Isabel Taylor, born 23 Aug 1891, baptized 22 Nov 1891 (sponsors: the parents and Cornelius Cole), confirmed 11 Dec 1910, died 18 (19?) Feb 1914, buried 21 Feb 1914; also see "Taylor Family," q.v. {Ref: Church Records, 1834-1903, pp. 10-11; Parish Register, 1903-1958, pp. 87, 110, 159; Tombstone inscription}

TAYLOR, R. Emory, born 27 Dec 1843, died 14 Mar 1903; also see "Fannie A. Taylor" and "Francis E. Taylor," q.v. {Ref: Tombstone inscription}

TAYLOR, Rachel, see "Charles H. Taylor" and "James A. Taylor" and "John R. Taylor" and "Lottie Taylor," q.v.

TAYLOR, Ralph Byrd, son of William T. and Maude R. Taylor, born 11 Sep 1898, baptized 15 Dec 1898 at home at "Union Farm," Maryland (sponsors: the parents and Mrs. Isabel Taylor). {Ref: Church Records, 1834-1903, pp. 14-15}

TAYLOR, Raymond, see "Taylor Family," q.v.

TAYLOR, Raymond Rouse, son of William T. and M. T. Taylor, born 24 Mar 1907, baptized 26 Apr 1908 at Perryman (sponsors: William T. Taylor, L. M. Taylor and I. May Byrd). {Ref: Parish Register, 1903-1958, pp. 30-31}

TAYLOR, Rebecca, see "Frances R. Taylor," q.v.

TAYLOR, Richard M., born 1835, married Margaret Ann Hopkins on 16 May 1861, died 1912; also see "Margaret Taylor," q.v. {Ref: Church Records, 1834-1903, p. 143; Tombstone inscription}

TAYLOR, Robert, see "Taylor Family," q.v.

TAYLOR, Robert Herman, son of Hammond and Georgia [Georgianna] Taylor, born 2 Aug 1870, baptized 14 Jul 1871, buried 16 Jul 1871. {Ref: Church Records, 1834-1903, pp. 38-39, 96}

TAYLOR, S. Lillian, buried 12 Jan 1890, age 18. {Ref: Church Records, 1834-1903, p. 101}

TAYLOR, Sarah Frances, widow of James Franklin Taylor, buried 23 Aug 1868; also see "Francis J. Taylor" and "John T. J. Taylor," q.v. {Ref: Church Records, 1834-1903, p. 95}

TAYLOR, Sarah L., see "Asa C. Taylor" and "Charles A. Taylor," q.v.

TAYLOR, Sarah Laura, daughter of Hammond and Georgianna Taylor, born 30 May 1861, baptized 10 Jul 1864. {Ref: Church Records, 1834-1903, pp. 34-35}

TAYLOR, Seth Buckley, son of James R. and Martha Taylor, born 26 Aug 1865, baptized 11 Nov 1866 at Hopewell. {Ref: Church Records, 1834-1903, pp. 36-37}

TAYLOR, Wesley, see "D. Wesley Taylor," q.v.

TAYLOR, Wesley Raymond, son of D. W. and Amelia Taylor, born ---- [blank], baptized 10 Apr 1887. {Ref: Church Records, 1834-1903, p. 9}

TAYLOR, William, see "Isabel Frances Taylor" and "Taylor Family," q.v.

TAYLOR, William H. (Mrs.), sponsored the baptism of Isabel Frances Taylor on 4 Jul 1906 and Asa Carr Taylor, John Robert Keen, III, and Ida Virginia Taylor on 1 Apr 1916. {Ref: Parish Register, 1903-1958, pp. 31, 33}

TAYLOR, William Henry (adult), born ---- [blank], baptized 17 Nov 1889; also see "Asa A. Taylor" and "Ida M. Taylor" and "Isabel Taylor" and "Lawrence M. Taylor" and "Norval C. Taylor" and "William T. Taylor" and "Willie T. Taylor" and "---- Taylor" and "Taylor Family," q.v. {Ref: Church Records, 1834-1903, p. 9}

TAYLOR, William Stephen, son of William T. and Maude R. Taylor, born 15 Apr 1897, private baptism on 3 Dec 1897 at home (sponsors: the parents and Mrs. Isabel Taylor). {Ref: Church Records, 1834-1903, pp. 12-13}

TAYLOR, William T., married Maude Rouse on 25 Jun 1896; sponsored the baptism of Raymond Rouse Taylor on 26 Apr 1908; also see "Ida V. Taylor" and "Isabel F. Taylor" and "Lawrence M. Taylor" and "Ralph B. Taylor" and "Raymond R. Taylor" and "William S. Taylor," q.v. {Ref: Church Records, 1834-1903, pp. 160-161; Parish Register, 1903-1958, p. 31}

TAYLOR, William Thomas, son of William H. and Isabel Taylor, born ---- [blank], baptized 1 May 1879. {Ref: Church Records, 1834-1903, pp. 42-43}

TAYLOR, Willie Thomas, son of William H. and Isabel Taylor, born ---- [blank], baptized 13 Aug 1882 (sponsors: the mother and Mrs. Annie Reynolds); also see "Taylor Family," q.v. {Ref: Church Records, 1834-1903, pp. 2-3}

TAYLOR, ---- [blank], "infant daughter of Martha and ---- Taylor," born ---- [blank], baptized 5 Jun 1879. {Ref: Church Records, 1834-1903, pp. 42-43}

TAYLOR, ---- [blank], infant daughter of William H. and Isabella Taylor, born ---- [blank], buried -- Apr 1879. {Ref: Church Records, 1834-1903, p. 97}

TEMPLE, Lee Powell, son of Dr. Thomas and Mary Temple. [*Ed. Note:* No date of birth or baptism was given, but the baptism was listed among several others in the register between 1872 and 1876]. {Ref: Church Records, 1834-1903, pp. 40-41}

213

TEMPLE, Mary Fontleroy, son of Dr. Thomas and Mary Temple. [*Ed. Note:* No date of birth or baptism was given, but the baptism was listed among several others in the register between 1872 and 1876]. {Ref: Church Records, 1834-1903, pp. 40-41}

TEMPLE, Thomas, son of Dr. Thomas and Mary Temple. [*Ed. Note:* No date of birth or baptism was given, but the baptism was listed among several others in the register between 1872 and 1876]. {Ref: Church Records, 1834-1903, pp. 40-41}

TEMPLE, Thomas P. (doctor), married Mary Keen on 29 Sep 1870. {Ref: Church Records, 1834-1903, p. 147}

THAYER, Nathaniel Howard (adult), born 1805, baptized 15 Mar 1840 (sponsor: James Preston), confirmed 15 Nov 1840. {Ref: Church Records, 1834-1903, pp. 20-21, 296}

THOMAS, Abraham J., died 31 Aug 1841, age 64; also see "Mary S. Higbee" and "Mary S. Thomas" and "Herman S. Thomas" and "John Thomas," q.v. {Ref: Tombstone inscription}

THOMAS, Abraham Jarrett, son of Abraham J. Thomas, died 4 Jul 1841, age 20. {Ref: Tombstone inscription}

THOMAS, Ann, wife of Oliver H. Thomas, born 1 Oct 1822, died 30 Jun 1882. {Ref: Tombstone inscription}

THOMAS, George W. (Mrs.), sponsored the baptisms of Mary Alice Henderson on 11 Jun 1916 and Evelyn Caldwell Hume on 14 Nov 1916. {Ref: Parish Register, 1903-1958, p. 33}

THOMAS, George William (reverend), rector from 1912 to 1945; sponsored the baptisms of Gladys Marie Kirby on 23 Apr 1914 and Herbert Malcolm Owens on 14 Oct 1917. {Ref: Parish Register, 1903-1958, pp. ii, 33}

THOMAS, Gertrude Edith, church member in March, 1912, transferred from St. Luke's; sponsored the baptisms of Marion Stockham on 11 May 1914 and Herbert Malcolm Owens on 14 Oct 1917. {Ref: Parish Register, 1903-1958, pp. 33, 110}

THOMAS, Gertrude S. (Mrs.), sponsored the baptism of Minor Porter Steele on 5 Sep 1920. {Ref: Parish Register, 1903-1958, p. 35}

THOMAS, Herman S., son of A. J. and Mary S. Thomas, fell in Battle of Monterey, Mexico on 23 Sep 1846, soldier of the Mexican War, and was "committed to the tomb" at Spesutia [St. George's Churchyard] on 5 Feb 1847. {Ref: Church Records, 1834-1903, p. 91; Tombstone inscription}

THOMAS, John, son of A. J. and Mary S. Thomas, died 9 Dec 1873, age 5 years, 3 months and 27 days. {Ref: Tombstone inscription}

THOMAS, Mary S., wife of A. J. Thomas, died 20 Sep 1826, age 29; also see "Mary S. Higbee," q.v. {Ref: Tombstone inscription}

THOMAS, Oliver H., died 23 Sep 1870, age 47; also see "Ann Thomas," q.v. {Ref: Tombstone inscription}

THOMAS, William T., son of A. J. and Mary S. Thomas, died 1850. {Ref: Tombstone inscription}

THOMPSON, Amelia, see "Virginia M. Thompson," q.v.

THOMPSON, Anna, see "Ethel E. Thompson" and "Naomi M. Thompson" and "Rosa M. Thompson," q.v.

THOMPSON, Charles Sumner (colored), son of George H. and Mary C. Thompson, born 3 Mar 1882, baptized 23 Apr 1882 (sponsors: the parents and Mrs. Wright). {Ref: Church Records, 1834-1903, pp. 2-3}

THOMPSON, Claude Melville Barnett, son of Melville and Elizabeth A. Thompson, born ---- [blank], baptized 10 Jun 1880. {Ref: Church Records, 1834-1903, pp. 42-43}

THOMPSON, Effie, daughter of Sally Thompson (servant of Mrs. A. Hall), born 28 Dec 1853, baptized 21 Sep 1854. {Ref: Church Records, 1834-1903, pp. 26-27}

THOMPSON, Elizabeth A., see "Claude M. B. Thompson," q.v.

THOMPSON, Ellen Casander, daughter of George W. and Mary Thompson, born 27 Sep 1859, baptized 13 Oct 1863. {Ref: Church Records, 1834-1903, pp. 32-33}

THOMPSON, Ethel Evana, daughter of George J. and Anna E. Thompson, born 15 Nov 1885, private baptism on 7 Feb 1886 (sick). {Ref: Church Records, 1834-1903, pp. 4-5}

THOMPSON, George H., see "Charles S. Thompson," q.v.

THOMPSON, George J., see "Ethel E. Thompson," q.v.

THOMPSON, George W., see "Ellen C. Thompson," q.v.

THOMPSON, George Washington, son of George W. and Mary Thompson, born -- Mar 1861, baptized 13 Oct 1863. {Ref: Church Records, 1834-1903, pp. 32-33}

THOMPSON, George Washington, son of Helen C. Thompson, born ---- [blank], baptized 7 Jul 1878. {Ref: Church Records, 1834-1903, pp. 42-43}

THOMPSON, Helen C., see "George W. Thompson," q.v.

THOMPSON, James Robert, son of Robert W. and Rosa A. Thompson, born 10 May 1895, baptized 5 Jun 1895 (sick) at home at "Medford" in Harford County. {Ref: Church Records, 1834-1903, pp. 12-13}

THOMPSON, Mary C., see "Charles S. Thompson," q.v.

THOMPSON, Melville, see "Claude M. B. Thompson" and "Virginia M. Thompson," q.v.

THOMPSON, Minnie, married George Cullum on 31 May 1905 in the church rectory. {Ref: Parish Register, 1903-1958, pp. 138-139}

THOMPSON, Naomi Matilda, daughter of Robert J. and Anna Thompson, Jr., born 20 Apr 1914, baptized 19 May 1914 in the church rectory (sponsors: mother and Mrs. P. M. Hall). {Ref: Parish Register, 1903-1958, pp. 32-33}

THOMPSON, Robert (Mrs.) Sr., sponsored the baptism of Rosa Margarite Thompson on 29 Mar 1916. {Ref: Parish Register, 1903-1958, p. 33}

THOMPSON, Robert J., see "Naomi M. Thompson" and "Rosa M. Thompson," q.v.

THOMPSON, Robert W., see "James R. Thompson," q.v.

THOMPSON, Rosa, see "James R. Thompson," q.v.

THOMPSON, Rosa Margarite, daughter of Robert J. and Anna Thompson, Jr., born 20 Feb 1916, baptized 29 Mar 1916 at Mr. P. M. Hall's farm (sponsors: Mrs. Hall and Mrs. Robert Thompson, Sr.). {Ref: Parish Register, 1903-1958, pp. 32-33}

THOMPSON, Sally, married Robert Kell on 31 May 1857. {Ref: Church Records, 1834-1903, p. 141}

THOMPSON, Stephen J., of Oakington, died 18 Oct 1855. {Ref: Church Records, 1834-1903, p. 92}

THOMPSON, Susan J., born 16 Nov 1792, died 18 Mar 1867. {Ref: Tombstone inscription}

THOMPSON, Virginia May, infant daughter of Melville and Amelia Thompson. [*Ed. Note:* No date of birth or baptism was given, but the baptism was listed among several others in the register between 1872 and 1876]; died in 1875 or 1876 [exact date not given]. {Ref: Church Records, 1834-1903, pp. 40-41, 97}

TILDEN, Delia, married James Griffin on 26 Jan 1859. {Ref: Church Records, 1834-1903, p. 142}

TILDEN, Henry (colored), married Jane Ringgold (colored) on 21 Jul 1867. {Ref: Church Records, 1834-1903, p. 146}

TILSON, Charles W. (colored), married Catherine Harris (colored) on 12 Aug 1869. {Ref: Church Records, 1834-1903, p. 147}

TINSON, Georgeanna (colored), married Abraham Lincoln Rice (colored) on 30 Sep 1886. {Ref: Church Records, 1834-1903, pp. 152-153}

TINSON, Jacob A. (colored), married Belle Brown (colored) on 2 Aug 1882 at Colored M. E. Church. {Ref: Church Records, 1834-1903, p. 150}

TINSON, Mary (colored), married Alfred Winfield (colored) ---- 1877. [*Ed. Note:* The date was blank, but the marriage was listed between June and December in the register]. {Ref: Church Records, 1834-1903, p. 148}

TOLEVER, Solomon, married Amanda Carter on 21 Oct 1880. {Ref: Church Records, 1834-1903, p. 149}

TOWNER FAMILY.

The following family information was entered in the church records under the heading of "Families" circa 1893-1903, but no relationships or ages were indicated, just names:
Jay F. Towner, Mrs. Gertrude B. Towner, Jay Ferdinand Towner, Rena Towner, J. Bonn Towner, Leonard F. Towner, and William LeRoy Towner. {Ref: Church Records, 1834-1903, p. 255}

TOWNER, Gertrude B., sponsored the baptism of Mary Ellen Michael on 11 Dec 1892; church member in 1903; also see "Joseph B. Towner" and "Leonard F. Towner" and "Rena Towner" and "William L. Towner" and "Towner Family," q.v. {Ref: Church Records, 1834-1903, p. 11; Parish Register, 1903-1958, p. 108}

TOWNER, Henrietta (neé Malcolm), Methodist, confirmed 18 Jun 1916, moved to Chestertown, Maryland in 1917. {Ref: Parish Register, 1903-1958, pp. 89, 111}

TOWNER, Jay Ferdinand, Jr., confirmed 29 Dec 1901, age 18. {Ref: Church Records, 1834-1903, p. 303}

TOWNER, Jay Ferdinand, Sr., confirmed 9 Jun 1893; church member in 1903; sponsored the baptisms of Wilbur Herman Flutka on 28 Aug 1910 and Marion Jeanette Emmord on 31 Dec 1913; Mr. & Mrs. J. F. Towner, Sr. sponsored the baptism of Marian Malcolm Towner on 20 Jun 1917; also see "Joseph B. Towner" and "Leonard F. Towner" and "Rena Towner" and "William L. Towner" and "Towner Family," q.v. {Ref: Church Records, 1834-1903, p. 301; Parish Register, 1903-1958, pp. 31, 33, 108}

TOWNER, Joseph Bonn, son of Jay F. and Gertrude B. Towner, born 27 Jan 1886, private baptism on 14 Mar 1886 (sick); confirmed 29 Dec 1901, age 16, church member in 1903, later removed to Chestertown, Maryland [date not given]; also see "Marian M. Towner" and "Towner Family," q.v. {Ref: Church Records, 1834-1903, pp. 4-5, 303; Parish Register, 1903-1958, p. 108}

TOWNER, Leonard Fair, son of Jay F. and Gertrude Towner, born ---- [blank], baptized 27 May 1888, confirmed 29 Dec 1901, age 14, died 28 Dec 1915, age 26, buried 30 Dec 1915; also see "Towner Family," q.v. {Ref: Church Records, 1834-1903, pp. 7, 303; Parish Register, 1903-1958, pp. 108, 159}

TOWNER, Marian Malcolm, son of J. Bonn and Henrietta Towner, born 22 Feb 1917, baptized 20 Jun 1917 (sponsors: Mr. & Mrs. J. F. Towner, Sr. and William L. Towner). {Ref: Parish Register, 1903-1958, pp. 32-33}

TOWNER, Rena, daughter of Jay F. and Gertrude B. Towner, born 24 Nov 1884, baptized 27 Sep 1885, confirmed 30 Apr 1899, age 14, church member in 1903, married William French [date not given]; also see "Towner Family," q.v. {Ref: Church Records, 1834-1903, pp. 4-5, 302; Parish Register, 1903-1958, p. 108}

TOWNER, William LeRoy, son of Jay Ferdinand and Gertrude B. Towner, born 29 Jun 1900, private baptism on 26 Aug 1900 (sick) at home (sponsors: the parents, Mrs. Honora B. Michael and A. G. Richards), confirmed 17 May 1914; sponsored the baptism of Marian Malcolm Towner on 20 Jun 1917; also see "Towner Family," q.v. {Ref: Church Records, 1834-1903, pp. 14-15; Parish Register, 1903-1958, pp. 33, 88, 110}

TOWSON, Rosanna, married Joseph Lee on 16 Jan 1851. {Ref: Church Records, 1834-1903, p. 140}

TRAUTNER, Herman August, sponsored the baptism of Wilbur Herman Flutka on 28 Aug 1910. {Ref: Parish Register, 1903-1958, p. 31}

TREDICK FAMILY.
    The following family information was entered in the church records under the heading of "Families" circa 1893-1903, but no relationships or ages were indicated, just names. Additional information shown in parenthesis was entered subsequently in the register:
    Mrs. ---- [blank] Treddick [sic] (removed), Mary Tredick (removed), Trafton Tredick (removed), Parker Tredick (removed), Wendell Tredick (removed), and Chandler Tredick (removed). A line was drawn diagonally through all the names. {Ref: Church Records, 1834-1903, p. 257}

TREDICK, John, Jr. (husband), formerly of New Hampshire, died 18 May 1881 in his 43rd year. {Ref: Tombstone inscription}

TREDICK, ----, see "Tredick Family," q.v.

TRIMBLE, George Marbury, son of Charles H. and Annie L. Trimble, born 29 Feb 1884, private baptism on 20 Jul 1884. {Ref: Church Records, 1834-1903, pp. 4-5}

TRIMBLE, Harry Walter, son of Charles H. and Annie L. Trimble, born 26 Feb 1881, private baptism on 20 Jul 1884. {Ref: Church Records, 1834-1903, pp. 4-5}

TRIMBLE, Phoebe Dwyer, age 73, buried 20 Jul 1914, buried at Loudon Park Cemetery in Baltimore. {Ref: Parish Register, 1903-1958, p. 159}

TRIMBLE, Susanna Silver, daughter of Charles and Annie Trimble, born 20 Oct 1886, baptized 13 Sep 1888. {Ref: Church Records, 1834-1903, p. 8}

TROTT, James E., died 12 Feb 1913, age 74, buried 15 Feb 1913. {Ref: Parish Register, 1903-1958, p. 158; Tombstone inscription}

TROTT, Martha Emily, born 1844, died 1927. {Ref: Tombstone inscription}

TROTT, Sarah E., died 2 Mar 1913. {Ref: Tombstone inscription}

TURNER, John Henry, son of Henry and Louisa Turner, born 1 Apr 1851, baptized 12 Feb 1853. {Ref: Church Records, 1834-1903, pp. 24-25}

TURNER, Lucy Ann, daughter of Henry and Louisa Turner, born 2 Aug 1845, baptized 4 Apr 1847. {Ref: Church Records, 1834-1903, pp. 22-23}

TURNER, Martha Caroline, daughter of Henry and Louisa Turner, born 4 Jan 1843, baptized 4 Apr 1847. {Ref: Church Records, 1834-1903, pp. 22-23}

TURNER, Mary Jane, daughter of Henry and Louisa Turner, born 22 Sep 1840, baptized 4 Apr 1847. {Ref: Church Records, 1834-1903, pp. 22-23}

TURNER, Samuel Henry Burkitt, son of Henry and Louisa Turner, born 22 Dec 1856, baptized 24 Sep 1857. {Ref: Church Records, 1834-1903, pp. 28-29}

TURNER, Thomas Edward, son of Henry and Louisa Turner, born 20 Jun 1845, baptized 16 Sep 1849. {Ref: Church Records, 1834-1903, pp. 22-23}

TURNER, William Charles, son of Henry and Louisa Turner, born 15 Aug 1854, baptized 22 Dec 1854. {Ref: Church Records, 1834-1903, pp. 26-27}

TURNER, William Fitzhugh, buried 5 Dec 1852. {Ref: Church Records, 1834-1903, p. 92}

TUTCHTON, Elizabeth, wife of Nathaniel Tutchton, died 13 Jul 1840. {Ref: Tombstone inscription}

TWONEY(?), Mary Adreine, Methodist, confirmed 10 Apr 1904. {Ref: Parish Register, 1903-1958, p. 87}

TYLER, Anner M. (Mrs.), removed to Haymarket, Virginia on 6 Apr 1900. {Ref: Church Records, 1834-1903, p. 203}

TYLER, Bailey, married Anner Moss Alrich on 6 Oct 1897. {Ref: Church Records, 1834-1903, pp. 160-161}

ULRICH, Michael, son of Michael and Juliana Pittner Ulrich, born 4 Aug 1864, baptized 14 Aug 1864. {Ref: Church Records, 1834-1903, pp. 34-35}

UNKLE, Elizabeth E. (mother), born 1843, died 1917. {Ref: Tombstone inscription}

UNKLE, George (father), born 1821, died 1879. {Ref: Tombstone inscription}

UPP, Rebecca Selinia, daughter of Francis and Cecelia Upp, born 1 Mar 1856, baptized 23 Nov 1856. {Ref: Church Records, 1834-1903, pp. 28-29}

VANBIBBER, Armfield Franklin, M.D., married Susanna Rebecca Michael on 16 Oct 1901. {Ref: Church Records, 1834-1903, pp. 162-163}

VANSICKLE, Elizabeth, wife of Henry Vansickle, died 29 May 1821, age 77. {Ref: Tombstone inscription}

VEASEY, Mary (Mrs.), buried 28 Mar 1849. {Ref: Church Records, 1834-1903, p. 91}

VEAZEY, George W. (of "Primrose"), died 12 Feb 1839. {Ref: Church Records, 1834-1903, p. 90}

VOGTS, Harriet L., born 1893, died 1907. {Ref: Tombstone inscription}

WACHSMUTH, Theresa, married William E. Lewis on 17 Sep 1899. {Ref: Church Records, 1834-1903, pp. 160-161}

WALKER, Albert Raymond, married Mary Stockham Taylor on 15 Oct 1902 at "Pleasant Hill" in Perryman; also see "Anna H. Walker" and "Taylor Family," q.v. {Ref: Church Records, 1834-1903, pp. 162-163}

WALKER, Anna Hazlett, daughter of Albert Raymond and Mary Taylor Walker, born 2 Oct 1903, baptized 3 Jul 1904 (sponsors: the parents, Joseph W. Taylor and Anna E. Taylor). {Ref: Parish Register, 1903-1958, pp. 30-31}

WALKER, Bessie, daughter of James T. and Fannie Walker, born ---- [blank], baptized 2 Apr 1879. {Ref: Church Records, 1834-1903, pp. 42-43}

221

WALKER, Elizabeth, see "Hugh C. Walker," q.v.

WALKER, Fannie, daughter of James T. and Fannie Walker, born ---- [blank], baptized 2 Apr 1879; also see "Bessie Walker" and "Mabel M. Walker," q.v. {Ref: Church Records, 1834-1903, pp. 42-43}

WALKER, George, Jr., married Susanna Cole on 2 Nov 1837. {Ref: Church Records, 1834-1903, p. 138}

WALKER, Hugh Christie, son of Robert and Elizabeth Walker, born 18 May 1846, baptized 21 Jun 1846. {Ref: Church Records, 1834-1903, pp. 22-23}

WALKER, James T., see "Bessie Walker" and "Fannie Walker" and "Mabel M. Walker," q.v.

WALKER, John Stein, Jr., born 13 Mar 1906. {Ref: Parish Register, 1903-1958, p. 44}

WALKER, Mabel Monroe, daughter of James T. and Fannie H. Walker, born 1 Aug 1883, baptized ---- [blank, but prob. Jan or Feb] 1884. {Ref: Church Records, 1834-1903, pp. 2-3}

WALKER, Mary Stockham Taylor, church member in 1903, married Lynn DeLancey Tanner on 29 Sep 1909; "by transfer to St. George's, May, 1914, removed to Suffolk, Virginia." {Ref: Parish Register, 1903-1958, pp. 108, 138-139}

WALKER, Mary T., see "Anna H. Walker," q.v.

WALKER, Raymond, buried 14 Apr 1906 [age not stated] in Grove Churchyard. {Ref: Parish Register, 1903-1958, p. 158}

WALKER, Robert, see "Hugh C. Walker," q.v.

WALLACE, Elizabeth W. (Miss), buried 26 May 1891, "age about 30." {Ref: Church Records, 1834-1903, p. 102}

WALLACE, Margaretta, daughter of Rosa Wallace (servant of Mrs. A. Hall), born 17 Mar 1854, baptized 21 Sep 1854. {Ref: Church Records, 1834-1903, pp. 26-27}

WALLIS, William Hawkins, born 1 Dec 1846, died 23 Oct 1916, age 70, buried 25 Oct 1916. {Ref: Parish Register, 1903-1958, p. 159; Tombstone inscription}

WALLIS, William Jolley [of Baltimore], married Annie Jolley Hawkins on 15 Jan 1846. {Ref: Church Records, 1834-1903, p. 139}

WARFIELD, Cassie (colored), married Robert Stansbury (colored) on 14 Mar 1867. {Ref: Church Records, 1834-1903, p. 146}

WARFIELD, Rebecca (colored), married William Stansbury (colored) on 28 Oct 1869. {Ref: Church Records, 1834-1903, p. 147}

WASHINGTON, Mary J., married Isaac Alexander Banks on 27 Jun 1862. {Ref: Church Records, 1834-1903, p. 144}

WATERS, Margaret C., see "John R. Denham," q.v.

WAY, Myrtle May, sponsored the baptism of Martha Viola Strong and James Thomas Strong on 6 Jul 1910. {Ref: Parish Register, 1903-1958, p. 31}

WEBB, David N., sponsored the baptism of Elmer Thomas Smith on 26 Apr 1908. {Ref: Parish Register, 1903-1958, p. 31}

WEBB, Ida C., see "Elmer T. Smith," q.v.

WEBB, John, sponsored the baptism of Elmer Thomas Smith on 26 Apr 1908. {Ref: Parish Register, 1903-1958, p. 31}

WEBSTER, Captain, see "Rachel Webster," q.v.

WEBSTER, Charles H., died 27 Jun 1849, age 28 years and 11 months, buried 29 Jun 1849. {Ref: Church Records, 1834-1903, p. 91; Tombstone inscription}

WEBSTER, Ellenora (colored), married George Howard Kennedy Rue (colored) on 9 Jun 1887. {Ref: Church Records, 1834-1903, pp. 154-155}

WEBSTER, George B., of Havre de Grace, died 6 May 1847 in his 29th year, buried 9 May 1847. {Ref: Church Records, 1834-1903, p. 91; Tombstone inscription}

WEBSTER, John (colored), married Mary E. Christie (colored) ---- 1877. [*Ed. Note:* The date was blank, but the marriage was listed between June and December in the register]. {Ref: Church Records, 1834-1903, p. 148}

WEBSTER, John Luster, married Susan Brown (of "Primrose") on 19 Dec 1839. {Ref: Church Records, 1834-1903, p. 138}

WEBSTER, Mary, died 1826, age 3 (5?) years. {Ref: Tombstone inscription}

WEBSTER, Mary M. (colored), married Philip Pinion (colored) on 2 Oct 1890. {Ref: Church Records, 1834-1903, pp. 156-157}

WEBSTER, Milkie, married Solomon J. Williams ---- 1878. [*Ed. Note:* The date was blank, but the marriage was listed between June and August in the register]. {Ref: Church Records, 1834-1903, p. 148}

WEBSTER, Rachel, wife of Capt. Webster, buried 5 Oct 1869. {Ref: Church Records, 1834-1903, p. 96}

WELCH, Isaac, married Harriet Lisby on 5 Nov 1863. {Ref: Church Records, 1834-1903, p. 145}

WELCH, Mary Jane (colored), married Levin H. Collins (colored) on 8 Dec 1864. {Ref: Church Records, 1834-1903, p. 145}

WELLS, Annie S., daughter of J. W. and S. R. Wells, died 9 Dec 1875, age 4. {Ref: Tombstone inscription}

WELLS, C. Elmer, son of James W. and Sarah R. Wells, died 8 Nov 1891, age 24 years, 10 months and 8 days. {Ref: Tombstone inscription}

WELLS, Charles W., born 17 Sep 1836, died 15 Jan 1884; also see "Elizabeth A. Wells," q.v. {Ref: Tombstone inscription}

WELLS, Edward Asels, son of Joseph and Matilda C. Wells, born 3 Sep 1872, baptized 10 Aug 1884 (sponsors: Mr. Joseph Wells and Mrs. Eliza McGill). {Ref: Church Records, 1834-1903, pp. 4-5}

WELLS, Elizabeth A., wife of Charles W. Wells, died 24 Oct 1873, age 42. {Ref: Tombstone inscription}

WELLS, Eva, daughter of J. W. and S. R. Wells, born 31 Aug 1865. died 20 Sep 1866, age 4. {Ref: Tombstone inscription}

WELLS, Herbert, son of J. W. and S. R. Wells, died 15 Dec 1875, age 7. {Ref: Tombstone inscription}

WELLS, James W., born 14 Oct 1842, died 30 Nov 1906; also see "Annie S. Wells" and "C. Elmer Wells" and "Eva Wells" and "Herbert Wells" and "Lillian M. Wells" and "Nettie V. Wells" and "Sarah R. Wells" and "W. Warren Wells," q.v. {Ref: Tombstone inscription}

WELLS, Joseph, see "Edward A. Wells," q.v.

WELLS, Joseph L., buried 24 Jun 1884, age 7 years and 8 days. {Ref: Church Records, 1834-1903, p. 100}

WELLS, Lillian M., daughter of J. W. and S. R. Wells, died 16 Aug 1878, age 2 months and 18 days. {Ref: Tombstone inscription}

WELLS, Margaret A., born 5 Apr 1860, died 14 Aug 1883. {Ref: Tombstone inscription}

WELLS, Matilda, see "Edward A. Wells," q.v.

WELLS, Nettie V., daughter of James W. and Sarah R. Wells, died 17 Mar 1877, age 2 months and 10 days. {Ref: Tombstone inscription}

WELLS, Sarah R., wife of James W. Wells, born 11 Sep 1840, died 2 May 1920; also see "Annie S. Wells" and "C. Elmer Wells" and "Eva Wells" and "Herbert Wells" and "Lillian M. Wells" and "Nettie V. Wells" and "W. Warren Wells," q.v. {Ref: Tombstone inscription}

WELLS, W. Warren, son of James W. and Sarah R. Wells, died 1 Oct 1881 1891, age 9 months. {Ref: Tombstone inscription}

WELSH, Mary (colored), married George Henry Miller (colored) on 4 Jun 1891. {Ref: Church Records, 1834-1903, pp. 156-157}

WEST, Annie, buried 11 Feb 1872 at Hopewell Cross Roads. {Ref: Church Records, 1834-1903, p. 96}

WETHERALL, Mary Isabella, daughter of James and Susan Wetherall, born 23 May 1844, baptized 22 Sep 1850; M. Isabel Wetheral married Robert R. Boarman on 15 Oct 1867 at Grace Church in Baltimore. {Ref: Church Records, 1834-1903, pp. 24-25, 146}

WHEELER, James (colored), married Eliza Hall (colored) on 25 Feb 1872. {Ref: Church Records, 1834-1903, p. 147}

WHEELER, Leonard, son of ---- [blank], born 21 Mar 1837, baptized 21 Jul 1837. {Ref: Church Records, 1834-1903, pp. 18-19}

WHEELER, Sophia, married Charles William Bowlyer ---- 1872 [blank, probably January]. {Ref: Church Records, 1834-1903, p. 147}

WHITE, Florence Lindsay, confirmed 21 Nov 1909, married John Henry Rowley on 15 Dec 1909 at Perryman. {Ref: Parish Register, 1903-1958, pp. 87, 109, 138-139}

WHITE, Frillas(?), married Hannah ---- [blank] on 4 Apr 1858. {Ref: Church Records, 1834-1903, p. 142}

WHITING, Carrie Eliza (Miss), received from Grace Memorial Church in Lynchburg, Virginia on 2 Oct 1900 and removed to Trinity Church at New Castle, Pennsylvania in March, 1902. {Ref: Church Records, 1834-1903, pp. 206-207}

WHITING FAMILY.
The following family information was entered in the church records under the heading of "Families" circa 1893-1903, but no relationships or ages were indicated, just names. Additional information shown in parenthesis was entered subsequently in the register:
Edward Whiting (Aberdeen, removed), Mrs. ---- [blank] Whiting (Aberdeen, removed), Mrs. ---- [blank] Whiting, Sr. (Aberdeen, removed), Miss Carrie Whiting (Aberdeen, removed), Miss Kate Whiting (Aberdeen, removed), Frederick Whiting (Aberdeen, removed), Hobart Whiting (Aberdeen, removed), and Mrs. Hobart Whiting (Aberdeen, removed). A line was drawn diagonally through all the names. {Ref: Church Records, 1834-1903, p. 258}

WHITING, Carrie, see "Whiting Family," q.v.

WHITING, Edward S., received from Waterbury, Connecticut on 23 Apr 1893; also see "William S. Whiting" and "Whiting Family," q.v. {Ref: Church Records, 1834-1903, p. 204}

WHITING, Frederick Keeler (Mr.), received from Grace Memorial Church in Lynchburg, Virginia on 2 Oct 1900 and removed to Trinity Church in New Castle, Pennsylvania in March, 1902; also see "Whiting Family," q.v. {Ref: Church Records, 1834-1903, pp. 206-207}

WHITING, Hobart, see "Whiting Family," q.v.

WHITING, Kate, see "Whiting Family," q.v.

WHITING, Marion Kate (Miss), received from Grace Memorial Church in Lynchburg, Virginia on 2 Oct 1900 and removed to Trinity Church in New Castle, Pennsylvania in March, 1902; also see "Whiting Family," q.v. {Ref: Church Records, 1834-1903, pp. 206-207}

WHITING, William Samuel, son of Edward S. and ---- [blank] Whiting, born 25 Nov 1893, baptized 2 Feb 1894 (sick) at home in Aberdeen. {Ref: Church Records, 1834-1903, pp. 12-13}

WHITMAN, Lizzie Evaline, daughter of John and Margaret Whitman, born 11 Jun 1869, baptized 24 Oct 1869. {Ref: Church Records, 1834-1903, pp. 38-39}

WHITMAN, John, married Margaret Hemless on 7 Sep 1869. {Ref: Church Records, 1834-1903, p. 147}

WHITSON, --?-- [first name was blank with a question mark in church register], child of ---- [blank], born ---- [blank], baptized 30 Jun 1839. {Ref: Church Records, 1834-1903, pp. 20-21}

WHITSON, Anna Frinetta, daughter of Burton and Mary Ann Whitson, born ---- [blank], baptized 6 Aug 1837 (sponsors: the parents). {Ref: Church Records, 1834-1903, pp. 18-19}

WHITSON, Benjamin, confirmed 15 Nov 1840. {Ref: Church Records, 1834-1903, p. 296}

WHITSON, Burt, see "Mary Ann Whitson," q.v.

WHITSON, John Henry, son of Burton and Mary Ann Whitson, born ---- [blank], baptized 6 Aug 1837 (sponsors: the parents). {Ref: Church Records, 1834-1903, pp. 18-19}

WHITSON, Mary Ann, wife of Burt Whitson, died 19 Aug 1843, age 37 years, 8 months and 9 days. {Ref: Tombstone inscription}

WHITSON, Mary Elizabeth, daughter of Burton and Mary Ann Whitson, born ---- [blank], baptized 6 Aug 1837 (sponsors: the parents), confirmed 15 Nov 1840. {Ref: Church Records, 1834-1903, pp. 18-19, 296}

WHITSON, Sarah Rebecca, daughter of Burton and Mary Ann Whitson, born ---- [blank], baptized 6 Aug 1837 (sponsors: the parents), confirmed 15 Nov 1840. {Ref: Church Records, 1834-1903, pp. 18-19, 296}

WHITSON, Susanna, daughter of Burton and Mary Ann Whitson, born ---- [blank], baptized 6 Aug 1837 (sponsors: the parents). {Ref: Church Records, 1834-1903, pp. 18-19}

WHITSON, William Amos, son of Burton and Mary Ann Whitson, born ---- [blank], baptized 6 Aug 1837 (sponsors: the parents). {Ref: Church Records, 1834-1903, pp. 18-19}

WHITTAKER, Charlotte, daughter of William P. C. and Mary K. Whittaker, born 24 Aug 1852, baptized 20 Mar 1853. {Ref: Church Records, 1834-1903, pp. 26-27}

WHITTAKER, Leila Gertrude, daughter of William P. C. and Mary K. Whittaker, born 22 Jul 1855, baptized 4 Mar 1857. {Ref: Church Records, 1834-1903, pp. 28-29}

WHITTAKER, Mary Elizabeth, daughter of William P. C. and Mary K. Whittaker, born 17 Apr 1850, baptized 20 Mar 1853. {Ref: Church Records, 1834-1903, pp. 26-27}

WILLIAM, George, see "George William ----," q.v.

WILLIAM, Isaac, see "Isaac William ----," q.v.

WILLIAMS, Andrew Harrison, married Amanda M. Lizby on 6 Feb 1862. {Ref: Church Records, 1834-1903, p. 144}

WILLIAMS, Annie (colored), married John Kenly (colored) on 15 Dec 1881. {Ref: Church Records, 1834-1903, p. 150}

WILLIAMS, Charles Samuel, son of "Levantia & Williams" *[sic]*, i.e., Henry and Levantia Williams, born ---- [blank], baptized 1 Sep 1878. {Ref: Church Records, 1834-1903, pp. 42-43}

WILLIAMS, Clarence Howard (colored), son of Henry and Levantia Williams, age 5 years, baptized 7 Oct 1890 (sponsors: the parents) near Perryman. {Ref: Church Records, 1834-1903, pp. 10-11}

WILLIAMS, Elizabeth, wife of George Williams, buried 19 Mar 1850. {Ref: Church Records, 1834-1903, p. 91}

WILLIAMS, George, see "Elizabeth Williams," q.v.

WILLIAMS, George (colored), married Ellen Gibson (colored) on 11 Dec 1892. {Ref: Church Records, 1834-1903, pp. 158-159}

WILLIAMS, George Edward (colored), son of Henry and Levantia Williams, born ---- [blank], baptized 13 Jun 1876. {Ref: Church Records, 1834-1903, pp. 40-41}

WILLIAMS, Harrison (colored), married Annie Harris (colored) on 6 Jan 1870. {Ref: Church Records, 1834-1903, p. 147}

WILLIAMS, Henry (colored), married Levantia Norton (colored) on 24 Dec 1868; also see "Charles S. Williams" and "Clarence H. Williams" and "George E. Williams" and "Ida E. Williams" and "Jacob H. Williams" and "Joseph S. Williams" and "Mary M. Williams" and "William S. Williams," q.v. {Ref: Church Records, 1834-1903, p. 147}

WILLIAMS, Ida Elizabeth (colored), daughter of Henry and Levantia Williams, born ---- [blank], baptized 13 Jun 1876. {Ref: Church Records, 1834-1903, pp. 40-41}

WILLIAMS, Jacob Henry (colored), son of Henry and Levantia Williams, born ---- [blank], baptized 13 Jun 1876. {Ref: Church Records, 1834-1903, pp. 40-41}

WILLIAMS, John, confirmed 27 Apr 1856 at St. John's Church in Havre de Grace. {Ref: Church Records, 1834-1903, p. 297}

WILLIAMS, Joseph Sovis (colored), son of Henry and Levantia Williams, age 6 years, baptized 7 Oct 1890 (sponsors: the parents) near Perryman. {Ref: Church Records, 1834-1903, pp. 10-11}

WILLIAMS, Levantia, see "Charles S. Williams" and "Clarence H. Williams" and "George E. Williams" and "Henry Williams" and "Ida E. Williams" and "Jacob H. Williams" and "Joseph S. Williams" and "Mary M. Williams" and "William S. Williams," q.v.

WILLIAMS, Martha (colored), married Henry Smith (colored) on 15 Sep 1869. {Ref: Church Records, 1834-1903, p. 147}

WILLIAMS, Mary (Mrs.), of Havre de Grace, buried 26 Aug 1857. {Ref: Church Records, 1834-1903, p. 93}

WILLIAMS, Mary Elizabeth, married John Isaiah Holland on 10 Oct 1861. {Ref: Church Records, 1834-1903, p. 143}

WILLIAMS, Mary Margaret (colored), daughter of Henry and Levantia Williams, age 1 year and 5 months, baptized 7 Oct 1890 (sponsors: the parents) near Perryman. {Ref: Church Records, 1834-1903, pp. 10-11}

WILLIAMS, Mavourneen, married James Frank Kenley, Jr. on 15 Sep 1914 at A. K. Williams' residence in Ijamsville, Maryland. {Ref: Parish Register, 1903-1958, pp. 138-139}

WILLIAMS, Rosa, married James Crawford Neilson on 2 Jun 1840 at Priestsford. {Ref: Church Records, 1834-1903, p. 138}

WILLIAMS, Solomon, married Mary Jane Lewis on 1 Mar 1862. {Ref: Church Records, 1834-1903, p. 144}

WILLIAMS, Solomon J., married Milkie Webster ---- 1878. [*Ed. Note:* The date was blank, but the marriage was listed between June and August in the register]. {Ref: Church Records, 1834-1903, p. 148}

WILLIAMS, Sydney (Miss), confirmed 27 Aug 1846. {Ref: Church Records, 1834-1903, p. 296}

WILLIAMS, William Henry, married Mary C. Curtis on 23 May 1861. {Ref: Church Records, 1834-1903, p. 143}

WILLIAMS, William Sidney (colored), son of Henry and Levantia Williams, age 2½ years, baptized 7 Oct 1890 (sponsors: the parents) near Perryman. {Ref: Church Records, 1834-1903, pp. 10-11}

WILLIS, Frances A. (neé Finlay), age 70, died 26 Nov 1899, buried 29 Nov 1899; also see "William F. Willis," q.v. {Ref: Church Records, 1834-1903, p. 104; Tombstone inscription}

WILLIS, George Newkirk ("Little George"), infant son of L. G. and A. M. Willis, born 7 Feb 1900, died 17 Nov 1903, age 3 years, 9 months and 10 days, buried 19 Nov 1903. {Ref: Parish Register, 1903-1958, p. 158; Tombstone inscription}

WILLIS, James N., infant son of Louis and A. Mary Willis, born 11 Apr 1910, died 4 Aug 1910. {Ref: Tombstone inscription}

WILLIS, James Newton, son of Louis and A. Mary Willis, died 4 Aug 1911. {Ref: Tombstone inscription}

WILLIS, Louis, see "George N. Willis" and "James N. Willis." q.v.

WILLIS, William Finlay, son of William L. and Frances A. Willis, born 13 Jan 1855, died 13 Apr 1864. {Ref: Tombstone inscription}

WILLIS, William Lewis, M.D., died 14 Jun 1959, age 29. {Ref: Tombstone inscription}

WILMER, Alice Ann, married Abraham Courtney on 7 Dec 1880. {Ref: Church Records, 1834-1903, p. 149}

WILMER, Aminta, married Washington Ringgold on 26 Dec 1857. {Ref: Church Records, 1834-1903, p. 141}

WILMER, Charles William Evans, son of William and Mary Wilmer, born 31 Aug 1863?, baptized 17 Apr 1864 [*Ed. Note:* Birth year was actually entered in the register as "1864?", but it was probably 1863]. {Ref: Church Records, 1834-1903, pp. 34-35}

WILMER, Harriet (colored), married Joshua Read (colored) ---- 1877. [*Ed. Note:* The date was blank, but the marriage was listed between June and December in the register]. {Ref: Church Records, 1834-1903, p. 148}

WILMER, Hester (colored), married Joseph Hall (colored) on 24 Jul 1892. {Ref: Church Records, 1834-1903, pp. 158-159}

WILMER, Horace, married Ruth Norton on 25 Jul 1858. {Ref: Church Records, 1834-1903, p. 142}

WILMER, James, married Sarah Lewis on 13 May 1866. {Ref: Church Records, 1834-1903, p. 146}

WILMER, Mary, see "Charles W. E. Wilmer," q.v.

WILMER, Mary (colored), of Hickory Ridge, buried 7 May 1872. {Ref: Church Records, 1834-1903, p. 96}

WILMER, Mary Jane (servant of J. S. Hall), born ---- [blank], baptized 25 Dec 1836. {Ref: Church Records, 1834-1903, pp. 16-17}

WILMER, Thomas (servant of J. S. Hall), born ---- [blank], baptized 25 Dec 1836. {Ref: Church Records, 1834-1903, pp. 16-17}

WILMER, William, married Mary Stewart on 17 Jan 1862; also see "Charles W. E. Wilmer," q.v. {Ref: Church Records, 1834-1903, p. 144}

WILMER, William, married Clara Bond on 6 Nov 1872. {Ref: Church Records, 1834-1903, p. 148}

WILMER, William H. (servant of J. S. Hall), born ---- [blank], baptized 25 Dec 1836. {Ref: Church Records, 1834-1903, pp. 16-17}

WILMORE, Sarah (colored), married Richard A. Brown (colored) on 1 Jan 1883 at Colored M. E. Church. {Ref: Church Records, 1834-1903, p. 150}

WILSON, Carrie E., daughter of W. H. and M. J. Wilson, died 12 Aug 1887, age 20 years and 4 months. {Ref: Tombstone inscription}

WILSON, Charles Augustus, son of James Roberts and Susan R. Wilson, born 4 Aug 1867, baptized 10 Jun 1868. {Ref: Church Records, 1834-1903, pp. 36-37}

WILSON, Doctor, see "Davis Family," q.v.

WILSON, Fannie E., church member in 1903. {Ref: Parish Register, 1903-1958, p. 108}

WILSON, Garret Vansickle (Mr.), buried 26 Dec 1850. {Ref: Church Records, 1834-1903, p. 91}

WILSON, George, buried 12 Mar 1863. {Ref: Church Records, 1834-1903, p. 94}

WILSON, George William, son of Thomas and Mary Wilson, born 5 Aug 1861, baptized 4 May 1862. {Ref: Church Records, 1834-1903, pp. 32-33}

WILSON, Henry B., M.D., husband of Frances Davis, born 25 Apr 1863, died 26 Sep 1900, buried 29 Sep 1900, age 37 years, 4 months and 25 days *[sic]*, in S. G. Mausoleum at St. George's. [*Ed. Note:* The church records indicated his middle name was "Betty" but perhaps they meant "Beaty"]. {Ref: Church Records, 1834-1903, p. 104; Cemetery records}

WILSON, James R., see "Charles A. Wilson," q.v.

WILSON, John, of Gunpowder Neck, buried 11 Oct 1850. {Ref: Church Records, 1834-1903, p. 91}

WILSON, Louisa, married Joseph M. Clay on 1 Jul 1855. {Ref: Church Records, 1834-1903, p. 140}

WILSON, M. J., born 28 Jan 1831, died 20 Mar 1913. {Ref: Tombstone inscription}

WILSON, Mary, see "George W. Wilson," q.v.

WILSON, Mary Wilson, daughter of William and Rachel Wilson, born 24 Dec 1827, baptized 22 Aug 1854. {Ref: Church Records, 1834-1903, pp. 26-27}

WILSON, Rachel, see "Mary W. Wilson" and "Sallie A. Wilson," q.v.

WILSON, Sallie Allen, daughter of William and Rachel Wilson, born 23 May 1830, baptized 22 Aug 1854. {Ref: Church Records, 1834-1903, pp. 26-27}

WILSON, Samuel E., died 21 Jul 1856, age 59. {Ref: Tombstone inscription}

WILSON, Susan R., see "Charles A. Wilson," q.v.

WILSON, Thomas, married Mary Quinn on 14 Jun 1860; also see "George W. Wilson," q.v. {Ref: Church Records, 1834-1903, p. 142}

WILSON, W. H., born 13 Mar 1826, died 22 Feb 1902. {Ref: Tombstone inscription}

WILSON, W. Henry, son of W. H. and M. J. Wilson, born 5 Oct 1859, died 24 Apr 1864. {Ref: Tombstone inscription}

WILSON, William, see "Mary W. Wilson" and "Sallie A. Wilson," q.v.

WILSON, William M., married Nannie E. Dawson on 27 Nov 1889 at Christ Church in Rockville, Maryland. {Ref: Church Records, 1834-1903, pp. 156-157}

WILTON, James, born 15 Mar 1890, died 14 Jul 1890. {Ref: Tombstone inscription}

WILTON, John, born 11 Mar 1898, died 19 Feb 1899. {Ref: Tombstone inscription}

WINCHESTER, Annie (colored), married Charles H. Brown (colored) on 11 Jun 1868. {Ref: Church Records, 1834-1903, p. 146}

WINCHESTER, Daniel (colored), married Caroline Monk (colored) on 7 Oct 1886. {Ref: Church Records, 1834-1903, pp. 152-153}

WINCHESTER, Lizzie (colored), married Daniel A. Smith (colored) on 10 Jun 1883. {Ref: Church Records, 1834-1903, p. 151}

WINCHESTER, Susan (colored), married Nathan Peters (colored) on 2 May 1883. {Ref: Church Records, 1834-1903, p. 150}

WINFIELD, Alfred (colored), married Mary Tinson (colored) ---- 1877. [*Ed. Note:* The date was blank, but the marriage was listed between June and December in the register]. {Ref: Church Records, 1834-1903, p. 148}

WIRSING, Roland Carl, son of Herman C. and Emma Wirsing, born 12 Sep 1913, baptized 1 Feb 1914 (sick) at Perryman (sponsors: the parents). {Ref: Parish Register, 1903-1958, pp. 32-33}

WOODHU, James Henry, son of James and Clarissa Woodhu, born -- Sep 1838, baptized 27 Dec 1838 (sponsors: the parents). {Ref: Church Records, 1834-1903, pp. 18-19}

WORTHINGTON, William, of Deer Creek Parish, died 6 Oct 1859. {Ref: Church Records, 1834-1903, p. 93}

WRIGHT, Alice Mildred, Methodist, confirmed 21 Nov 1909. {Ref: Parish Register, 1903-1958, p. 87}

WRIGHT, Amelia, see "Annie C. Wright" and "Charles H. Wright" and "George E. Wright" and "Mary L. Wright" and "William T. Wright," q.v.

WRIGHT, Avarilla, married William Gallion ---- 1878. [*Ed. Note:* The date was blank, but the marriage was listed between March and June in the register]. {Ref: Church Records, 1834-1903, p. 148}

WRIGHT, Annie Crawford, daughter of John W. and Amelia Ann Wright, born 8 Dec 1867, baptized 10 Jun 1868. {Ref: Church Records, 1834-1903, pp. 36-37}

WRIGHT, Charles Henry, son of John W. and Amelia Ann Wright, born 12 Jan 1872, baptized 1 Feb 1872. {Ref: Church Records, 1834-1903, pp. 38-39}

WRIGHT, Daniel G. (judge), sponsored the baptism of Louise Trezevant Wigfall Marshall on 12 Sep 1916. {Ref: Parish Register, 1903-1958, p. 33}

WRIGHT, Emma E. (Mrs.), Methodist, confirmed 17 May 1914. {Ref: Parish Register, 1903-1958, pp. 88, 110}

WRIGHT, Emma Elizabeth (Miss), Methodist, confirmed 13 Jun 1915. {Ref: Parish Register, 1903-1958, pp. 88, 111}

WRIGHT, George Edward, son of John W. and Amelia Ann Wright, born 15 May 1867, baptized 10 Jun 1868. {Ref: Church Records, 1834-1903, pp. 36-37}

WRIGHT, George Edward, Jr., Methodist, confirmed 13 Jun 1915. [*Ed. Note:* One entry listed his name as Sr. and another as Jr., but they both gave the same confirmation date]. {Ref: Parish Register, 1903-1958, pp. 88, 110-111}

WRIGHT, George Edward, Sr., confirmed 17 May 1914. [*Ed. Note:* One entry listed his name as Sr. and another as Jr., but they both gave the same confirmation date]. {Ref: Parish Register, 1903-1958, pp. 88, 110}

WRIGHT, Grace (Holland) Mrs., received from Grace Chapel, Hickory, on 5 May 1918. {Ref: Parish Register, 1903-1958, p. 111}

WRIGHT, Helen Opall, Methodist, confirmed 21 Nov 1909, married Lee Webster Selfe on 5 May 1917 at Mr. Wright's residence in Stepney. {Ref: Parish Register, 1903-1958, pp. 87, 109, 138-139}

WRIGHT, Howard, confirmed 19 Aug 1917. {Ref: Parish Register, 1903-1958, p. 89}

WRIGHT, J. W., buried 6 Oct 1886, "age circa 60 years." {Ref: Church Records, 1834-1903, p. 101}

WRIGHT, John W., see "Annie C. Wright" and "Charles H. Wright" and "George E. Wright" and "Mary L. Wright" and "William T. Wright," q.v.

WRIGHT, Mary Louisa, daughter of John W. and Amelia Ann Wright, born 8 Feb 1865, baptized 10 Jun 1868. {Ref: Church Records, 1834-1903, pp. 36-37}

WRIGHT, Mrs., buried 31 Nov [sic] 1879. {Ref: Church Records, 1834-1903, p. 97}

WRIGHT, Mrs., sponsored baptism of Charles Sumner Thompson (colored) on 23 Apr 1882. {Ref: Church Records, 1834-1903, p. 3}

WRIGHT, William Thomas, son of John W. and Amelia Ann Wright, born 22 Oct 1869, baptized 1 Feb 1872. {Ref: Church Records, 1834-1903, pp. 38-39}

YARNALL FAMILY.
The following family information was entered in the church records under the heading of "Families" circa 1893-1903, but no relationships or ages were indicated, just names. Additional information shown in parenthesis was entered subsequently in the register:
Mrs. ---- Yarnall, Anna M. Yarnall, Robert B. Yarnall (Wilmington), and Harriet E. Yarnall. {Ref: Church Records, 1834-1903, p. 256}

YARNALL, Annie (Anna) Malcolm, age 14, confirmed 18 Nov 1900; also see "Yarnall Family," q.v. {Ref: Church Records, 1834-1903, p. 303}

YARNALL, Harriet E. (Mrs.), confirmed 9 Jun 1893, church member in 1903, later removed [date not given]; also see "Yarnall Family," q.v. {Ref: Church Records, 1834-1903, p. 301; Parish Register, 1903-1958, p. 108}

YARNALL, Harriet Ellen, daughter of Jacob P. and Harriet E. Yarnall, born 24 Mar 1890, baptized 2 Nov 1890 (sponsors: the mother, Miss Georgie K. Malcolm and James W. Malcolm), confirmed 7 Dec 1902, age 13 [sic]; sponsored the baptism of Paul Nettleton Richards on 10 May 1903; church member in 1903, later removed [date not given]; also see "Robert B. Yarnall" and "Yarnall Family," q.v. {Ref: Church Records, 1834-1903, pp. 10-11, 17, 303; Parish Register, 1903-1958, p. 108}

YARNALL, Jacob P., married Hattie E. Malcolm on 15 Jan 1884; sponsored the baptism of Malcolm Yarnall Tarring on 1 Jun 1913; also see "Harriet E. Yarnall" and "Robert B. Yarnall," q.v. {Ref: Church Records, 1834-1903, p. 151; Parish Register, 1903-1958, p. 33}

YARNALL, M. G., sponsored the baptism of Henry Tarring on 19 Jul 1908. {Ref: Parish Register, 1903-1958, p. 31}

YARNALL, Robert Bruce, son of Jacob P. and Harriet E. Yarnall, born 15 Aug 1887, baptized 2 Nov 1890 (sponsors: the mother, Miss Georgie K. Malcolm and

James W. Malcolm), confirmed 29 Dec 1901, age 14; church member in 1903, later removed [date not given]; also see "Yarnall Family," q.v. {Ref: Church Records, 1834-1903, pp. 10-11, 303; Parish Register, 1903-1958, p. 108}

YORK, John (servant belonging to Mr. E. Griffith), buried 5 May 1864. {Ref: Church Records, 1834-1903, p. 94}

YORK, Harriet, see "John H. York" and "Stepney York," q.v.

YORK, John Henry (an infant child of color), son of Stepney and Harriet York (servants to Edward Griffith), born ---- [blank], baptized 5 Oct 1856, buried 14 Jan 1858. {Ref: Church Records, 1834-1903, pp. 28-29, 93}

YORK, Milly (servant of Mr. Ed. Griffith), buried 9 May 1858. {Ref: Church Records, 1834-1903, p. 93}

YORK, Sarah (colored), buried 2 Jul 1872. {Ref: Church Records, 1834-1903, p. 96}

YORK, Stepney, son of Stepney and Harriet York (servants of Mr. E. Griffith), born ---- [blank], baptized 8 Aug 1858; also see "John H. York," q.v. {Ref: Church Records, 1834-1903, pp. 28-29}

YORK, Stepney, married Harriet Steward on 27 May 1855. {Ref: Church Records, 1834-1903, p. 140}

ZEIGLER, Oscar Woodward (reverend), rector from 1 Dec 1904 to Sep 1907; removed [place and date not given]. {Ref: Parish Register, 1903-1958, pp. ii, 109}

----, Aminta, daughter of Emily ---- [blank], servant of Mr. Keen, born ---- [blank], baptized 1 Aug 1858. {Ref: Church Records, 1834-1903, pp. 28-29}

----, Ann, daughter of Ann ---- (servant of Mrs. Davidge), born -- Jan 1837, baptized 19 Jan 1840 at "The Dairy." {Ref: Church Records, 1834-1903, pp. 20-21}

----, Ann Rebecca (servant of Miss Adaline Hall), born 17 Apr 1857, baptized 22 Sep 1863. {Ref: Church Records, 1834-1903, pp. 32-33}

----, Elizabeth, daughter of Elizabeth ---- (servant of Mrs. Davidge), born -- Jan 1838, baptized 19 Jan 1840 at "The Dairy." {Ref: Church Records, 1834-1903, pp. 20-21}

----, Fanny, daughter of Harriet ---- [blank], servant of Mrs. J. A. Perryman, born ---- [blank], baptized 7 Nov 1858. {Ref: Church Records, 1834-1903, pp. 28-29}

----, George (servant of Mr. E. Griffith), buried 14 Jul 1860. {Ref: Church Records, 1834-1903, p. 93}

----, George William (a child), buried 7 Mar 1864. {Ref: Church Records, 1834-1903, p. 94}

----, Hannah, married Frillas(?) White on 4 Apr 1858. {Ref: Church Records, 1834-1903, p. 142}

----, Harriet, married Charles Jones on 28 Nov 1847. {Ref: Church Records, 1834-1903, p. 139}

----, Harriet Amanda (servant of Miss Adaline Hall), born 30 Dec 1857, baptized 22 Sep 1863. {Ref: Church Records, 1834-1903, pp. 32-33}

----, Isaac William (colored), son of Maria ---- (servant of Mr. Edw. Griffith). {Ref: Church Records, 1834-1903, p. 94}

----, James (colored), son of Eliza and Delpha ---- [blank], born 10 Jan 1848, baptized 16 May 1868. {Ref: Church Records, 1834-1903, pp. 36-37}

----, Katy Lea, a child about 9 years old, buried 28 Aug 1868. {Ref: Church Records, 1834-1903, p. 95}

----, Laura Frances (servant of Miss Adaline Hall), born 16 Sep 1853, baptized 22 Sep 1863. {Ref: Church Records, 1834-1903, pp. 32-33}

----, Lucy, daughter of Rachel ---- (servant of Dr. J. A. and C. Preston), born -- Nov 1838, baptized 3 Feb 1840. {Ref: Church Records, 1834-1903, pp. 20-21}

----, Margaret (an aged servant of Mr. E. Griffith), buried 9 Mar 1863. {Ref: Church Records, 1834-1903, p. 94}

----, Martha Susan, colored child of Septimus D. and Maria L. Sewell, born -- Feb 1853, baptized 30 Dec 1859. {Ref: Church Records, 1834-1903, pp. 30-31}

----, May Jane (servant of Miss Adaline Hall), born 9 Feb 1863, baptized 22 Sep 1863. {Ref: Church Records, 1834-1903, pp. 32-33}

----, Permela Ann (servant of Miss Adaline Hall), born 29 Sep 1859, baptized 22 Sep 1863. {Ref: Church Records, 1834-1903, pp. 32-33}

----, Rosetta, daughter of Rosetta ---- (servant of Mrs. Davidge), born -- Nov 1838, baptized 19 Jan 1840 at "The Dairy." {Ref: Church Records, 1834-1903, pp. 20-21}

----, Stewart, "a youth," died in 1875 or 1876 [exact date not given]. {Ref: Church Records, 1834-1903, p. 97}

----, [blank], "a colored infant," baptized 4 Jul 1880 [name of parents and date of birth were not given]. {Ref: Church Records, 1834-1903, pp. 42-43}

----, [blank], "a youth, 16 years, at the Dairy Farm," died in 1875 or 1876 [exact date not given]. {Ref: Church Records, 1834-1903, p. 97}

----, [blank], an infant (not named), died in 1874 [exact date not given]. {Ref: Church Records, 1834-1903, p. 97}

Other Heritage Books by Henry C. Peden, Jr. :

A Closer Look at St. John's Parish Registers [Baltimore County, Maryland], 1701–1801

A Collection of Maryland Church Records

A Guide to Genealogical Research in Maryland: 5th Edition, Revised and Enlarged

Abstracts of the Ledgers and Accounts of the Bush Store and Rock Run Store, 1759–1771

Abstracts of the Orphans Court Proceedings of Harford County, 1778–1800

Abstracts of Wills, Harford County, Maryland, 1800–1805

Baltimore City [Maryland] Deaths and Burials, 1834–1840

Baltimore County, Maryland, Overseers of Roads, 1693–1793

Bastardy Cases in Baltimore County, Maryland, 1673–1783

Bastardy Cases in Harford County, Maryland, 1774–1844

Bible and Family Records of Harford County, Maryland Families: Volume V

Children of Harford County: Indentures and Guardianships, 1801–1830

Colonial Delaware Soldiers and Sailors, 1638–1776

Colonial Families of the Eastern Shore of Md.: Vols. 5, 6, 7, 8, 9, 11, 12, 13, 14, and 16

Colonial Maryland Soldiers and Sailors, 1634–1734

Dr. John Archer's First Medical Ledger, 1767–1769, Annotated Abstracts

Early Anglican Records of Cecil County

Early Harford Countians, Individuals Living in Harford Co., Md. in Its Formative Years Volume 1: A to K, Volume 2: L to Z, and Volume 3: Supplement

Harford County Taxpayers in 1870, 1872 and 1883

Harford County, Maryland Divorce Cases, 1827–1912: An Annotated Index

Heirs and Legatees of Harford County, Maryland, 1774–1802

Heirs and Legatees of Harford County, Maryland, 1802–1846

Inhabitants of Baltimore County, Maryland, 1763–1774

Inhabitants of Cecil County, Maryland, 1649–1774

Inhabitants of Harford County, Maryland, 1791–1800

Inhabitants of Kent County, Maryland, 1637–1787

Joseph A. Pennington & Co., Havre De Grace, Maryland Funeral Home Records: Volume II, 1877–1882, 1893–1900

Maryland Bible Records, Volume 1: Baltimore and Harford Counties

Maryland Bible Records, Volume 2: Baltimore and Harford Counties

Maryland Bible Records, Volume 3: Carroll County

Maryland Bible Records, Volume 4: Eastern Shore

Maryland Deponents, 1634–1799

Maryland Deponents: Volume 3, 1634–1776

Maryland Public Service Records, 1775–1783: A Compendium of Men and Women of Maryland Who Rendered Aid in Support of the American Cause against Great Britain during the Revolutionary War

Marylanders to Carolina: Migration of Marylanders to North Carolina and South Carolina prior to 1800

Marylanders to Kentucky, 1775–1825

Methodist Records of Baltimore City, Maryland: Volume 1, 1799–1829

Methodist Records of Baltimore City, Maryland: Volume 2, 1830–1839

Methodist Records of Baltimore City, Maryland: Volume 3, 1840–1850 (East City Station)

More Maryland Deponents, 1716–1799

More Marylanders to Carolina: Migration of Marylanders to North Carolina and South Carolina prior to 1800

More Marylanders to Kentucky, 1778–1828

Outpensioners of Harford County, Maryland, 1856–1896

Presbyterian Records of Baltimore City, Maryland, 1765–1840

Quaker Records of Baltimore and Harford Counties, Maryland, 1801–1825

Quaker Records of Northern Maryland, 1716–1800

Quaker Records of Southern Maryland, 1658–1800

Revolutionary Patriots of Anne Arundel County, Maryland

Revolutionary Patriots of Baltimore Town and Baltimore County, 1775–1783

Revolutionary Patriots of Calvert and St. Mary's Counties, Maryland, 1775–1783

Revolutionary Patriots of Caroline County, Maryland, 1775–1783

Revolutionary Patriots of Cecil County, Maryland

Revolutionary Patriots of Charles County, Maryland, 1775–1783

Revolutionary Patriots of Delaware, 1775–1783

Revolutionary Patriots of Dorchester County, Maryland, 1775–1783

Revolutionary Patriots of Frederick County, Maryland, 1775–1783

Revolutionary Patriots of Harford County, Maryland, 1775–1783

Revolutionary Patriots of Kent and Queen Anne's Counties

Revolutionary Patriots of Lancaster County, Pennsylvania

Revolutionary Patriots of Maryland, 1775–1783: A Supplement

Revolutionary Patriots of Maryland, 1775–1783: Second Supplement

Revolutionary Patriots of Montgomery County, Maryland, 1776–1783

Revolutionary Patriots of Prince George's County, Maryland, 1775–1783

Revolutionary Patriots of Talbot County, Maryland, 1775–1783

Revolutionary Patriots of Worcester and Somerset Counties, Maryland, 1775–1783

Revolutionary Patriots of Washington County, Maryland, 1776–1783

St. George's (Old Spesutia) Parish, Harford County, Maryland: Church and Cemetery Records, 1820–1920

St. John's and St. George's Parish Registers, 1696–1851

Survey Field Book of David and William Clark in Harford County, Maryland, 1770–1812

The Crenshaws of Kentucky, 1800–1995

The Delaware Militia in the War of 1812

Union Chapel United Methodist Church Cemetery Tombstone Inscriptions, Wilna, Harford County, Maryland

www.ingramcontent.com/pod-product-compliance
Lightning Source LLC
Chambersburg PA
CBHW060123170426
43198CB00010B/1015